S. R. Riggs.

MARY AND I.

Forty Years with the Sioux.

BY

STEPHEN R. RIGGS, D.D., LL. D.,

Missionary of the A. B. C. F. M; and Author of
"Dakota Grammar and Dictionary," and
"Gospel Among the Dakotas," etc.

With an Introduction

BY

REV. S. C. BARTLETT, D.D.,

President of Dartmouth College.

CORNER HOUSE PUBLISHERS
WILLIAMSTOWN, MASSACHUSETTS 01267
1971

Copyrighted, March, 1880.
BY STEPHEN R. RIGGS.

REPRINTED 1971
BY
CORNER HOUSE PUBLISHERS

Printed in the United States of America

TO

MY CHILDREN,

ALFRED, ISABELLA, MARTHA, ANNA,

THOMAS, HENRY, ROBERT,

CORNELIA AND EDNA;

Together with all the

GRANDCHILDREN

Growing up into the

MISSIONARY INHERITANCE

OF THEIR FATHERS AND MOTHERS,

This Book is inscribed,

By the Author.

PREFACE.

This book I have INSCRIBED to my own family. It will be of interest to them, as, in part, a history of their father and mother, in the toils, and sacrifices, and rewards, of commencing and carrying forward the work of evangelizing the Dakota people.

Many others, who are interested in the uplifting of the Red Men, may be glad to obtain glimpses, in these pages, of the inside of Missionary Life in what was, not long since, the Far West; and to trace the threads of the inweaving of a Christ-life into the lives of many of the Sioux nation.

"Why don't you tell more about yourselves?" is a question, which, in various forms, has been often asked me, during these last four decades. Partly as the answer to questions of that kind, this book assumes somewhat the form of a personal narrative.

Years ago it was an open secret, that our good and noble friend, SECRETARY S. B. TREAT, contemplated a History of the American Board's Indian Missions, as DR. ANDERSON had made of the missions beyond the seas. When MR. TREAT had gone up higher, DR. N. G. CLARK sent me a note of inquiry—could I undertake that work? For reasons quite satisfactory to myself, and I presume also to him, I declined. At that time I said, "The Da-

PREFACE.

kota mission is the only one of the American Board's Indian missions of which I could undertake to give a history." The suggestion was a winged seed. By and by, thought took form and substance, and the result is this book.

While I do not claim, even at this evening time of my life, to be freed from the desire that good Christian readers will think favorably of this effort of mine, I cannot expect that the appreciation with which my Dakota Grammar and Dictionary was received, by the literary world, more than a quarter of a century ago, will be surpassed by this humbler effort.

Moreover, the chief work of my life has been the part I have been permitted, by the good Lord, to have in giving the entire Bible to the Sioux Nation. This book is only "the band of the sheaf." If, by weaving the principal facts of our Missionary work, its trials and joys, its discouragements and grand successes, into this personal narrative of "MARY AND I," a better judgment of Indian capabilities is secured, and a more earnest and intelligent determination to work for their Christianization and final Citizenship, I shall be quite satisfied.

Since the historical close of " Forty Years with the Sioux," some important events have transpired, in connection with our missionary work, which are grouped together in an Appendix, in the form of Monographs.

S. R. R.

Beloit, Wis., January, 1880.

INTRODUCTION.

The churches owe a great debt of gratitude to their missionaries, first, for the noble work they do, and, secondly, for the inspiring narratives they write. There is no class of writings more quickening to piety at home than the sober narratives of these labors abroad. The faith and zeal, the wisdom and patience, the enterprise and courage, the self-sacrifice and Christian peace which they record, as well as the wonderful triumphs of grace and the simplicity of native piety which they make known, bring us nearer, perhaps, to the spirit and the scenes of Apostolic times than any other class of literature. How the churches could, or can ever, dispense with the reactionary influence from the Foreign Mission field, it is difficult to understand. Doubtless, however, when the harvest is all gathered, the Lord of the Harvest will, in his wisdom, know how to supply the lack.

Some narratives are valuable chiefly for their interest of style and manner, while the facts themselves are of minor account. Other narratives secure attention by the weight of their facts alone. The author of "Mary and I; Forty Years with the Sioux," has our thanks for giving us a story attractive alike from the present significance of its theme, and from the frank and fresh simplicity of its method.

It is a timely contribution. Thank God, the attention

INTRODUCTION.

of the whole nation is at length beginning to be turned in good earnest to the chronic wrongs inflicted on the Indian race, and is, though slowly and with difficulty, comprehending the fact, long known to the friends of missions, that these tribes, when properly approached, are singularly accessible and responsive to all the influences of Christianity and its resultant civilization. Slowest of all to apprehend this truth, though with honorable exceptions, are our military men. The officer who uttered that frightful maxim, "No good Indian but a dead Indian"—if indeed it ever fell from his lips—needs all the support of a brilliant and gallant career in defense of his country to save him from a judgment as merciless as his maxim. Such principles, let us believe, have had their day. They and their defenders are assuredly to be swept away by the rising tide of a better sentiment slowly and steadily pervading the country. The wrongs of the African have been, in part, redressed, and now comes the turn of the Indian. He must be permitted to have a home in fee simple, a recognized citizenship, and complete protection under a settled system of law. The gospel will then do for him its thorough work, and show once more that God has made all nations of one blood. He is yet to have them. It is but a question of time. And the Indian tribes are doubtless not to fade away, but to be rescued from extinction by the gospel of Christ working in them and for them.

The reader who takes up this volume will not fail to read it through. He will easily believe that Anna Baird Riggs was "a model Christian woman,"—the mother who could bring up her boy in a log cabin where once the bear looked in at the door, or in the log school-house with its newspaper windows, "slab benches" and drunken teacher, and could train him for his work of faith and perseverance in that dreary and forbidding missionary region, and in what men thought that forlorn hope. And he will learn—unless he knew it already—that a lad who in early life hammered on the anvil, can strike a strong and steady stroke for God and man.

The reader will also recognize in the "Mary" of this story, now gone to her rest, a worthy pupil of Mary Lyon and Miss Z. P. Grant. With her excellent education, culture and character, how cheerfully she left her home in Massachusetts to enter almost alone on a field of labor which she knew perfectly to be most fraught with self-sacrifice, least attractive, not to say most repulsive, of them all. How hopefully she journeyed on thirteen days, from the shores of Lake Harriet, to plunge still farther into the wilderness at Lac-qui-parle. How happily she found a "home" for five years in the upper story of Dr. Williamson's log house, in a room eighteen feet by ten, occupied in due time by three children also. How quietly she glided into all the details and solved all the difficulties of that primitive life, bore with the often revolting habits of the aborigines, taught their boys English, and persevered and persisted till she had taught their women "the gospel of soap." How bravely she bore up in that terrible midnight flight from Hazelwood, and the long exhausting journey to St. Paul, through the pelting rains and wet swamp-grass, and with murderous savages upon the trail. But it was the chief test and glory of her character to have brought up a family of children, among all the surroundings of Indian life, as though amid the homes of civilization and refinement. All honor to such a woman, wife and mother. Her children rise up and call her blessed. Forty-one years after her departure from the station at Lake Harriet, the present writer stood upon the

INTRODUCTION.

pleasant shore where the tamarack mission houses had long disappeared, and felt that this was consecrated ground.

The other partner in this firm of "Mary and I" needs no words of mine. He speaks here for himself, and his labors speak for him. His Dakota Dictionary and Bible are lasting monuments of his persevering toil, while eleven churches with a dozen native preachers and eight hundred members, and a flourishing Dakota Home Missionary Society, bear witness to the Christian work of himself and his few co-laborers. "Forty Years Among the Sioux," he writes. "Forty Years in the Turkish Empire," was the story of Dr. Goodell. Fifty Years in Ceylon, was the life-work of Levi Spalding. What records are these of singleness of aim, of energy, of Christian work, and of harvests gathered and gathering for the Master. Would that such a holy ambition might be kindled in the hearts of many other young men as they read these pages. How invigorating the firm assurance: "During the years of my preparation there never came to me a doubt of the rightness of my decision. At the end of forty years' work I am abundantly satisfied with the way in which the Lord has led me." How many of those who embark in other lines of life and action can say the same?

And how signally was the spirit of the parents transmitted to the children. Almost a whole family in the mission work: six sons and daughters among the Dakotas, the seventh in China. I know not another instance so marked as this. And what a power for good to the Dakota race, past, present and future, is gathered up in one undaunted, single-hearted family of Christian toilers. A part of this family it has been the writer's privilege to know, and of two of the sons he had the pleasure to be

INTRODUCTION.

the teacher in the original tongues of the word of God. And he deems it an additional pleasure and privilege thus to connect his name with theirs and their mission. For not alone the dusky Dakotas, but all the friends of the Indian tribes and lovers of the Missionary cause, are called on to honor the names of Pond, Williamson, and Riggs.

S. C. BARTLETT.

Dartmouth College.

CONTENTS.

CHAPTER I.

1837.—Our Parentage.—My Mother's Bear Story.—Mary's Education.—Her First School Teaching.—School Houses and Teachers in Ohio.—Learning the Catechism.—Ambitions.—The Lord's Leading —Mary's Teaching in Bethlehem.—Life Threads Coming Together.—Licensure.—Our Decision as to Life Work.—Going to New England.—The Hawley Family. —Marriage.—Going West.—From Mary's Letters.—Mrs. Isabella Burgess.—"Steamer Isabella."—At St. Louis.—The Mississippi.—To the City of Lead.—Rev. Aratus Kent.—The Lord Provides —Mary's Descriptions.—Upper Mississippi.—Reaching Fort Snelling..................................1

CHAPTER II.

1837.—First Knowledge of the Sioux.—Hennepin and Du Luth.—Fort Snelling.—Lakes Harriet and Calhoun.—Three Months at Lake Harriet.—Samuel W. Pond.—Learning the Language.—Mr. Stevens.—Temporary Home.—That Station Soon Broken Up.—Mary's Letters.—The Mission and People. —Native Customs.—Lord's Supper.—" Good Voice."—Description of our Home.—The Garrison.—Seeing St. Anthony.—Ascent of the Saint Peters.—Mary's Letters.—Traverse des Sioux.—Prairie Traveling.—Reaching Lac-qui-parle.—T. S. Williamson.—A Sabbath Service.—Our Upper Room.—Experiences.—Church at Lac-qui-parle.—Mr. Pond's Marriage.—Mary's Letters.—Feast........................16

CONTENTS.

CHAPTER III.

1837–1839.—The Language.—Its Growth.—System of Notation.—After Changes.—What we Had to Put into the Language.—Teaching English, and Teaching Dakota.—Mary's Letter.—Fort Renville.—Translating the Bible.—The Gospels of Mark and John.—"Good Bird" Born.—Dakota Names.—The Lessons we Learned.—Dakota Washing.—Extracts from Letters.—Dakota Tents.—A Marriage.—Visiting the Village.—Girls, Boys and Dogs.—G. H. Pond's Indian Hunt.—Three Families Killed.—The Village Wail.—The Power of a Name.—Post-Office Far Away.—The Coming of the Mail.—S. W. Pond Comes Up.—My Visit to Snelling.—Lost My Horse.—Dr. Williamson Goes to Ohio.—The Spirit's Presence.—Prayer.—Mary's Reports............ 35

CHAPTER IV.

1838–1840.—"Eagle Help."—His Power as War Prophet.—Makes No-Flight Dance.—We Pray Against It.—Unsuccessful on the War Path.—Their Revenge.—Jean Nicollet and J. C. Fremont.—Opposition to Schools.—Progress in Teaching.—Method of Counting.—"Lake that Speaks."—Our Trip to Fort Snelling.—Incidents of the Way.—The Changes There.—Our Return Journey.—Birch Bark Canoe.—Mary's Story.—"Le Grand Canoe."—Baby Born on the Way.—Walking Ten Miles.—Advantages of Travel.—My Visit to the Missouri River.—"Fort Pierre."—Results.......................53

CHAPTER V.

1840—1843.—Dakota Braves.—Simon Anawangmane.—Mary's Letter.—Simon's Fall.—Maple Sugar.—Adobe Church.—Catharine's Letter.—Another Letter of Mary's.—Left Hand's Case.—The Fifth Winter.—Mary to her Brother.—The Children's Morning Ride.—Visit to Hawley and Ohio.—Dakota Printing.—New Recruits.—Return.—Little Rapids.

CONTENTS.

—Traverse des Sioux.—Stealing Bread.—Forming a New Station.—Begging.—Opposition.—Thomas L. Longley.—Meeting Ojibwas.—Two Sioux Killed.—Mary's Hard Walk. 65

CHAPTER VI.

1843-1846.—Great Sorrow.—Thomas Drowned.—Mary's Letter.—The Indians' Thoughts.—Old Grey-Leaf.—Oxen Killed.—Hard Field.—Sleepy Eyes' Horse.—Indian in Prison.—The Lord keeps us.—Simon's Shame.—Mary's Letter.—Robert Hopkins and Agnes.—Le Bland.—White Man Ghost.—Bennett.—Sleepy Eyes' Camp.—Drunken Indians.—Making Sugar.—Military Company.—Dakota Prisoners.—Stealing Melons.—Preaching and School.—A Canoe Voyage.—Red Wing..80

CHAPTER VII.

1846-1851.—Returning to Lac-qui-parle.—Reasons Therefor.—Mary's Story.—"Give me my Old Seat, Mother."—At Lac-qui-parle.—New Arrangements.—Better Understanding.—Buffalo Plenty.—Mary's Story.—Little Samuel Died.—Going on the Hunt.—Vision of Home.—Building House.—Dakota Camp.—Soldiers' Lodge.—Wakanmane's Village.—Making a Presbytery.—New Recruits.—Meeting at Kaposia.—Mary's Story.—Varied Trials.—Sabbath Worship.—"What is to Die?"—New Stations.—Making a Treaty.—Mr. Hopkins Drowned.—Personal Experience........................99

CHAPTER VIII.

1851-1854.—Grammar and Dictionary.—How it grew.—Publication.—Minnesota Historical Society.—Smithsonian Institution.—Going East.—Mission Meeting at Traverse de Sioux.—Mrs. Hopkins.—Death's Doings.—Changes in the Mode of

CONTENTS.

Writing Dakota.—Completed Book.—Growth of the Language.—In Brooklyn and Philadelphia.—The Misses Spooner.—Changes in the Mission.—The Ponds and Others Retire.—Dr. Williamson at Pay-zhe-hoo-ta-ze.—Winter Storms.—Andrew Hunter.—Two Families Left.—Children Learning Dakota.—Our House burned.—The Lord Provides...117

CHAPTER IX.

1854–1856.—Simon Anawangmane.—Rebuilding after the Fire. —Visit of Secretary Treat.—Change of Plan.—Hazelwood Station.—Circular Saw-Mill.—Mission Buildings.—Chapel. —Civilized Community.—Making Citizens.—Boarding School.—Educating our own Children.—Financial Difficulties.—The Lord Provides.—A Great Affliction.—Smith Burgess Williamson.—"Aunt Jane."—Bunyan's Pilgrim in Dakota..129

CHAPTER X.

1857–1861.—Spirit Lake.—Massacres by Inkpadoota.—The Captives.—Delivery of Mrs. Marble and Miss Gardner.—Excitement.—Inkpadoota's Son Killed.—U. S. Soldiers.—Maj. Sherman.—Indian Councils.—Great Scare.—Going Away.— Indians Sent after Scarlet End.—Quiet Restored.—Children at School.—Quarter-Century Meeting.—John P. Williamson at Red Wood.—Dedication of Chapel..................138

CHAPTER XI.

1861–1862.—Republican Administration.—Its Mistakes.—Changing Annuities.—Results.—Returning from General Assembly. —A Marriage in St. Paul.—D. Wilson Moore and Wife.— Delayed Payment.—Difficulty with the Sissetons.—Peace

CONTENTS.

Again.—Recruiting for the Southern War.—Seventeenth of August, 1862.—The Outbreak.—Remembering Christ's Death. —Massacres Commenced.—Capt. Marsh's Company.—Our Flight.—Reasons Therefor.—Escape to an Island.—Final Leaving.—A Wounded Man.—Traveling on the Prairie.— Wet Night.—Taking a Picture.—Change of Plan.—Night Travel.—Going around Fort Ridgely.—Night Scares.—Safe Passage.—Four Men Killed.—The Lord Leads Us.—Sabbath.—Reaching the Settlements.—Mary at St. Anthony. 147

CHAPTER XII.

1862.—Gen. Sibley's Expedition.—I Go as Chaplain.--At Fort Ridgely.—The Burial Party.—Birch Coolie Defeat.—Simon and Lorenzo Bring in Captives.—March to Yellow Medicine. —Battle of Wood Lake.—Indians Flee.—Camp Release.— A Hundred Captives Rescued.—Amos W. Huggins Killed.— We Send for His Wife and Children.—Spirit Walker has Protected Them.—Martha's Letter......................164

CHAPTER XIII.

1862-1863.—Military Commission.—Excited Community.—Dakotas Condemned.—Moving Camp.—The Campaign Closed.— Findings sent to the President.—Reaching my Home in St. Anthony.—Distributing Alms on the Frontier.—Recalled to Mankato.—The Executions.—Thirty-eight Hung.—Difficulty of Avoiding Mistakes.—Round Wind.—Confessions.—The next Sabbath's Service.—Dr. Williamson's Work.—Learning to Read.—The Spiritual Awakening.—The Way it Came.— Mr. Pond Invited up.—Baptisms in the Prison.—The Lord's Supper.—The Camp at Snelling.—A like Work of Grace.— John P. Williamson.—Scenes in the Garret.—One Hundred Adults Baptized.—Marvelous in our Eyes...............179

CONTENTS.

CHAPTER XIV.

1863-1866.—The Dakota Prisoners taken to Davenport.—Camp McClellan.—Their Treatment.—Great Mortality.—Education in Prison.—Worship.—Church Matters.—The Camp at Snelling Removed to Crow Creek.—John P. Williamson's Story.—Many Die.—Scouts' Camp.—Visits to Them.—Family Threads.—Revising the New Testament.—Educating Our Children.—Removal to Beloit.—Family Matters.—Little Six and Medicine Bottle.—With the Prisoners at Davenport.
................................193

CHAPTER XV.

1866-1869.—Prisoners meet their Families at the Niobrara.—Our Summer's Visitation.—At the Scouts' Camp.—Crossing the Prairie.—Killing Buffalo.—At Niobrara.—Religious Meetings.—Licensing Natives.—Visiting the Omahas.—Scripture Translating.—Sisseton Treaty at Washington.—Second visit to the Santees.—Artemas and Titus Ordained.—Crossing to the Head of the Coteau.—Organizing Churches and Licensing Dakotas.—Solomon, Robert, Louis, Daniel.—On Horseback in 1868.—Visit to the Santees, Yanktons, and Brules.—Gathering at Dry Wood.—Solomon Ordained.—Writing "Takoo Wakan."—Mary's Sickness.—Grand Hymns.—Going through the Valley of the Shadow.—Death!....203

CHAPTER XVI.

1869-1870.—Home Desolate.—At the General Assembly.—Summer Campaign.—A. L. Riggs.—His Story of Early Life.—Inside View of Missions.—Why Missionaries' Children Become Missionaries.—No Constraint Laid on Them.—A. L. Riggs Visits the Missouri Sioux.—Up the River.—The Brules.—Cheyenne and Grand River.—Starting for Fort Wadsworth.—Sun Eclipsed.—Sisseton Reserve.—Deciding to Build there.—In the Autumn Assembly.—My Mother's Home.—Winter Visit to Santee.—Julia La Framboise. 217

CONTENTS.

CHAPTER XVII.

1870-1871.—Beloit Home Broken up.—Building on the Sisseton Reserve.—Difficulties and Cost.—Correspondence with Washington.—Order to Suspend Work.—Disregarding the Taboo.—Anna Sick at Beloit.—Assurance.—Martha Goes in Anna's Place.—The Dakota Churches.—Lac-qui-parle, Ascension.—John B. Renville.—Daniel Renville.—Houses of Worship.—Eight Churches.—The "Word Carrier."—Annual Meeting on the Big Sioux.—Homestead Colony.—How it Came about.—Joseph Iron Old Man.—Perished in a Snow Storm.—The Dakota Mission Divides.—Reasons Therefor............229

CHAPTER XVIII.

1870-1873.—A. L. Riggs Builds at Santee.—The Santee High School.—Visit to Fort Sully.—Change of Agents at Sisseton.—Second Marriage.—Annual Meeting at Good Will.—Grand Gathering.—New Treaty Made at Sisseton.—Nina Foster Riggs.—Our Trip to Fort Sully.—An Incident by the Way.—Stop at Santee.—Pastor Ehnamane.—His Deer Hunt.—Annual Meeting in 1873.—Rev. S. J. Humphrey's Visit.—Mr. Humphrey's Sketch.—Where They Come From.—Morning Call.—Visiting the Teepees.—The Religious Gathering.—The Moderator.—Questions Discussed.—The *Personnel.*—Putting Up a Tent.—Sabbath Service.—Mission Reunion.........243

CHAPTER XIX.

1873-1874.—The American Board at Minneapolis.—The *nidus* of the Dakota Mission.—Large Indian Delegation.—Ehnamane and Mazakootemane.—"Then and Now."—The Woman's Meeting.—Nina Foster Riggs and Lizzie Bishop.—Miss Bishop's Work and Early Death.—Manual Labor Boarding School at Sisseton.—Building Dedicated.—M. N. Adams, Agent.—School Opened.—Mrs. Armor and Mrs. Morris.—"My Darling in God's Garden."—Visit to Fort Berthold.—Mandans, Rees and Hidatsa.—Dr. W. Matthews' Hidatsa

CONTENTS.

Grammar.—Beliefs.—Missionary Interest in Berthold.—Down the Missouri.—Annual Meeting at Santee.—Normal School.—Dakotas Build a Church at Ascension.—Journey to the Ojibwas with E. P. Wheeler.—Leech Lake and Red Lake.—On the Gitche Gumme.—"The Stoneys."—Visit to Odanah.—Hope for Ojibwas.................................261

CHAPTER XX.

1875-1876.—Annual Meeting of 1875.—Homestead Settlement on the Big Sioux.—Interest of the Conference.—"Iapi Oaye."—Inception of Native Missionary Work.—Theological Class.—The Dakota Home.—Charles L. Hall ordained.—Dr. Magoun, of Iowa.—Mr. and Mrs. Hall sent to Berthold by the American Board.—The "Word Carrier's" good words to them.—The Conference of 1876.—In J. B. Renville's Church.—Coming to the Meeting from Sully.—Miss Whipple's Story.—"Dakota Missionary Society."—Miss Collins' Story.—Impressions of the Meeting.......................................281

CHAPTER XXI.

1871-1877.—The Wilder Sioux.—Gradual Openings.—Thomas Lawrence.—Visit to the Land of the Teetons.—Fort Sully.—Hope Station.—Mrs. Gen. Stanley in the Evangelist.—Work by Native Teachers.—Thomas Married to Nina Foster.—Nina's First Visit to Sully. - Attending the Conference and American Board.—Miss Collins and Miss Whipple.—Bogue Station.—The Mission Surroundings.—Chapel Built.—Mission Work.—Church Organized.—Sioux War of 1876.—Community Excited.—Schools.—"Waiting for a Boat."—Miss Whipple Dies at Chicago.—Mrs. Nina Riggs' Tribute.—The Conference of 1877 at Sully.—Questions Discussed.—Grand Impressions..298

CONTENTS.

APPENDIX.

MONOGRAPHS.

Mrs. Nina Foster Riggs	316
Rev. Gideon H. Pond	329
Solomon	339
Dr. T. S. Williamson	345
A Memorial	358
The Family Reunion	365

Mary and I.

Mary and I.

Forty Years with the Sioux.

MARY AND I.

FORTY YEARS WITH THE SIOUX.

CHAPTER I.

1837.—Our Parentage.—My Mother's Bear Story.—Mary's Education.—Her First School Teaching.—School Houses and Teachers in Ohio.—Learning the Catechism.—Ambitions.—The Lord's Leading.—Mary's Teaching in Bethlehem.—Life Threads Coming Together.—Licensure.—Our Decision as to Life Work.—Going to New England.—The Hawley Family.—Marriage.—Going West.—From Mary's Letters.—Mrs. Isabella Burgess.—"Steamer Isabella"—At St. Louis.—The Mississippi.—To the City of Lead.—Rev. Aratus Kent.—The Lord Provides —Mary's Descriptions —Upper Mississippi.—Reaching Fort Snelling.

Forty years ago this first day of June, 1877, MARY and I came to Fort Snelling. She was from the Old Bay State, and I was a native-born Buckeye. Her ancestors were the Longleys and Taylors of Hawley and Buckland, names honorable and honored in the western part of Massachusetts. Her father, Gen. Thomas Longley, was for many years a member of the General Court and had served in the war of 1812, while her grandfather, Col. Edmund Longley, had been a soldier of the Revolution, and had served under Washington. Her maternal grandfather, Taylor, had held a civil commission under George the Third. In an early day both families had settled in the hill country west of the Connecticut River. They were the true and worthy representatives of New England.

As it regards myself, my father, whose name was Stephen Riggs, was a blacksmith, and for many years an elder in the Presbyterian church of Steubenville, Ohio, where I was born. He had a brother, Cyrus, who was a preacher in Western Pennsylvania; and he traced his lineage back, through the Riggs families of New Jersey, a long line of godly men, ministers of the gospel and others, to *Edward Riggs who came over from Wales in the first days of Colonial history. My mother was Anna Baird, a model Christian woman, as I think, of a Scotch Irish family, which in the early days settled in Fayette County, Pa. Of necessity they were pioneers. When they had three children they removed up into the wild wooded country of the Upper Allegheny. My mother could tell a good many bear stories. At one time she and those first three children were left alone in an unfinished log cabin. The father was away hunting food for the family. When, at night, the fire was burning in the old-fashioned chimney, a large black bear pushed aside the quilt that served for the door, and sitting down on his haunches, surveyed the scared family within. But as God would have it, to their great relief, he retired without offering them any violence.

Mary's education had been carefully conducted. She had not only the advantages of the common town school

*Heretofore, we have supposed the first progenitor of the Riggs Family in America was MILES; but the investigations of Mr. J. H. Wallace, of New York, show that it was EDWARD, who settled in Roxbury, Mass., about the year 1635. The name of MILES comes in later. He was the progenitor of one branch of the family.

and home culture, but was a pupil of Mary Lyon, when she taught in Buckland, and afterward of Miss Grant, at Ipswich. At the age of sixteen she taught her first school, in Williamstown, Mass. As she used to tell the story, she taught for a dollar a week, and, at the end of her first quarter, brought the $12 home and gave it to her father, as a recognition of what he had expended for her education.

To me it was a joy to meet, the other day in Chicago, Mrs. Judge Osborne, who was one of the scholars in this school, as it was in her father's family; and who spoke very affectionately of Mary Ann Longley, her teacher.

Contrasted with the present appliances for education in all the towns, and many of the country districts also, the common schools in Ohio, when I was a boy, were very poorly equipped. My first school-house was a log cabin, with a large open fire-place, a window with four lights of glass where the master's seat was; on the other two sides a log was cut out and old newspapers pasted over the hole through which the light was supposed to come, and the seats were benches made of slabs. One of my first teachers was a drunken Irishman, who often visited the tavern near by and came back to sleep the greater part of the afternoon. This gave us a long play spell. But he was a terrible master for the remainder of the day. Notwithstanding these difficulties in the way of education we managed to learn a good deal. Sabbath-schools had not reached the efficiency they now have; but we children were taught carefully at home. We were obliged to commit to memory the Shorter Catechism, and every few months the good minister came around to see how well we could repeat it. All through my life this summary of Christian doctrine—not perfect indeed, and not to be quoted as authority equal to the Scriptures, as it sometimes is—has been to me of incalculable advantage. What I understood not then, I have come to understand better since, with the opening of the Word and the illumination of the Holy Spirit. If I were a boy again, I would learn the Shorter Catechism.

My ambition was to learn some kind of a trade. But I had wrought enough with my father at the anvil not to choose that. It was hard work, and not over clean work. Something else would suit me better, I thought. About that time my sister Harriet married William McLaughlin, who was a well-to-do harness maker in Steubenville. This suited my ideas of life better. But that sister died soon after her marriage, and my father removed from that part of the country to the southern part of the State. There in Ripley, a Latin school was opened about that time, and the Lord appeared to me in a wonderful manner, making discoveries of himself to my spiritual apprehension, so that from that time and onward my path lay in the line of preparation for such service as He should call me unto. My father, as he said many years afterward, had intended to educate my younger brother James; but he was taken away suddenly, and I came in his place. Thus the Lord opened the way for a commencement, and by the help of friends I was enabled to continue until I finished the course at Jefferson College, and afterward spent a year at the Western Theological Seminary at Allegheny.

MARY had been educated for a teacher. She was well fitted for the work. And while she was still at Ipswich, a benevolent gentleman in New York City, who had interested himself in establishing a seminary in Southern Indiana, sent to Miss Grant for a teacher to take charge of the school near Bethlehem, in the family of Rev. John M. Dickey. It was far away, but it seemed just the opening she had been desiring. But a young woman needed company in traveling so far westward. It was at the time of the May meetings in New York. Clergymen and others were on East from various parts of the West. In several instances, however, she failed of the company she hoped for, by what seemed singular providences. And at last, it was her lot to come West under the protection of Rev. Dyer Burgess, of West Union, Ohio. Mr. Burgess was what was called in those days, "a rabid abolitionist," and had taken a fancy to help me along, because, as he said, I was " of the same craft." And so it was that during his absence I was living in his family. This is the way in which the threads of our two lives, Mary's and mine, were brought together. A year and a half after this I was licensed to preach the gospel by the Chillicothe Presbytery, and we were on our way to her mountain home in Massachusetts.

Before starting to New England, the general plan of our life-work was arranged. Early in my course of education, I had considered the claims of the heathen upon us Christians, and upon myself personally as a believer in Christ; and with very little hesitation or delay, the decision had been reached, that, God willing, I would go somewhere among the unevangelized. And, during the years of my preparation, there never came to me a doubt of the rightness of my decision. Nay, more, at the end of forty years' work, I am abundantly satisfied with the way in which the Lord has led me. If China had been then open to the gospel, as it was twenty years afterward, I should have probably elected to go there.

But Dr. Thomas S. Williamson, of Ripley, Ohio, had started for the Dakota field the same year that I graduated from college. His representations of the needs of these aborigines, and the starting out of Whitman and Spalding with their wives to the Indians of the Pacific coast, attracted me to the westward. And Mary was quite willing, if not enthusiastic, to commence a life-work among the Indians of the Northwest, which at that time involved more of sacrifice than service in many a far-off foreign field. Hitherto, the evangelization of our own North American Indians had been, and still is, in most parts of the field, essentially a foreign mission work. It has differed little, except, perhaps, in the element of greater self-sacrifice, from the work in India, China or Japan. And so, with a mutual good understanding of the general plan of life's campaign, with very little appreciation of what its difficulties might be, but with a good faith in ourselves, and more faith in Him who has said, "Lo, I am with you all days," Mary left her school in Bethlehem, to which she had become a felt necessity, and I gathered up such credentials as were necessary to the consummation of our acceptance as missionaries of the American Board of Commissioners for Foreign Missions, and we went eastward.

Railroads had hardly been thought of in those days, and so what part of the way we were not carried by steamboats, we rode in stages. It was only the day before Thanksgiving, and a stormy evening it was, when we hired a very ordinary one-horse wagon to carry us and our baggage from Charlemont up to Hawley. I need not say that in the old house at home, the sister and the daughter and granddaughter found a warm reception, and I, the western stranger, was not long overlooked.

It was indeed a special Thanksgiving and time of family rejoicing, when the married sister and her family were gathered, with the brothers, Alfred and Moses and Thomas and Joseph, and the little sister Henrietta, and the parents and grandparents, then still living. Since that time, one by one, they have gone to the beautiful land above, and only two remain.

Well, the winter, with its terrible storms and deep snows, soon passed by. It was all too short for Mary's preparation. I found work waiting for me in preaching to the little church in West Hawley. They were a primitive people, with but little of what is called wealth, but with generous hearts; and the three months I spent with them were profitable to me.

On the 16th of February, 1837, there was a great gathering in the old meeting-house on the hill; and after the service was over, Mary and I received the congratulations of hosts of friends. Soon after this the time of our departure came. The snow drifts were still deep on the hills, when, in the first days of March, we commenced our hegira to the far West. It was a long and toilsome journey—all the way to New York City by stage, and then again from Philadelphia across the mountains to Pittsburgh in the same manner, through the March rains and mud, we traveled on, day and night. It was quite a relief to sleep and glide down the beautiful Ohio on a steamer. And there we found friends in Portsmouth and Ripley and West Union, with whom we rested, and by whom we were refreshed, and who greatly forwarded our preparations for life among the Indians.

Of the journey Mary wrote under date, City of Penn, March 3, 1837: "We were surprised to find sleighing here, when there was little at Hartford and none at New

Haven and New York. We expect to spend the Sabbath here; and may the Lord bless the detention to ourselves and others. Oh for a heart more engaged to labor by the way—to labor *any* and *everywhere.*"

In West Union, Ohio, she writes from Anti-Slavery Palace, April 5: "Brother Joseph Riggs made us some valuable presents. His kindness supplied my lack of a good English merino, and Sister Riggs had prepared her donation and laid it by, as the Apostle directs,—one pair of warm blankets, sheets and pillow cases. My new nieces also seemed to partake of the same kind spirit, and gave us valuable mementoes of their affection.

"We found Mrs. Burgess not behind, and perhaps before most of our friends, in her plans and gifts. Besides a cooking stove and furniture, she has provided a fine blanket and comforter, sheets, pillow cases, towels, dried peaches, etc. Perhaps you will fear that with so many kind friends we shall be furnished with too many comforts. Pray, then, that we may be kept very humble and receive these blessings thankfully from the Giver of every good and perfect gift."

Mrs. Isabella Burgess, the wife of my friend Rev. Dyer Burgess, we put into lasting remembrance by the name we gave to our first daughter, who is now living by the great wall of China. By and by we found ourselves furnished with such things as we supposed we should need for a year to come, and we bade adieu to our Ohio friends, and embarked at Cincinnati for St. Louis.

"Steamer Isabella, Thursday Eve, May 4.

"We have been highly favored thus far on our way down the Ohio. We took a last look of Indiana about noon, and saw the waters of the separating Wabash join those of the Ohio, and yet flow on without commingling for ten or twelve miles, marking their course by their blue tint and purer shade. The banks are much lower here than nearer the source, sometimes gently sloping to the water's edge, and bearing such marks of inundation as trunks and roots of trees half imbedded in the sand, or cast higher upon the shore. At intervals we passed some beautiful bluffs, not very high, but very verdant, and others more precipitous. Bold, craggy rocks with evergreen tufted tops, and a few dwarf stragglers on their sides. One of them contained a cave apparently dark enough for deeds of darkest hue, and probably it may have witnessed many perpetrated by those daring bandits that prowled about these bluffs during the early settlement of Illinois.

"Friday Eve.—This morning when we awoke, we found ourselves in the muddy waters of the broad Mississippi. They are quite as muddy as those of a shallow pond after a severe shower. We drink it, however, and find the taste not quite as unpleasant as one might suppose from its color, though quite warm. The river is very wide here, and beautifully spotted with large islands. Their sandy points, the muddy waters, and abounding snags render navigation more dangerous than on the Ohio. We have met with no accident yet, and I am unconscious of fear. I desire to trust in Him who rules the water as well as the lands."

"St. Louis, May 8, 1837.

"Had you been with us this morning you would have sympathized with us in our supposed detention from our distant unfound home in the wilderness, when we heard that the Fur Company's boat left for Fort Snelling last week. You can imagine our feelings, our doubts, our hopes, our fears rushing to our hearts, but soon quieted with the conviction that the Lord would guide us in his own time to the field where he would have us labor. We feel that we have done all in our power to hasten on our journey and to gain information in reference to the time of leaving this city. Having endeavored to do this, we have desired to leave the event with God, and he will still direct. We now have some ground for hope that another boat will ascend the river in a week or two, and if so, we shall avail ourselves of the opportunity. Till we learn something more definitely in regard to it, we shall remain at Alton, if we are prospered in reaching there."

In those days the Upper Mississippi was still a wild and almost uninhabited region. Such places as Davenport and Rock Island, which now together form a large center of population, had then, all told, only about a dozen houses. The lead mines of Galena and Dubuque had gathered in somewhat larger settlements. Above them there was nothing but Indians and military. So that a steamer starting for Fort Snelling was a rare thing. It was said that less than half a dozen in a season reached that point. Indeed, there was nothing to carry up but goods for the Indian trade and army supplies. Some friends at Alton invited us to come and spend the intervening time. There we were kindly entertained in the family of Mr. Winthrop S. Gilman, who has since been one of the substantial Christian business men in New York City. On our leaving, Mr. Gilman bade us "Look Upward," which has ever been one of our Life Mottoes.

At that time, a steamer from St. Louis required at least two full weeks to reach Fort Snelling. It was an object with us not to travel on the Sabbath, if possible. So we planned to go up beforehand, and take the up-river boat at the highest point. It might be, we thought, that the Lord would arrange things for us so that we should reach our mission field without traveling on the Day of Rest. With this desire we embarked for Galena. But Saturday night found us passing along by the beautiful country of Rock Island and Davenport. In the latter place Mary and I spent a Sabbath, and worshiped with a few of the pioneer people who gathered in a school-house. By the middle of the next week we had reached the city of lead. There we found the man who had said to the Home Missionary Society, "If you have a place so difficult that no one wants to go to it, send me there." And they sent the veteran, Rev. Aratus Kent, to Galena, Illinois.

Some of the scenes and events connected with our ascent of the Mississippi are graphically described by Mary's facile pen:

"STEAMBOAT OLIVE BRANCH, May 17.

"We are now on our way to Galena, where we shall probably take a boat for St. Peters. We pursue this course, though it subjects us to the inconvenience of changing boats, that we may be able to avoid Sabbath traveling, *if possible.* One Sabbath at least will be rescued in this way, as the *Pavillion*, the only boat for St. Peters at present, leaves St. Louis on Sunday! This we felt would not be right for us, consequently we left Alton to-day, trusting that the Lord of the Sabbath would speed us on our journey of 3,000 miles, and enable us to keep his Sabbath holy unto the end thereof.

"Of the scenery we have passed this afternoon, and are still passing, I can give you no just conceptions. It beggars description, and yet I wish you could imagine the Illinois shore lined with high semi-circular rocks, embosomed by trees of most delicate green, and crowned with a grassy mound of the same tint, or rising more perpendicularly and towering more loftily in solid columns, defying art to form or demolish works so impregnable, and at the same time so grand and beautiful. I have just been gazing at these everlasting rocks mellowed by the soft twilight. A bend in the river and an island made them apparently meet the opposite shore. The departing light of day favored the illusion of a splendid city reaching for miles along the river, built of granite and marble, and shaded by luxurant groves, all reflected in the quiet waters. This river bears very little resemblance to itself (as Geographies name it,) after its junction with the Missouri. To me it seems a misnomer to name a river from a branch which is so dissimilar. The waters here are comparatively pure and the current mild. Below, they are turbid and impetuous, rolling on in their power, and sweeping all in their pathway onward at the rate of five or six miles an hour.

"Just below the junction we were astonished and amused to see large spots of muddy water surrounded by those of a purer shade, as if they would retain their distinctive character to the last; but in vain, for the lesser was contaminated and swallowed up by the greater. I might moralize on this, but will leave each one to draw his own inferences."

"STEPHENSON (now Davenport), May 22.

"We left the *Olive Branch* between 10 and 11 on Saturday night. The lateness of the hour obliged us to accept of such accommodations as presented themselves first, and even made us thankful for them, though they were the most wretched I ever endured. I do not allude to the house or table, though little or nothing could be said in their praise, but to the horrid profanity. Connected with the house and adjoining our room was a grocery, a devil's den indeed, and so often were the frequent volleys of dreadful oaths, that our hearts grew sick, and we shuddered and sought to shut our ears. Notwithstanding all this, we were happier than if we had been traveling on God's holy day. Our consciences approved resting according to the commandment, though they did not chide for removing, even on the Sabbath, to a house where God's name is not used so irreverently—so profanely."

"GALENA, May 23.

"This place, wild and hilly as it is, we reached this afternoon, and have been very kindly received by some Yankee Christian friends, where we feel ourselves quite at home, though only inmates of this hospitable mansion a few hours. Surely the Lord has blessed us above measure in providing warm Christian hearts to receive us. Mr. and Mrs. Fuller, where we are, supply the place of the Gilmans of Alton. We hope to leave in a day or two for Fort Snelling."

"GALENA, ILL., May 25, 1837.

"A kind Providence has so ordered our affairs that we are detained here still, and I hope our stay may promote the best interests of the mission. It seems desirable that Christians in these villages of the Upper Mississippi should become interested in the missionaries and the missions among the northern Indians, that their prejudices may be overcome and their hearts made to feel the claims those dark tribes have upon their sympathies, their charities and their prayers."

"STEAMER PAVILLION—UPPER MISSISSIPPI, May 31.

"We are this evening (Wednesday) more than 100 miles above Prairie du Chien, on our way to St. Peters, which we hope to reach before the close of the week, that we may be able to keep the Sabbath on shore. You will rejoice with us that we have been able, in all our journey of 3,000 miles, to rest from traveling on the Sabbath. Last Saturday, however, our principles and feelings were tried by this boat, for which we had waited three weeks, and watched anxiously for the last few days, fearing it would subject us to Sabbath traveling. Saturday eve, after sunset, when our wishes had led us to believe it would not leave, if it should reach Galena until Monday, we heard a boat, and soon our sight confirmed our ears. Mr. Riggs hastened on board and ascertained from the captain that he should leave Sabbath morning. The inquiry was, shall we break one command in fulfilling another? We soon decided that it was not our duty to commence a journey under these circumstances even, and retired to rest, confident the Lord would provide for us. Notwithstanding our prospects were rather dark, I felt a secret hope that the Lord would detain the *Pavillion* until Monday. If I had any faith it was very weak, for I felt deeply conscious we were entirely undeserving such a favor. But judge of our happy surprise, morning and afternoon, on our way to and from church, to find the *Pavillion* still at the wharf. We felt that it was truly a gracious providence. On Monday morning we came on board."

This week on the Upper Mississippi was one of quiet joy. We had been nearly three months on our way from Mary's home in Massachusetts. God had prospered us all the way. Wherever we had stopped we had found or made friends. The Lord, as we believed, had signally interfered in our behalf, and helped us to "Remember the Sabbath day," and to give our testimony to its sacred observance. The season of the year was inspiring. A resurrection to new life had just taken place. All external nature had put on her beautiful garments. And day after day,—for the boat tied up at night,—we found ourselves passing by those grand old hills and wonderful escarpments of the Upper Mississippi. We were in the wilds of the West, beyond the cabins of the pioneer. We were passing the battle fields of Indian story. Nay, more, we were already in the land of the Dakotas, and passing by the *teepees* and the villages of the Red man, for whose enlightenment and elevation we had left friends and home. Was it strange that this was a week of intense enjoyment, of education, of growth in the life of faith and hope? And so, as I said in the beginning, on the first day of June, 1837, Mary and I reached, in safety, the mouth of the Minnesota, in the land of the Dakotas.

CHAPTER II.

1837.—First Knowledge of the Sioux.—Hennepin and Du Luth.—Fort Snelling.—Lakes Harriet and Calhoun.—Three Months at Lake Harriet.—Samuel W. Pond.—Learning the Language.—Mr. Stevens.—Temporary Home.—That Station Soon Broken Up.—Mary's Letters.—The Mission and People. Native Customs.—Lord's Supper.—" Good Voice."—Description of our Home.—The Garrison.—Seeing St. Anthony.—Ascent of the Saint Peters.—Mary's Letters.—Traverse des Sioux —Prairie Traveling.—Reaching Lac-qui-parle. —T. S. Williamson.—A Sabbath Service.—Our Upper Room.—Experiences.—Church at Lac-qui-parle.—Mr. Pond's Marriage.—Mary's Letters.—Feast.

About two hundred and forty years ago, the French voyagers and fur traders, as they came from Nouvelle, France, up the Saint Lawrence and the Great Lakes, began to hear, from Indians farther east, of a great and warlike people, whom they called NADOUWE or NADOWAESSI, *enemies*. Coming nearer to them, both trader and priest met, at the head of Lake Superior representatives of this nation, "numerous and fierce, always at war with other tribes, pushing northward and southward and westward," so that they were sometimes called the "Iroquois of the West."

But really not much was known of the Sioux until the summer of 1680, when Hennepin and Du Luth met in a camp of Dakotas, as they hunted buffalo in what is now northwestern Wisconsin. Hennepin had been captured by a war-party, which descended the Father of waters in their canoes, seeking for scalps among their enemies, the Miamis and Illinois. They took him and his companions of the voyage up to their villages on the head waters of Rum River, and around the shores of Mille Lac and Knife Lake. From the former of these the eastern band of the Sioux nation named themselves Mdaywakantonwan, *Spirit Lake Villagers;* and from the latter, they inherited the name of Santees (Isanyati), *Dwellers on Knife.*

These two representative Frenchmen, thus brought together, at so early a day, in the wilds of the West, visited the home of the Sioux, as above indicated, and to them we are indebted for much of what we know of the Dakotas two centuries ago.

The Ojibwas and Hurons were then occupying the southern shores of Lake Superior, and, coming first into communication with the white race, they were first supplied with fire arms, which gave them such an advantage over the more-warlike Sioux, that, in the next hundred years, we find the Ojibwas in possession of all the country on the head waters of the Mississippi, while the Dakotas had migrated southward and westward.

The general enlistment of the Sioux, and indeed of all these tribes of the northwest, on the side of the British in the war of 1812, showed the necessity of a strong military garrison in the heart of the Indian country. Hence the building of Fort Snelling nearly sixty years ago. At the confluence of the Minnesota with the Mississippi, and on the high point between the two, it has an admirable outlook. So it seemed to us as we approached it on that first day of June, 1837. On our landing we became the guests of Lieut. Ogden and his excellent wife, who was the daughter of Major Loomis. To us, Mary and me, every thing was new and strange. We knew nothing of military life. But our sojourn of a few days was made pleasant and profitable by the Christian sympathy which met us there—the evidence of the Spirit's presence, which, two years before, had culminated in the organization of a Christian church in the garrison, on the arrival of the first missionaries to the Dakotas.

The FALLS OF SAINT ANTHONY and the beautiful MINNEHAHA have now become historic, and MINNETONKA has become a place of summer resort. But forty years ago it was only now and then that the eyes of a white man, and still more rarely the eyes of a white woman, looked upon the Falls of Curling Water; and scarcely any one knew that the water in Little Falls Creek came from Minnetonka Lake. But nearer by were the beautiful lakes, CALHOUN and HARRIET. On the first of these was the Dakota Village, of which *Cloudman* and *Drifter* were then the chiefs; and on whose banks the brothers Pond had erected the first white man's cabin; and on the north bank of the latter was a mission station of the American Board, commenced two years before by Rev. Jedediah D. Stevens.

Here Mary and I were to make a home for the next three months. It was a delightful spot, and we very much enjoyed the commencement of our missionary life. There we were in daily contact with the Dakota men, women and children. There we began to listen to the strange sounds of the Dakota tongue; and there we made our first laughable efforts in speaking the language.

We were fortunate in meeting there Rev. Samuel W. Pond, the older of the brothers, who had come out from Connecticut three years previous, and, in advance of all others, had erected their missionary cabin on the margin of Lake Calhoun. Mr. Pond's knowledge of Dakota was quite a help to us who were just commencing to learn it. Before we left the States, it had been impressed upon us by Secretary David Greene, that whether we were successful missionaries or not depended much on our acquiring a free use of the Language. And the teaching of my own experience and observation is, that if one fails to make a pretty good start the first year, in its acquisition, it will be a rare thing if he ever masters the language. And so, obedient to our instructions, we made it our first work to get our ears opened to the strange sounds, and our tongues made cunning for their utterance. Often times we laughed at our own blunders, as when I told Mary, one day, that *pish* was the Dakota for *fish*. A Dakota boy was trying to speak the English word. Mr. Stevens had gathered, from various sources, a vocabulary of five or six hundred words. This formed the commencement of the growth of the Dakota Grammar and Dictionary which I published fifteen years afterward.

Mr. and Mrs. Stevens were from Central New York, and were engaged as early as 1827, in missionary labors on the Island of Mackinaw. In 1829, Mr. Stevens and Rev. Mr. Coe made a tour of exploration through the wilds of Northern Wisconsin, coming as far as Fort Snelling. For several years thereafter, Mr. Stevens was connected with the Stockbridge mission on Fox Lake; and, in the summer of 1835, he had commenced this station at Lake Harriet. At the time of our arrival he had made things look quite civilized. He had built two houses of tamarack logs, the larger of which his own family occupied; the lower part of the other was used for the school and religious meetings. Half a dozen boarding scholars, chiefly half-breed girls, formed the nucleus of the school, which was taught by his niece, Miss Lucy C. Stevens, who was afterward married to Rev. Daniel Gavan, of the Swiss mission to the Dakotas.

As the mission family was already quite large enough for comfort, Mary and I, not wishing to add to any one's burdens, undertook to make ourselves comfortable in a part of the school-building. Our stay there was to be only temporary, and hence it was only needful that we take care of ourselves, and give such occasional help in the way of English preaching and otherwise as we could. The Dakotas did not yet care to hear the gospel. The Messrs. Pond had succeeded in teaching one young man to read and write, and occasionally a few could be induced to come and listen to the good news. It was seed-sowing time. Many seeds fell by the wayside, or on the hard path of sin. Most fell among thorns. But some found good ground, and lying dormant a full quarter of a century, then sprang up and fruited in the prison at Mankato. Also of the girls in that first Dakota boarding-school, quite a good proportion became Christian women and the mothers of Christian families.

But the mission at Lake Harriet was not to continue long. In less than two years from the time we were there, two Ojibwa young men avenged the killing of their father by waylaying and killing a prominent man of the Lake Calhoun Village. A thousand Ojibwas had just left Fort Snelling to return to their homes by way of Lake St. Croix and the Rum River. Both parties were followed by the Sioux, and terrible slaughter ensued. But the result of their splendid victory was, that the Lake Calhoun people were afraid to live there any longer, and so they abandoned their village and plantings and settled on the banks of the Minnesota.

During our three-months' stay at Lake Harriet, everything we saw and heard was fresh and interesting, and Mary could not help telling of them to her friends in Hawley. The grandfather was ninety years old, to whom she thus wrote:

"LAKE HARRIET, June 22, 1837.

"We are now on missionary ground, and are surrounded by those dark people of whom we often talked at your fireside last winter. I doubt not you will still think and talk about them, and pray for them also. And surely your grandchildren will not be forgotten.

"We reached this station two weeks since, after enjoying Lieut. Ogden's hospitality a few days, and were kindly welcomed by Mr. Stevens' family, with whom we remain until a house, now occupied by the school, can be prepared, that we can live in a part. Then we shall feel still more at home, though I hope our rude habitation will remind us that we are pilgrims on our way to a house not made with hands, eternal in the heavens.

"The situation of the mission houses is very beautiful—on a little eminence, just upon the shore of a lovely lake skirted with trees. About a mile north of us is Lake Calhoun, on the margin of which is an Indian village of about twenty lodges. Most of these are bark houses, some of which are twenty feet square, and others are tents of skin or cloth. Several days since I walked over to the village and called at the house of one of the chiefs. He was not at home, but his daughters smiled very good naturedly upon us. We seated ourselves on all the bed, sofa and chairs they had, which was a frame extending on three sides of the house, and covered with skins.

"Since our visit at the village, two old chiefs have called upon us. One said this was a very bad country—

ours was a good country—we had left a good country, and come to live in his bad country, and he was glad. The other called on Sabbath evening, when Mr. Riggs was at the Fort, where he preaches occasionally. He inquired politely how I liked the country, and said it was bad. What could a courtier have said more?

"The Indians come here at all hours of the day without ceremony, sometimes dressed and painted very fantastically, and again with scarcely any clothing. One came in yesterday dressed in a coat, calico shirt and cloth leggins, the only one I have seen with a coat, excepting two boys who were in the family when we came. The most singular ornament I have seen was a large striped snake fastened among the painted hair, feathers, and ribbons of an Indian's head-dress, in such a manner that it could coil round in front and dart out its snake head, or creep down upon the back at pleasure. During this the Indian sat perfectly at ease, apparently much pleased at the astonishment and fear manifested by some of the family."

"June 26.

"Yesterday Mr. Riggs and myself commemorated a Savior's love, for the first time on missionary ground. The season was one of precious interest, sitting down at Jesus' table with a little band of brothers and sisters, one of whom was a Chippewa convert who accompanied Mr. Ayer from Pokeguma. One of the Methodist missionaries, Mr. King, with a colored man, and the members of the church from the Fort and the mission, completed our band of *fifteen*. Two of these were received on this occasion. Several Sioux were present and gazed on the strange scene before them. A medicine man, *Howashta* by name, was present with a long pole in his hand, having his head decked with a stuffed bird of brilliant plumage, and the tail of another of dark brown. His name means "Good Voice," and he is building him a log house not far from the mission. If *he* could be brought into the fold of the Kind Shepherd, and become a humble and devoted follower of Jesus, he might be instrumental of great good to his people. He might indeed be a *Good Voice* bringing glad tidings to their dark souls."

TO HER MOTHER.

"HOME, July 8, 1837.

"Would that you could look in upon us; but as you cannot, I will try and give you some idea of our *home*. The building fronts the lake, but our part opens upon the woodland back of its western shore. The lower room has a small cooking-stove, given us by Mrs. Burgess, a few chairs and a small table, a box and barrel containing dishes, etc., a small will-be pantry when completed, under the stairs, filled with flour, corn meal, beans and stove furniture. Our chamber is low and nearly filled by a bed, a small bureau and stand, a table for writing made of a box, and the rest of our half-dozen chairs and one rocking chair, cushioned by my mother's kind forethought.

"The rough, loose boards in the chamber are covered with a coarse and cheap hair-and-tow carpeting, to save labor. The floor below will require some cleaning, but I shall not try to keep it white. I have succeeded very well, according to my judgment, in household affairs— that is, very well for me.

"Some Indian women came in yesterday bringing strawberries, which I purchased with beans. Poor creatures, they have very little food of any kind at this season of the year, and we feel it difficult to know how much it is our duty to give them.

"We are not troubled with all the insects which used to annoy me in Indiana, but the musquitoes are far more abundant. At dark, swarms fill our room, deafen our ears, and irritate our skin. For the last two evenings we have filled our house with smoke, almost to suffocation, to disperse these our officious visitors."

"July 31.

"Until my location here, I was not aware that it was so exceedingly common for officers im the army to have two wives or more,—but one of course legally so. For instance, at the Fort, before the removal of the last troops, there were but two officers who were not known to have an Indian woman, if not half-Indian children. You remember I used to cherish some partiality for the military, but I must confess the last vestige of it has departed. I am not now thinking of its connection with the Peace question, but with that of moral reform. Once in my childhood's simplicity, I regarded the army and its discipline as a school for gentlemanly manners, but now it seems a sink of iniquity, a school of vice."

With the month of September came the time of our departure for Lac-qui-parle. But Mary had not yet seen the Falls of Saint Anthony. And so, we harnessed up a horse and cart, and had a pleasant ride across the prairie to the government saw-mill, which, with a small dwelling for the soldier occupant, was then the only sign of civilization on the present site of Minneapolis. Then we had our household goods packed up and put on board Mr. Prescott's Mackinaw boat to be carried up to Traverse des Sioux. Mr. Prescott was a white man with a Dakota wife, and had been for years engaged in the fur trade. He had on board his winter outfit. Mary and I took passage with him and his family, and spent a week of new life on what was then called the Saint Peter's River. The days were very enjoyable, and the nights were quite comfortable, for we had all the advantages of Mr. Prescott's tent, and conveniences for camp life. His propelling force was the muscles of five Frenchmen, who worked the oars and the poles, sometimes paddling and sometimes pushing, and often, in the upper part of the voyage, wading to find the best channel over a sand bar. But they enjoyed their work and sang songs by the way.

FROM MARY'S LETTERS.

"Sept. 2, 1837.

"Dr. Williamson arrived at Lake Harriet after a six days' journey from home, and assured us of their kindest wishes, and their willingness to furnish us with corn and potatoes, and a room in their house. We have just breakfasted on board our Mackinaw, and so far on our way have had cause for thankfulness that God so overruled events, even though some attendant circumstances were unpleasant. It is also a great source of comfort that we have so good accommodations and Sabbath-keeping company. You recollect my mentioning the marriage of Mr. and Mrs. Prescott, and of his uniting with the church at Lake Harriet, in the summer.

"Perhaps you may feel some curiosity respecting our appearance and that of our barge. Fancy a large boat of forty feet in length, and perhaps eight in width in the middle, capable of carrying five tons, and manned by five men, four at the oars and a steersman at the stern. Near the center are our sleeping accommodations nicely rolled up, on which we sit, and breakfast and dine on bread, cold ham, wild fowl, etc. We have tea and coffee for breakfast and supper. Mrs. Prescott does not pitch and strike the tent, as the Indian women usually do; but it is because the boatmen can do it, and her husband does not require as much of her as an Indian man. They accommodate us in their tent, which is similar to a soldier's tent, just large enough for two beds. Here we take our supper, sitting on or by the matting made by some of these western Indians, and then, after worship, lie down to rest."

"Monday, Sept. 4.

"Again we are on our way up the crooked Saint Peter's, having passed the Sabbath in our tent in the wilderness, far more pleasantly than the Sabbath we spent in St. Louis. Last Saturday I became quite fatigued sympathizing with those who drew the boat on the Rapids, and following my Indian guide, Mrs. Prescott, through the woods, to take it after ascending them. The fall I should think two feet, at this stage of water, and nearly perpendicular, excepting a very narrow channel, where it was oblique. The boat being lightened, all the men attempted to force it up this channel, some by the rope attached to the boat, and others by pulling and pushing it as they stood by it on the rocks and in the water. Both the first and second attempts were fruitless. The second time the rope was lengthened and slipped round a tree on the high bank, where the trader's wife and I were standing. Her husband called her to hold the end of the rope, and, as I could not stand idle, though I knew I could do no good, I joined her, watching the slowly ascending boat with the deepest interest. A moment more and the toil would have been over, when the rope snapped, and the boat slid back in a twinkling. It was further lightened and the rope doubled, and then it was drawn safely up and re-packed, in about two hours and a half from the time we reached the Rapids."

"Tuesday, Sept. 5.

"In good health and spirits, we are again on our way. As the river is shallow and the bottom hard, poles have been substituted for oars; boards placed along the boat's sides serve for a footpath for the boatmen, who propel the boat by fixing the pole into the earth at the prow and pushing until they reach the stern.

At Traverse des Sioux our land journey, of one hundred and twenty-five miles to Lac-qui-parle, commenced. Here we made the acquaintance of a somewhat remarkable French Trader, by name Louis Provencalle, but commonly called Le Bland. The Indians called him Skadan, *Little White.* He was an old voyager, who could neither read nor write, but, by a certain force of character, he had risen to the honorable position of trader. He kept his accounts with his Indian creditors by a system of hieroglyphics.

For the next week we were under the convoy of Dr. Thomas S. Williamson and Mr. Gideon H. Pond, who met us with teams from Lac-qui-parle. The first night of our camping on the prairie, Dr. Williamson taught me a lesson which I never forgot. We were preparing the tent for the night, and I was disposed to let the roughness of the surface remain, and not even gather grass for a bed, which the Indians do; on the ground, as I said, that it was for *only one night.* "But," said the doctor, "there will be a *great many one nights.*" And so I have found it. It is best to make the tent comfortable for ONE NIGHT.

This was our first introduction—Mary's and mine—to the broad prairies of the West. At first, we kept in sight of the woods of the Minnesota, and our road lay among and through little groves of timber. But by and by we emerged into the broad savannahs—thousands of acres of meadow unmowed, and broad rolling country covered, at this time of year, with yellow and blue flowers. Every thing was full of interest to us, even the Bad Swamp—Wewe Shecha—which so bent and shook under the tramp of our teams, that we could almost believe it would break through and let us into the earth's center. For years after, this was the great *fear* of our prairie traveling, always reminding us very forcibly of Bunyan's description of the "Slough of Despond." The only accident of this journey was the breaking of the axle of one of Mr. Pond's loaded carts. It was Saturday afternoon. Mr. Pond and Dr. Williamson remained to make a new one, and Mary and I went on to the stream where we were to camp, and made ready for the Sabbath.

"ON THE BROAD PRAIRIE OF 'THE FAR WEST.'
"Saturday Eve., Sept. 9, 1837.
"*My Ever Dear Mother:*

Just at twilight I seat myself upon the ground by our fire, with the wide heavens above for a canopy, to commune with her whose yearning heart follows her children wherever they roam. This is the second day we have traveled on this prairie, having left Traverse des Sioux late Thursday afternoon. Before leaving that place, a little half-Indian girl, daughter of the trader where we stopped, brought me nearly a dozen of eggs (the first I had seen since leaving the States), which afforded us a choice morsel for the next day. To-morrow we rest, it being the Sabbath, and may we and you be in the Spirit on the Lord's day.

"LAC-QUI-PARLE, Sept. 18.

"The date will tell you of our arrival at this station where we have found a *home*. We reached this place on

Wednesday last, having been thirteen days from Fort Snelling, a shorter time than is usually required for such a journey, the Lord's hand being over us to guide and prosper us on our way. Two Sabbaths we rested from our travels, and the last of them was peculiarly refreshing to body and spirit. Having risen and put our tent in order, we engaged in family worship, and afterward partook of our frugal meal. Then all was still in that wide wilderness, save at intervals, when some bird of passage told us of its flight and bade our wintry clime farewell.

"Before noon we had a season of social worship, lifting up our hearts with one voice in prayer and praise, and reading a portion of God's word. It was indeed pleasant to think that God was present with us, far away as we were from any human being but ourselves. The day passed peacefully away, and night's refreshing slumbers succeeded. The next morning we were on our way before the sun began his race, and having rode fifteen or sixteen miles, according to our best calculations, we stopped for breakfast and dinner at a lake where wood and water could both be obtained, two essentials which frequently are not found together on the prairie.

"Thus, you will be able to imagine us with our two one-ox carts and a double wagon, all heavily laden, as we have traveled across the prairie."

THOMAS SMITH WILLIAMSON had been ten years a practicing physician in Ripley, Ohio. There he had married MARGARET POAGE, of one of the first families. One after another their children had died. Perhaps that led them to think that God had a work for them to do elsewhere. At any rate, after spending a year in the Lane Theological Seminary, the doctor turned his thoughts toward the Sioux, for whom no man seemed to care. In the spring of 1834, he made a visit up to Fort Snelling. And in the year following, as has already been noted, he came as a missionary of the A. B. C. F. M., with his wife and one child, accompanied by MISS SARAH POAGE, Mrs. Williamson's sister, and MR. ALEXANDER G. HUGGINS and his wife, with two children.

This company reached Fort Snelling a week or two in advance of Mr. Stevens, and were making preparations to build at Lake Calhoun; but Mr. Stevens claimed the right of selection, on the ground that he had been there in 1829. And so Dr. Williamson and his party accepted the invitation of Mr. Joseph Renville, the Bois Brule trader at Lac-qui-parle, to go two hundred miles into the interior. All this was of the Lord, as it plainly appeared in after years. At the time we approached the mission at Lac-qui-parle, they had been two full years in the field, and, under favorable auspices, had made a very good beginning. About the middle of September, after a pretty good week of prairie travel, we were very glad to receive the greetings of the mission families.

A few days after our arrival, Mary wrote: "The evening we came, we were shown *a little chamber*, where we spread our bed and took up our abode. On Friday, Mr. Riggs made a bedstead, by boring holes and driving slabs into the logs, across which boards are laid. This answers the purpose very well, though rather uneven. Yesterday was the Sabbath, and such a Sabbath as I never before enjoyed. Although the day was cold and stormy, and much like November, twenty-five Indians and part-bloods assembled at eleven o'clock in our school-room for public worship. Excepting a prayer, all the exercises were in Dakota and French, and most of them in the former language. Could you have seen these Indians kneel with stillness and order, during prayer, and rise and engage in singing hymns in their own tongue, led by one of their own tribe, I am sure your heart would have been touched. The hymns were composed by Mr. Renville the trader, who is probably three-fourths Sioux."

Doctor Williamson had erected a log house a story and a half high. In the lower part was his own living room, and also a room with a large open fireplace, which then, and for several years afterward, was used for the school and Sabbath assemblies. In the upper part, there were three rooms, still in an unfinished state. The largest of these, ten feet wide and eighteen feet long, was appropriated to our use. We fixed it up with loose boards overhead, and quilts nailed up to the rafters, and improvised a bedstead, as we had been unable to bring ours farther than Fort Snelling.

That room we made our home for five winters. There were some hardships about such close quarters, but, all in all, Mary and I never enjoyed five winters better than those spent in that upper room. There our first three children were born. There we worked in acquiring the language. There we received our Dakota visitors. There I wrote and wrote again my ever growing dictionary. And then, with what help I could obtain, I prepared for the printer the greater part of the New Testament in the language of the Dakotas. It was a consecrated room.

Well, we had set up our cooking-stove in our upper room, but the furniture was a hundred and twenty-five miles away. It was not easy for Mary to cook with nothing to cook in. But the good women of the mission came to her relief with kettle and pan. More than this, there were some things to be done now which neither Mary nor I had learned to do. She was not an adept at making light bread, and neither of us could milk a cow. She grew up in New England, where the men alone did the milking, and I in Ohio, where the women alone milked in those days. At first it took us both to milk a cow, and it was poorly done. But Mary succeeded best. Nevertheless, application and perseverance succeeded, and, although never boasting of any special ability in that line of things, I could do my own milking, and Mary became very skillful in bread-making, as well as in other mysteries of housekeeping.

The missionary work began now to open before us. The village at Lac-qui-parle consisted of about 400 persons, chiefly of the Wahpaton, or Leaf-village band of the Dakotas. They were very poor and very proud. Mr. Renville, as a half-breed and fur trader, had acquired an unbounded influence over many of them. They were willing to follow his leading. And so the young men of his soldier's lodge were the first, after his own family, to learn to read. On the Sabbath, there gathered into this lower room twenty or thirty men and women, but mostly women, to hear the Word as prepared by Dr. Williamson with Mr. Renville's aid. A few Dakota hymns had been made, and were sung under the leadership of Mr. Huggins or young Mr. Joseph Renville. Mr. Renville and Mr. Pond made the prayers in Dakota. Early in the year 1836, a church had been organized, which, at this time, contained seven native members, chiefly from Mr. Renville's household. And in the winter which followed our arrival, nine were added, making a native church of sixteen, of which one half were full-blood Dakota women, and in the others the Dakota blood greatly predominated.

One of the noted things that took place in those autumn days, was the marriage of MR. GIDEON HOLISTER

Pond and Miss Sarah Poage. That was the first couple I married, and I look back to it with great satisfaction. The bond has been long since sundered by death, but it was a true covenant entered into by true hearts, and receiving, from the first, the blessing of the Master. Mr Pond made a great feast, and "called the poor, and the maimed, and the halt and the blind," and many such Dakotas were there to be called. *They* could not recompense him by inviting him again, and it yet remains that "he shall be recompensed at the resurrection of the just."

"Nov. 2.

"Yesterday the marriage referred to was solemnized. Could I paint the assembly, you would agree with me that it was deeply and singularly interesting. Fancy, for a moment, the audience who were witnesses of the scene. The rest of our missionary band sat near those of our number who were about to enter into the new and sacred relationship, while most of the room was filled with our dark-faced guests, a blanket or a buffalo robe their chief "wedding garment," and coarse and tawdry beads, brooches, paint and feathers, their wedding ornaments. Here and there sat a Frenchman or half-breed, whose garb bespoke their different origin. No turkey or eagle feathers adorned the hair, or party-colored paint the face, though even *their* appearance and attire reminded us of our location in this wilderness.

"Mr. Riggs performed the marriage ceremony, and Dr. Williamson made the concluding prayer, and, through Mr. Renville, briefly explained to the Dakotas the ordinance and its institution. After the ceremony, Mr. Renville and family partook with us of our frugal meal, leaving the Indians to enjoy their feast of potatoes, turnips and bacon, to which the poor, the lame and the blind had been invited. As they were not aware of the supper that was provided, they did not bring their dishes, as is the Indian custom, so that they were scantily furnished with milk pans, etc. This deficiency they supplied very readily by emptying the first course, which was potatoes, into their blankets, and passing their dishes for a supply of turnips and bacon.

"I know not when I have seen a group so novel, as I found on repairing to the room where these poor creatures were promiscuously seated. On my left sat an old man nearly blind; before me, the woman who dipped out the potatoes from a five-pail boiler, sat on the floor; and near her was an old man dividing the bacon, clenching it firmly in his hand, and looking up occasionally to see how many there were requiring a share. In the corner sat a lame man eagerly devouring his potatoes, and around were scattered women and children.

"When the last ladle was filled from the large pot of turnips, one by one they hastily departed, borrowing dishes to carry home the supper, to divide with the children who had remained in charge of the tents."

CHAPTER III.

1837–1839.—The Language.—Its Growth.—System of Notation.—After Changes.—What we Had to Put into the Language.—Teaching English, and Teaching Dakota.—Mary's Letter.—Fort Renville.—Translating the Bible.—The Gospels of Mark and John.—"Good Bird" Born.—Dakota Names.—The Lessons we Learned.—Dakota Washing.—Extracts from Letters.—Dakota Tents.—A Marriage.—Visiting the Village.—Girls, Boys and Dogs.—G. H. Pond's Indian Hunt.—Three Families Killed.—The Village Wail.—The Power of a Name.—Post-Office Far Away.—The Coming of the Mail.—S. W. Pond Comes Up.—My Visit to Snelling.—Lost My Horse.—Dr. Williamson Goes to Ohio.—The Spirit's Presence.—Prayer.—Mary's Reports.

To learn an unwritten language, and to reduce it to a form that can be seen as well as heard, is confessedly a work of no small magnitude. Hitherto it has seemed to exist only in sound. But it has been, all through the past ages, worked out and up by the forges of human hearts. It has been made to express the lightest thoughts as well as the heart throbs of men and women and children in their generations. The human mind, in its most untutored state, is God's creation. It may not stamp purity nor even goodness on its language, but it always, I think, stamps it with the deepest philosophy. So far at least, language is of divine origin. The unlearned Dakota may not be able to give any definition for any single word that he has been using all his lifetime—he may say, "It means that, and can't mean anything else," —yet, all the while, in the mental workshop of the people, unconsciously and very slowly it may be, but no less very surely, these words of air are newly coined. No angle can turn up, but by and by it will be worn off by use. No ungrammatical expression can come in, that will not be rejected by the best thinkers and speakers. New words will be coined to meet the mind's wants; and new forms of expression, which at the first are bungling descriptions only, will be pared down and tucked up so as to come into harmony with the living language.

But it was no part of our business to make the Dakota language. It was simply the missionary's work to report it faithfully. The system of notation had in the main been settled upon before Mary and I joined the mission. It was of course to be phonetic, as nearly as possible. The English alphabet was to be used as far as it could be. These were the principles that guided and controlled the writing of Dakota. In their application it was soon found that only five pure vowel sounds were used. So far the work was easy. Then it was found that x, and v, and r, and g, and j, and f, and c, with their English powers, were not needed. But there were four *clicks* and two *gutturals* and a *nasal* that must in some way be expressed. It was then, even more than now, a matter of pecuniary importance, that the language to be printed should require as few new characters as possible. And so "n" was taken to represent the nasal; "q" represented one of the clicks; "g" and "r" represented the gutterals; and "c" and "j" and "x" were used to represent "ch," "zh" and "sh." The other clicks were represented by marked letters. Since that time, some changes have been made; x and r have been discarded from the purely Dakota alphabet. In the Dakota grammar and dictionary, which was published fifteen years afterward, an effort was made to make the notation philosophical, and accordant with itself. The changes which have since been adopted, have all been in the line of the dictionary.

When we missionaries had gathered and expressed and arranged the words of this language, what had we to put into it, and what great gifts had we for the Dakota people? What will you give me? has always been their cry. We brought to them the Word of Life, the Gospel of Salvation through faith in Jesus Christ our Lord, as contained in the Bible. Not to preach Christ to them only, that they might have life, but to engraft His living words into their living thoughts, so that they might grow into His spirit more and more, was the object of our coming. The labor of writing the language was undertaken as a means to a greater end. To put God's thoughts into their speech, and to teach them to read in their own tongue the wonderful works of God, was what brought us to the land of the Dakotas. But they could not appreciate this. Ever and anon came the question, What will you give me? And so when we would proclaim the "Old, old Story" to those proud Dakota men at Lac-qui-parle, we had to begin with kettles of boiled pumpkins, turnips and potatoes. The bread that perisheth could be appreciated—the Bread of Life was still beyond their comprehension. But by and by it was to find its proper nesting place.

It was very fortunate for the work of education among the Dakotas that it had such a staunch and influential friend as Joseph Renville, Sr., of Lac-qui-parle. It was never certainly known whether Mr. Renville could read his French Bible or not. But he had seen so much of the advantages of education among the white people, that he greatly desired his own children should learn to read and write, both in Dakota and English, and through his whole life gave his influence in favor of Dakota education. Sarah Poage, afterward Mrs. G. H. Pond, had come as a teacher, and had, from their first arrival at Lac-qui-parle, been so employed. Mr. Renville had four daughters, all of them young women, who had with some other half-breeds, made an English class. They had learned to read the language, but understood very little of it, and were not willing to speak even what they understood. All through these years the teaching of English, commenced at the beginning of our mission work, although found to be very difficult and not producing much apparent fruit, has never been abandoned. But for the purposes of civilization, and especially of Christianization, we have found culture in the native tongue indispensable.

To teach the classes in English was in Mary's line of life. She at once relieved Miss Poage of this part of her work, and continued in it, with some intervals, for several years. Often she was greatly tried, not by the inability of her Dakota young lady scholars, but by their unwillingness to make such efforts as to gain the mastery of English.

Teaching in Dakota was a different thing. It was their own language. The lessons printed with open type and a brush on old newspapers, and hung round the walls of the school-room, were words that had a meaning even to a Dakota child. It was not difficult. A young man has sometimes come in, proud and unwilling to be taught, but by sitting there and looking and listening to others, he has started up with the announcement, "I am able." Some small books had already been printed. Others were afterward provided. But the work of works, which in some sense took precedence of all others, was then commencing, and has not yet been quite completed—that of putting the Bible into the language of the Dakotas.

"Nov. 18, 1837.

"I make very slow progress in learning Dakota, and could you hear the odd combinations of it with English which we allow ourselves, you would doubtless be somewhat amused, if not puzzled to guess our meaning, though our speech would betray us, for the little Dakota we can use we cannot speak like the Indians. The peculiar tone and ease are wanting, and several sounds I have been entirely unable to make; so that in my case at least, there would be 'shibboleths' not a few. And these cause the Dakota pupils to laugh very frequently when I am trying to explain, or lead them to understand some of the most simple things about arithmetic. Perhaps you will think them impolite, and so should I if they had been educated in a civilized land, but now I am willing to bear with them, if I can teach them anything in the hour which is alotted for this purpose.

"As yet, I have devoted no time to any except those who are attempting to learn English, and my class will probably consist of five girls, and two or three boys. Two of the boys whom we hope will learn English are full Dakotas, and if their hearts were renewed, might be very useful as preachers of the Gospel to their own degraded people."

Fort Renville, as it was sometimes called, was a stockade, made for defense in case of an invasion by the

Ojibwas, who had been, from time immemorial, at war with the Sioux. Inside of this stockade stood Mr. Renville's hewed log house, consisting of a storehouse and two dwellings. Mr. Renville's reception room was of good size, with a large open fire-place, in which his Frenchmen, or "French-boys" as they were called by the Indians, piled an enormous quantity of wood of a cold day, setting it up on end, and thus making a fire to be felt as well as seen. Here the chief Indian men of the village gathered to smoke and talk. A bench ran almost around the entire room on which they sat or reclined. Mr. Renville usually sat on a chair in the middle of the room. He was a small man with rather a long face and head developed upward. A favorite position of his was to sit with his feet crossed under him like a tailor. This room was the place of Bible translating. Dr. Williamson and Mr. G. H. Pond had both learned to read French. The former usually talked with Mr. Renville in French, and, in the work of translating, read from the French Bible, verse by verse. Mr. Renville's memory had been specially cultivated by having been much employed as interpreter between the Dakotas and the French. It seldom happened that he needed to have the verse re-read to him. But it often happened that we, who wrote the Dakota from his lips, needed to have it repeated in order that we should get it exactly and fully. When the verse or sentence was finished, the Dakota was read by one of the company. We were all only beginners in writing the Dakota language, and I more than the others. Sometimes Mr. Renville showed, by the twinkle of his eye, his conscious superiority to us, when he repeated a long and difficult sentence, and found that we had forgotten the beginning. But ordinarily he was patient with us and ready to repeat. By this process, continued from week to week during that first winter of ours at Lac-qui-parle, a pretty good translation of the Gospel of Mark was completed, besides some fugitive chapters from other parts. In the two following winters the Gospel of John was made in the same way.

Besides giving these portions of the Word of God to the Dakotas sooner than it could have been done by the missionaries alone, these translations were invaluable to us as a means of studying the structure of the language, and as determining, in advance of our own efforts in this line, the forms or molds of many new ideas which the Word contains. In after years we always felt safe in referring to Mr. Renville as authority in regard to the form of a Dakota expression.

During this first year that Mary and I spent in the Dakota country, there were coming to us continually new experiences. One of the most common, and yet one of the most thrilling and abiding, was in the birth of our first born. In motherhood and fatherhood are found large lessons in life. The mother called her first born child Alfred Longley, naming him for a very dear brother of hers. The Dakotas named this baby boy of ours Good Bird (Zitkadan washtay). They said that was a good name. In those days it was a habit with them to give names to the white people who came among them. Dr. Williamson they called *Payjehoota wechasta*—Medicine man, or more literally Grass-root man—that is *Doctor*. To Mr. G. H. Pond they gave the name Matohota, Grizzly-bear. Mr. S. W. Pond was Wamdedoota, Red-eagle. To me they gave the name of Tamakoche, *His country*. They said some good Dakota long ago had borne that name. To Mary they gave the name of Payuha. At first they gutteralized the "h," which made it mean *Curly-head*—her black hair did curl a good deal; but afterward they naturalized the "h," and said it meant *Having-a-head*.

The winter as it passed by had other lessons for us. For me it was quite a chore to cut and carry up wood enough to keep our somewhat open upper room cozy and comfortable. Mary had more ambition than I had to get native help. She had not been accustomed to do a day's washing. It came hard to her. The other women of the mission preferred to wash for themselves rather than train natives to do it. And indeed, at the beginning, that was found to be no easy task. For in the first place, Dakota women did not wash. Usually they put on a garment and wore it until it rotted off. This was pretty much the rule. No good, decent woman could be found willing to do for white people what they did not do for themselves. We could hire all the first women of the village to hoe corn or dig potatoes, but not one would take hold of the wash-tub. And so it was that Mary's first washer-women were of the lowest class and not very reputable characters. But she persevered and conquered. Only a few years had passed when the wash-women of the mission were of the best women of the village. And the effort proved a great public benefaction. The gospel of soap was indeed a necessary adjunct and outgrowth of the Gospel of Salvation.

"Dec. 13.

"My first use of the pen since the peculiar manifestation of God's loving kindness, we have so recently experienced, shall be for you, my dear parents. That you will with us bless the Lord, as did the Psalmist in one of my favorite Psalms, the 103d, we do not doubt; for I am sure you will regard my being able so soon to write as a proof of God's tender mercy. I have been very comfortable most of the time during the past week. As our little one cries, and I am now his chief nurse, I must lay aside my pen and paper and attend to his wants, for Mr. Riggs is absent, procuring, with Dr. W. and Mr. Pond, the translation of Mark, from Mr. Renville."

"Dec. 28.

"Yesterday our dear little babe was three weeks old. I washed with as little fatigue as I could expect, still I should have thought it right to have employed some one; was there any one to be employed who could be trusted. But the Dakota women, besides not knowing how to wash, need constant and vigilant watching. Poor creatures, thieves from habit, and from a kind of necessity, though one of their own creating!"

"Jan. 10.

"The Dakota tent is formed of buffalo skins, stretched on long poles placed on the ground in a circle, and meeting at the top, where a hole is left from which the smoke of the fire in the center issues. Others are made of bark tied to the poles placed in a similar manner. A small place is left for a door of skin stretched on sticks and hinged with strings at the top, so that the person entering raises it from the bottom and crawls in. At this season of the year the door is protected by a covered passage formed by stakes driven into the ground several feet apart, and thatched with grass. Here they keep their wood which the women cut this cold weather, the thermometer at eighteen to twenty degrees below zero. And should you lift the little door, you would find a cold, smoky lodge about twelve feet in diameter, a mother and her child, a blanket or two, or a skin, a kettle, and possibly a sack of corn in some of them."

"Thursday Eve., Jan. 11.

"Quite unexpectedly, this afternoon, we received an invitation to a wedding at Mr. Renville's, one of his daughters marrying a Frenchman. We gladly availed ourselves of an ox-sled, the only vehicle we could command, and a little before three o'clock we were in the guest chamber. Mr. Renville, who is part Dakota, received us with French politeness, and soon after the rest of the family entered. These, with several Dakota men and women seated on benches, or on the floor around the room, formed not an uninteresting group. The marriage ceremony was in French and Dakota, and was soon over. Then the bridegroom rose, shook hands with his wife's relations, and kissed her mother, and she also kissed all her father's family.

"When supper was announced as ready, we repaired to a table amply supplied with beef and mutton, potatoes, bread and tea. Though some of them were not prepared as they would have been in the States, they did not seem as singular as a dish that I was unable to determine what it could be, until an additional supply of *blood* was offered me. I do not know how it was cooked, though it might have been fried with pepper and onions, and I am told it is esteemed as very good. The poor Indians throw nothing away, whether of beast or bird, but consider both inside and outside delicious broiled on the coals."

"April 5th.

"Yesterday afternoon Mrs. Pond and myself walked to 'the lodges.' As the St. Peter's now covers a large part of the bottom, we wound our way in the narrow Indian path on the side of the hill. An Indian woman, with her babe fastened upon its board at her back, walked before us, and as the grass on each side of the foot path made it uncomfortable walking side by side, we conformed to Dakota custom, one following the other. For a few moments we kept pace with our guide, but she soon outstripping us, turned a corner and was out of sight. As we wished for a view of the lake and river, we climbed the hill. There we saw the St. Peter's, which in the summer is a narrow and shallow stream, extending over miles of land, with here and there a higher spot peeping out as an island in the midst of the sea. The haze prevented our having a good view of the lake.

"After counting thirty lodges stretched along below us, we descended and entered one, where we found a sick woman, who said she had not sat up for a long time, lying on a little bundle of hay. Another lodge we found full of corn, the owners having subsisted on deer and other game while absent during the winter.

"When we had called at Mr. Renville's, which was a little beyond, we returned through the heart of the village, attended by such a retinue as I have never before seen, and such strange intermingling of laughing and shouting of children and barking of dogs as I never heard. Amazed, and almost deafened by the clamor, I turned to gaze upon the unique group. Some of the older girls were close upon our heels, but as we stopped they also halted, and those behind slackened their pace. Boys and girls of from four to twelve years of age, some wrapped in their blankets, more without, and quite a number of boys almost or entirely destitute of clothing, with a large number of dogs of various sizes and colors, presented themselves in an irregular line. As all of the Indians here have pitched their lodges together, I suppose there might have been thirty or forty children in our train. When we reached home I found little Alfred happy and quiet in the same place on the bed I had left him more than two hours previous, his father having been busy studying Dakota.

"This evening two Indian women came and sat a little while in our happy home. One of them had a babe about the age of Alfred. You would have smiled to see the plump, undressed child peeping out from its warm blanket like a little unfledged bird from its mossy nest."

Mr. Pond had long been yearning to see inside of an Indian. He had been wanting to be an Indian, if only for half an hour, that he might know how an Indian felt, and by what motives he could be moved. And so when the early spring of 1838 came, and the ducks began to come northward, a half dozen families started out from Lac-qui-parle to hunt and trap on the upper part of the Chippewa River, in the neighborhood of where is now the town of Benson, in Minnesota. Mr. Pond went with them, and was gone two weeks. It was in the first of April, and the streams were flooded, and the water was cold. There should have been enough of game easily obtained to feed the party well. So the Indians thought. But it did not prove so. A cold spell came on, the ducks disappeared, and Mr. Pond and his Indian hunters were reduced to scanty fare, and sometimes to nothing, for a whole day. But Mr. Pond was seeing inside of Indians, and was quite willing to starve a good deal in the process. However, his stay with them, and their hunt for that time as well, was suddenly terminated.

It appears that during the winter some rumors of peace

visits from the Ojibwas had reached the Dakotas, so that this hunting party were somewhat prepared to meet Ojibwas who should come with this announced purpose. The half dozen teepees had divided. Mr. Pond was with Round Wind, who had removed from the three teepees that remained. On Thursday evening there came Hole-in-the-day, an Ojibwa chief, with ten men. They had come to smoke the peace-pipe, they said. The three Dakota tents contained but three men and ten or eleven women and children. But, while starving themselves, they would entertain their visitors in the most royal style. Two dogs were killed and they were feasted, and then all lay down to rest. But the Ojibwas were false. They arose at midnight and killed their Dakota hosts. In the morning but one woman and a boy remained alive of the fourteen in the three teepees the night before, and the boy was badly wounded. It was a cowardly act of the Ojibwas, and one that was terribly avenged afterward. When Mr. Pond had helped to bury the dead and mangled remains of these three families, he started for home, and was the first to bring the sad news to their friends at Lac-qui-parle. To him quite an experience was bound up in those two weeks, and the marvel was, why he was not then among the slain. To Mary and me it opened a whole storehouse of instruction, as we listened to the wail of the whole village, and especially when the old women came with disheveled heads and ragged clothes, and cried and sang around our house, and *begged in the name of our first born.* We discovered all at once the power of a name. And if an earthly name has such power, much more the Name that is above every name—much more the Name of the Only Begotten of the Heavenly Father.

Lac-qui-parle was in those days much shut out from the great world. We were two hundred miles away from our post-office at Fort Snelling. We seldom received a letter from Massachusetts or Ohio in less than three months after it was written. Often it was much longer, for there were several times during our stay at Lac-qui-parle when we passed three months, and once five months, without a mail. We used to pray that the mail would not come in the evening. If it did, good-bye sleep! If it came in the early part of the day we could look it over and become quieted by night. Our communication with the post-office was generally through the men engaged in the fur trade. Some of them had no sympathy with us as missionaries, but they were ever willing to do us a favor as men and Americans. Sometimes we sent and received our mail by Indians. That was a very costly way. The postage charged by the government—although it was then twenty-five cents on a letter—was no compensation for a Dakota in those days. It is fortunate for them that they have learned better the value of work.

Once a year, at least, it seemed best that one of ourselves should go down to the mouth of the Minnesota. Our annual supplies were to be brought up, and various matters of business transacted. I was sent down in the spring of 1838, and I considered myself fortunate in having the company of Rev. S. W. Pond. This was Mr. Pond's second visit to Lac-qui-parle on foot. The first was made over two years before in midwinter. That was a fearful journey. What with ignorance of the country, and deep snows, and starvation, and an ugly Indian for his guide, Mr. Pond came near reaching the spirit land before he came to Lac-qui-parle.

This second time he came under better auspices, and having spent several weeks with us, during which many questions of interest with regard to the language and the mission work were discussed, he and I made a part of Mr. Renville's caravan to the fur depot of the American Fur Company at Mendota, in charge of H. H. Sibley, a manly man, since that time occupying a prominent position in Minnesota.

To make this trip I was furnished by the mission with a valuable young horse, gentle and kind, but not possessed of much endurance. At any rate, he took sick while I was away and never reached home. The result may have been owing a good deal to my want of skill in taking care of horses, and in traveling through the bogs and quagmires of this new country. I could not but be profoundly sorry when obliged to leave him, as it entailed upon me other hardships for which I was not well prepared. Reaching the Traverse des Sioux on foot, I found Joseph R. Brown, even then an old Indian trader, coming up with some led horses. He kindly gave me the use of two with which to bring up my loaded cart. That was a really Good Samaritan work, which I have always remembered with gratitude.

When the first snows were beginning to fall in the coming winter, and not till then, Dr. Williamson was ready to make his trip on to Ohio. The Gospel of Mark and some smaller portions of the Bible he had prepared for the press. The journey was undertaken a few weeks too late, and so it proved a very hard one. They thought to go down the Mississippi in a Mackinaw boat, but were frozen in before they reached Lake Pepin. From that point the entire journey to Ohio was made by land in the rigors of winter.

The leaving of Dr. Williamson entailed upon me the responsibility of taking care of the Sabbath service. Mr. G. H. Pond was not then a minister of the Gospel, but his superior knowledge of the Dakota fitted him the best to communicate religious instruction. But it was well for me to have the responsibility, as it helped me in the use of the native tongue. I was often conscious of making mistakes, and doubtless made many that I knew not of. Mr. Pond and Mr. Renville were ever ready to help me out, and, moreover, we had with us that winter Rev. Daniel Gavan, one of the Swiss missionaries, who had settled on the Mississippi River at Red Wing and Wabashaw's villages. Mr. G. came up to avail himself of the better advantages in learning the language, and so for the winter he was a valuable helper.

It pleased God to make this winter one of fruitfulness. Mr. Renville was active in persuading those under his influence to attend the religious meetings, the schoolroom was crowded on Sabbaths, and the Word, imperfectly as it was spoken, was used by the Spirit upon those dark minds. There was evidently a quickening of the church. They were interested in prayer. What is prayer—and how shall we pray? became questions of interest with them. One woman who had received at her baptism the name of Catherine, and who still lives a believing life at the end of forty years, was then troubled to know how prayer could reach God. I told her in this we were all little children. God recognized our condition in this respect, and had told us that, as earthly fathers and mothers were willing, and desirous of giving good gifts to their children, He was more willing to give the Holy Spirit to them that ask Him. Besides, He made the ear, and shall He not hear? He made, in a large sense, all language, and shall He not be able to understand Dakota words? The very word for "pray" in the Dakota language was "to cry to"—*chakiya*. Prayer was now, as through all ages it had been, the child's cry in the ear of the Great Father. So there appeared to be a working upward of many hearts. Early in February Mr. Pond, Mr. Renville and Mr. Huggins, Mr. Gavan and myself, after due examination and instruction, agreed to receive ten Dakotas into the church—all women. I baptized them and their children—twenty-eight in all—on one Sabbath morning. It was to us a day of cheer. To these Dakota gentiles also God had indeed opened the door of faith. Blessed be his name for ever and ever.

"Dec. 6, 1838.

"This is our little Alfred's natal day. He of course has received no birthday sugar or earthen toys, and his only gift of such a kind has been a very small bow and arrow, from an Indian man, who is a frequent visitor. The bow is about three-eights of a yard long and quite neatly made, but Alfred uses it as he would any other little stick. I do not feel desirous that he should prize a bow or a gun, as do these sons of the prairie. My prayer is, that he may early become a lamb of the Good Shepherd's fold, that while he lives he may be kept from the fierce wolf and hungry lion, and at length be taken home to the green pastures and still waters above."

"Feb. 9, 1839.

"We mentioned in our last encouraging prospects here. The forenoon schools, which are for misses and children, have some days been crowded during the few past weeks, and a Sabbath-school recently opened has been so well attended as to encourage our hopes of blessed results. Last Lord's day we had a larger assembly than have ever before met for divine worship in this heathen land. More than eighty were present."

As Mr. Gavan was a native Frenchman and a scholar, we expected much from his presence with us, during the winter, in the way of obtaining translations. He and Mr. Renville could communicate fully and freely through that language, and we believed he would be able to explain such words as were not well understood by the other. And so we commenced the translation of the Gospel of John from the French. But it soon became apparent that the perfection of knowledge, of which they both supposed themselves possessed, was a great bar to progress. And by the time we had reached the end of the seventh chapter, the relations of the two Frenchmen were such as to entirely stop our work. We were quite disappointed. But this event induced us the sooner to gird ourselves for the work of translating the Bible from the original tongues, and so was, in the end, a blessing.

CHAPTER IV.

1838–1840.—" Eagle Help."—His Power as War Prophet.—Makes No-Flight Dance.—We Pray Against It.—Unsuccessful on the War Path.—Their Revenge.—Jean Nicollet and J. C. Fremont.—Opposition to Schools.—Progress in Teaching.—Method of Counting.—" Lake that Speaks "—Our Trip to Fort Snelling.—Incidents of the Way.—The Changes There. —Our Return Journey.—Birch Bark Canoe.—Mary's Story.— " Le Grand Canoe."—Baby Born on the Way.—Walking Ten Miles.—Advantages of Travel.—My Visit to the Missouri River.—"Fort Pierre."—Results.

" Eagle Help " was a good specimen of a war prophet and war leader among the Dakotas. At the time of the commencement of the mission he was a man of family and in middle age, but he was the first man to learn to read and write his language. And from the very first, no one had clearer apprehensions of the advantages of that attainment. He soon became one of the best helps in studying the Dakota, and the best critical helper in translations. He wanted good pay for a service, but he was ever ready to do it, and always reliable. When my horse failed me, on the trip up from Fort Snelling, and I had walked fifty miles, Eagle Help was ready for a consideration (my waterproof coat), to go on foot and bring up the baggage I had left. And in the early spring of 1839, when Mr. Pond would remove his family—wife and child—to join his brother in the work near Fort Snelling,

Eagle Help was the man to pilot his canoe down the Minnesota.

But notwithstanding his readiness to learn and to impart, to receive help and give help—notwithstanding his knowledge of the "new way," of which his wife was a follower, and his near relations to us in our missionary work, he did not, at once, abandon his Dakota customs, one of which was going on the war path.

As a war prophet, he claimed to be able to get into communication with the spirit world, and thus to be made a *seer*. After fasting and praying and dancing the circle dance, a *vision* of the enemies he sought to kill would come to him. He was made to see in this trance, or dream, whichever it might be, the whole panorama, the river or lake, the prairie or wood, and the Ojibwas in canoes or on the land, and the spirit in the vision said to him, "Up Eagle Help and kill." This vision and prophecy had heretofore never failed, he said.

And so when he came back from escorting Mr. Gavan and Mr. Pond to the Mississippi River, he determined to get up a war party. He made his "yoomne wachepe" (circle dance), in which the whole village participated—he dreamed his dream, he saw his vision, and was confident of a successful campaign. About a score of young men painted themselves for the war; they fasted and feasted and drilled by dancing the no-flight dance, and made their hearts firm by hearing the brave deeds of older warriors, who were now "*hors de combat*" by age.

In the mean time, the thought that our good friend Eagle Help should lead out a war party to kill and mangle Ojibwa women and children, greatly troubled us. We argued and entreated, but our words were not heeded. Among other things we said we would pray that the war party might not be successful. That was too much of a menace. Added to this they came and asked Mr. Huggins to grind corn for them on our little ox-power mill, which he refused to do. They were greatly enraged, and just before they started out, they killed and ate two of the mission cows. After a rather long and difficult tramp they returned without having seen an Ojibwa. Their failure they attributed entirely to our prayers, and so, as they returned ashamed, they took off the edge of their disgrace by killing another of our unoffending animals.

After this it was some months before Eagle Help could again be our friend and helper. In the meantime, Dr. Williamson and his family returned from Ohio, bringing with them Miss Fanny Huggins, to be a teacher in the place of Mrs. Pond. Miss Huggins afterward became Mrs. Jonas Pettijohn, and both she and her husband were for many years valuable helpers in the mission work. Also, this summer brought to Lac-qui-parle such distinguished scientific gentlemen as Mons. Jean Nicollet and J. C. Fremont. Mr. Nicollet took an interest in our war difficulty, and of his own motion made arrangements, in behalf of the Indians, to pay for the mission cattle destroyed. And so that glory and that shame were alike forgotten. In after years Eagle Help affirmed that his power of communicating with the spirit world, as a war prophet, was destroyed by his knowledge of letters and the religion of the Bible. Shall we accept that as true? And if so, what shall we say of modern spiritism? Is it in accord with living a true Christian life?

Thus events succeeded each other rapidly. But Mary and I and the baby boy, "Good Bird," lived still in the "upper chamber," and were not ashamed to invite the

French savant, Jean Nicollet, to come and take tea with us.

During these first years of missionary work at Lac-qui-parle, the school was well attended. It was only once in a while that the voice of opposition was raised against the children. Occasionally some one would come up from below and tell about the fight that was going on there *against* the Treaty appropriation for Education.

The missionaries down there were charged with wanting to get hold of the Indians' money; and so the provision for education, made by the treaty of 1837, effectually blocked all efforts at teaching among those lower Sioux. What should have been a help became a great hindrance. Indians and traders joined to oppose the use of that fund for the purpose it was intended, and finally the government yielded and turned over the accumulated money to be distributed among themselves. The Wahpatons of Lac-qui-parle had no interest in that treaty; and had yet made no treaty with the government; and had not a red cent of money anywhere that missionaries could, by any hook or crook, lay hold of: nevertheless it was easy to get up a fear and belief; for was it possible that white men and women would come here and teach year after year, and not expect, in some way and at some time, to get money out of them? If they ever made a treaty, and sold land to the government, would not the missionaries bring in large bills against them? It was easy to work up this matter in their own minds, and make it all seem true, and the result was, the soldiers were ordered to stop the children from coming to school. There were some such moods as this and our school had a vacation. But the absurdity appeared pretty soon and the children were easily induced to come back.

Mr. and Mrs. Pond were now gone. For the next winter, Mary and Miss Fanny Huggins took care of the girls and younger boys, and Mr. Huggins, with such assistance as I could give, took care of the boys and young men. The women also undertook, under the instruction of Mrs. Huggins and Miss Fanny, to spin, and knit, and weave. Mr. Renville had already among his flock some sheep. The wool was here and the flax was soon grown. Spinning-wheels and knitting-needles were brought on, and Mr. Huggins manufactured a loom. They knit socks and stockings, and wove skirts and blankets, while the little girls learned to sew patchwork and make quilts. All this was of advantage as education.

My own special effort in the class-room during the first years was in teaching a knowledge of figures. The language of counting in Dakota was limited. The "wan-cha, nonpa, yamne"—one, two, three, up to ten, every child learned, as he bent down his fingers and thumbs until all were gathered into two bunches, and then let them loose as geese flying away. Eleven was *ten more one*, and so on. Twenty was *ten twos* or *twice ten*, and thirty, *ten threes*. With each ten the fingers were all bent down, and one was kept down to remember the ten. Thus when ten tens were reached, the whole of the two hands was bent down, each finger meaning ten. This was the perfected "bending down." It was opawinge—one hundred. Then when the hands were both bent down for hundreds, the climax was supposed to be reached, which could only be expressed by "again also bending down." When something larger than this was reached, it was a *great count*—something which they nor we can comprehend—a million.

On the other side of *one* the Dakota language is still

more defective. Only one word of any definiteness exists—*hankay*, half. We can say hankay-hankay—*the half of a half*. But it does not seem to have been much used. Beyond this there was nothing. A *piece* is a word of uncertain quantity, and is not quite suited to introduce among the certainties of mathematics. Thus the poverty of the language has been a great obstacle in teaching arithmetic. And that poorness of language shows their poverty of thought in the same line. The Dakotas are not, as a general thing, at all smart in arithmetic.

Before the snows had disappeared or the ducks come back to this northern land, in the spring of 1840, a baby girl had been added to the little family in the upper chamber. By the first of June, Mary was feeling well, and exceedingly anxious to make a trip across the prairie. She had been cooped up here now nearly three years. There was no where to go. Lac-qui-parle is the "Lake that speaks," but who could be found around it? And no one had any knowledge of any great Indian talk held there that might have justified the name. But the romance was all taken out of the French name by the criticism of Eagle Help, that the Dakota name "Mdaeyaydan," did not mean "Lake that talks," but "Lake that connects." And so Lac-qui-parle had no historic interest. It was not a good place to go on a picnic. She had been to the Indian village frequently, but that was not a place to visit for pleasure. And on the broad prairie there was no objective point. Where could she go for a pleasure trip, but to Fort Snelling?

And so we made arrangements for the journey. The little boy "Good Bird" was left behind, and the baby Isabella must go along of course. We were with Mr. Renville's annual caravan going to the fur-trader's Mecca.

The prairie journey was pleasant and enjoyable, though somewhat fatiguing. We had our own team and could easily keep in company with the long line of wooden carts, carrying buffalo robes and other furs. It was indeed rather romantic. But when we reached the Traverse des Sioux, we were at our wit's end how to proceed further. That was the terminus of the wagon road. It was then regarded as absolutely impossible to take any wheeled vehicle through by land to Fort Snelling. Several years after this we began to do it, but it was very difficult. Then it was not to be tried. Mr. Sibley's fur boat, it was expected, would have been at the Traverse, but it was not. And a large canoe which was kept there had gotten loose and floated away. Only a little crazy canoe, carrying two persons, was found to cross the stream with. Nothing remained but to abandon the journey or to try it on horseback. And for that not a saddle of any kind could be obtained. But Mary was a plucky little woman. She did not mean to use the word "fail" if she could help it. And so we tied our buffalo robe and blanket on one of the horses, and she mounted upon it, with a rope for a stirrup. Many a young woman would have been at home there, but Mary had not grown up on horseback. And so at the end of a dozen miles, when we came to the river where Le Sueur now is, she was very glad to learn that the large canoe had been found. In that she and baby Isabella took passage with Mr. Renville's girls and an Indian woman or two to steer and paddle. The rest of the company went on by land, managing to meet the boat at night and camp together. This we did for the next four nights. It was a hard journey for Mary. The current was not swift. The canoe was heavy and required hard paddling to make it move onward. The Dakota young women did not care to work, and their helm's-woman was not in a condition to do it. On the fourth day out they ran ashore somewhat hurriedly and put up their tent, where the woman pilot gave birth to a baby girl. They named it "By-the-way." One day they came in very hungry to an Indian village. The Dakota young women were called to a tent to eat sugar. Then Mary thought they might have called "the white woman" also, but they did not. She did not consider that they were relatives.

By and by the mouth of the Minnesota was reached, through hardship and endurance. But then it was to be "a pleasure trip," and this was the way in which the pleasure came.

Since we had last seen him, S. W. Pond had married Miss Cordelia Eggleston, a sister of Mrs. J. D. Stevens. The station at Lake Harriet had been abandoned, the Indians having left Lake Calhoun first. Mr. Stevens had gone down to Wabashaw's village, and the Pond brothers with their families were occupying what was called the "Stone House," within a mile of the Fort. Mary found an old school friend in the garrison, and so the two weeks spent in this neighborhood were pleasant and profitable.

We now addressed ourselves to the return journey. The fur boat had gone up and come down again. We were advised to try a birch-bark canoe, and hire a couple of French voyagers to row it. In the first part of the river we went along nicely. But after awhile we began to meet with accidents. The strong arms of the paddlers would ever and anon push the canoe square on a snag. The next thing to be done was to haul ashore and mend the boat. By and by our mending material was all used up. It was Saturday morning, and we could reach

Traverse that day if we met with no mishap. But we did meet with a mishap. Suddenly we struck a snag which tore such a hole in our bark craft, that it was with difficulty we got ashore. By land, it was eight or ten miles to the Traverse. The Frenchmen were sent on for a cart to bring up the baggage. But rather than wait for them, Mary and I elected to walk and carry baby Bella. To an Indian woman that would have been a mere trifle—not worth speaking of. But to me it meant work. I had no strap to tie her on my back, and the little darling seemed to get heavier every mile we went. But then, Mary had undertaken the trip for pleasure and so we must not fail to find in it all the pleasure we could. And we did it. Altogether, that trip to Fort Snelling was a thing to be remembered and not regretted.

MARY'S STORY.

"FORT SNELLING, June 19, 1840.

"We left Lac-qui-parle June 1, and reached Le Bland's the Saturday following, having enjoyed as pleasant a journey across the prairie as we could expect or hope. We had expected to find at that place a barge, but we could not even procure an Indian canoe. With no other alternative we mounted our horses on Monday, with no other saddles than our baggage. Mine was a buffalo robe and blanket fastened with a trunk strap. My spirits sank within me as I gave our little Isabella to an Indian woman, to carry perched up in a blanket behind, and clung to my horse's mane as we ascended and descended the steep hills, and thought a journey of seventy miles by land was before us.

I rode thus nearly ten miles, and then walked a short distance to rest myself, to the place where our company took lunch. There, to our great joy, a Frenchman exclaimed, "Le grand canoe, le grand canoe!" and we found that the Indian, who had been commissioned to search, had found and brought it down the river thus far. I gladly exchanged my seat on the horse for one in the canoe, with two Indian women and Mr. Renville's daughters. Our progress was quite comfortable, though slow, as some of our party were invited to Indian lodges to feast occasionally, while the rest of us were sunning by the river's bank.

On the fourth day we had an addition to our party. The woman at the helm said she was sick—and we went on shore perhaps three-quarters of an hour on account of the rain, and when it ceased, she was ready with her infant to step into the canoe and continue rowing, although she did not resume her seat in the stern until the next morning. This is a specimen of Indian life.

We have found Dr. and Mrs. Turner in the garrison here; she was formerly Mary Stuart, of Mackinaw.

"Traverse des Sioux, July 4.

"The canoe (birch bark) which we praised so highly, failed us about eight miles below this place, in consequence of not having a supply of gum to mend a large rent made by a snag early this morning. Not thinking it was quite so far, I chose to try walking, husband carrying Isabella, the Frenchmen having hastened on to find our horses to bring up the baggage. We reached the river and found there was no boat here with which to cross. Mr. Riggs waded with Isabella, the water being about two and a half feet deep, and an Indian woman came to carry me over, when our horses were brought up. Husband mounted without any saddle, and I, quivering like an aspen, seated myself behind, clinging so tightly that I feared I should pull us both off. I do not think it was fear, at least not entirely, for I am still exceedingly fatigued and dizzy, but I have reason to be gratified that I did not fall into the river from faintness, as husband thought I was in danger of doing. Isabella's face is nearly blistered, and mine almost as brown as an Indian's."

"LAC-QUI-PARLE MISSION, July 27, 1840.

"We are once more in the quiet enjoyment of home, and are somewhat rested from the fatigue of our journey. The repetition of that parental injunction, " Mary, do be careful of your health," recalled your watchful care most forcibly. How often have I heard these words, and perhaps too often have regarded them less strictly than an anxious mother deemed necessary for my highest welfare. And even now, were it not that the experience of a few years may correct my *notions* about health, I should be so unfashionable as to affirm, that necessary exposures, such as sleeping on the prairie in a tent drenched with rain, and walking some two or three miles in the dewy grass, where the water would gush forth from our shoes at every step, and then continuing our walk until they were more than comfortably dry, as we did on the morning our canoe failed us, are not as injurious to the health as the unnecessary exposures of fashionable life."

The Sioux on the Mississippi and Minnesota Rivers were known to be but a small fraction of the Dakota people. We at Lac-qui-parle had frequent intercourse with the Sissetons of Lake Traverse. Sometimes, too, we had visits from the Yanktonais, who followed the buffalo on the great prairies this side of the Missouri River. But more than half of the Sioux nation were said to be Teetons, who lived beyond the Big Muddy. So it seemed very desirable that we extend our acquaintance among them.

About the first of September, Mr. Huggins and I, having prepared ourselves with a small outfit, started for the Missouri. We had one pony for the saddle, and one horse and cart to carry the baggage. At first we joined a party of wild Sioux from the Two Woods, whose leader was "Thunder Face." He was a great scamp, but had promised to furnish us with guides to the Missouri, after we had reached the Coteau. The party were going out to hunt buffalo, and moved by short days' marches. In a week we had only made fifty miles. After some vexatious delays and some coaxing and buying, we succeeded in getting started ahead with two young men, the principal one being "Sacred Cow." The first day brought us into the region of buffalo, one of which Sacred Cow killed. This came near spoiling our journey. The young men now wanted to turn about and join the hunt. An additional bargain had to be made. In about two weeks from Lac-qui-parle we reached the Missouri, striking it near Fort Pierre. To this trading fort we crossed, and there spent a good part of a week. Forty or fifty teepees of Teetons were encamped there. They treated us kindly (inviting us to a dog feast on one occasion), as did also the white people and half-breeds of the Post. We gathered a good deal of information in regard to the western bands of the Sioux nation; we communicated to them something of the object of our missionary work, and of the good news of salvation, and then returned home pretty nearly by the way we went. We had been gone a month. The result of our visit was the conclusion that we could not do much, or attempt much, for the civilization and Christianization of those roving bands of Dakotas.

CHAPTER V.

1840–1843.—Dakota Braves.—Simon Anawangmane.—Mary's Letter.—Simon's Fall.—Maple Sugar.—Adobe Church.—Catharine's Letter.—Another Letter of Mary's.—Left Hand's Case.—The Fifth Winter.—Mary to her Brother.—The Children's Morning Ride.—Visit to Hawley, and Ohio.—Dakota Printing.—New Recruits.—Return.—Little Rapids.—Traverse des Sioux.—Stealing Bread.—Forming a New Station.—Begging.—Opposition.—Thomas L. Longley.—Meeting Ojibwas.—Two Sioux Killed.—Mary's Hard Walk.

Among the encouraging events of 1840 and 1841, was the conversion of SIMON ANAWANGMANE. He was the first full-blood Dakota man to come out on the side of the new religion. Mr. Renville and his sons had joined the church, but the rest were women. It came to be a taunt that the men used when we talked with them, and asked them to receive the gospel, "Your church is made up of women;" and, "If you had gotten us in first it would have amounted to something, but now they are only women. Who would follow after women?" Thus the proud Dakota braves turned away.

But God's truth has sharp arrows in it, and the Holy Spirit knows how to use them in piercing even Dakota hearts.

Anawangmane (Walks galloping on) was at this time not far from thirty years old. He was not a bright scholar —rather dull and slow in learning to read. But he had a very strong will-power and did not know what fear was. He had been a very dare-devil on the war path. The Dakotas had a curious custom of being *under law* and *above law*. It was always competent for a Dakota soldier to punish another man for a misdemeanor, if the other man did not rank above him in savage prowess. As for example: If a Dakota man had braved an Ojibwa with a loaded gun pointed at him, and had gone up and killed him, he ranked above all men who had not done a like brave deed. And if no one in the community had done such an act of bravery, then this man could not be punished for anything, according to Dakota custom.

Under date of Feb. 24, 1841, Mary writes:—"Last Sabbath was Isabella's birth-day. She has been a healthy child, for which we have cause of gratitude. But this was not our, only or principal, cause of joy on last Sabbath. Five adults received the baptismal rite preparatory to the celebration of the Lord's Supper on next Sabbath. One of them was a man, the first in the nation—a full-blooded Sioux, that has desired to renounce all for Christ. May God enable him to adorn his profession. His future life will doubtless exert a powerful influence either for or against Christ's cause here. Three years since he was examined by the church session, but then he acknowledged that the 6th and 7th commandments were too broad in their restrictions for him. Now he professes a desire and determination to keep them also. His wife, whom he is willing to marry, with her child, and three children by two other wives he has had, stood with him, and at the same time received the seal of the new covenant. As they all wished English names, we gave 'Hetta' to a white, grey-eyed orphan girl who was baptized on account of her grandmother."

This young man, Anawangmane, had reached that enviable position of being above Dakota law. He had not only attained to the "first three," but he was the chief. And so when he came out on the side of the Lord and Christianity, there was a propriety in calling him Simon, when he was baptized. He was ordinarily a quiet man —a man of deeds and not of words. But once in a while he would get roused up, and his eyes would flash, and his words and gestures were powerful. Simon immediately put on white-man's clothes, and made and planted a field of corn and potatoes adjoining the mission field. No Dakota brave dared to cut up his tent or kill his dog or break his gun; but this did not prevent the boys, and women too, from pointing the finger at him, and saying, "There goes the man who has made himself a woman." Simon seemed to care for it no more than the bull dog does for the barking of a puppy. He apparently brushed it all aside as if it was only a straw. So far as any sign from him, one looking on would be tempted to think that he regarded it as glory. But it did not beget pride. He did indeed become stronger thereby.

And yet, as time rolled by, it was seen by the unfolding of the divine plan, that Simon could not be built up into the best and noblest character without suffering. Naturally, he was the man who would grow into self-sufficiency. There were weak points in his character which he perhaps knew not of. It was several years after this when Simon visited us at the Traverse, and made our hearts glad by his presence and help. But alas! he came there to stumble and fall! "You are a brave man—no man so brave as you are," said the Indians at the Traverse to him. And some of them were distantly related to him. While they praised and flattered him, they asked him to drink whiskey with them. Surely he was man enough for that. How many times he refused Simon never told. But at last he yielded, and then the very energy of his character carried him to great excess in drinking "spirit water."

"LAC-QUI-PARLE, March 27, 1841.

"Until this, the seasons for sugar-making have been very unfavorable since we have resided here. But this spring the Indian women have been unusually successful, and several of them have brought us a little maple sugar, which, after melting and straining, was excellent, and forcibly reminded us of *home sugar*. However, it does not always need purifying, as some are much more cleanly than others, here as well as in civilized lands. Sugar is a luxury for which these poor women are willing to toil hard, and often with but small recompense. Their camps are frequently two or three miles from their lodges. If they move to the latter, they must also pack corn for their families; and if not, with kettle in hand they go to their camps, toil all day, and often at night return with their syrup or sugar and a back load of wood for their husband's use the next day. Thus sugar is to them a hard-earned luxury. But they have also others, which they sometimes offer us, such as muskrats, beaver's tails and tortoises. I have never tried muskrats, but husband says they are as good as *polecats*—another delicacy!"

But I must leave these broken threads, and take up the thread of my story. At Lac-qui-parle the school-room in Dr. Williamson's log house became too straight for our religious gatherings. We determined to build a church. The Dakota women volunteered to come and dig out, in the side of the hill, the place where it should stand. Building materials were not abundant nor easily obtained, and so we decided to build an *adobe*. We made our bricks and dried them in the sun, and laid them up into the walls. We sawed our boards with the whip-saw, and made our shingles out of the ash-trees. We built our house without much outlay of money. The heavy Minnesota rains washed its sides, and we plastered one and clapboarded another. It was a comfortable house, and one in which much preaching and teaching were done; moreover, when, in after years, our better framed house was burned to the ground, this adobe church still stood for us to take refuge in. There we were living when Secretary S. B. Treat visited us in 1854, and in one corner of that, we fenced off with bed-quilts a little place for him to sleep. In this adobe house we first made trial of an instrument in song worship. Miss Lucy Spooner, afterward Mrs. Drake, took in her melodeon. But the Dakota voices fell so much below the instrument that she gave it up in despair. By all these things we remember the old adobe church at Lac-qui-parle. And not less by the first consecration of it. That was a feast made by Dr. Williamson for the *men*. The floor was not yet laid, but a hundred Dakota men gathered into it and sat on the sleepers, and ate their potatoes and bread and soup gladly, and then we talked to them about Christ.

Of this church when commenced, Catherine Totiduta-win wrote: "Now are we to have a church, and on that account we rejoice greatly. In this house we shall pray to the Great Spirit. We have dug ground two days already. We have worked having the Great Spirit in our thoughts. We have worked praying. When we have this house we shall be glad. In it, if we pray he will have mercy upon us, and if he hears what we say, he will make us glad. As yet we do what he hates. In this house we will confess these things to him—our thoughts, our words, our actions—these we will tell to him. His Son will dwell in this house and pardon all that is bad. God has mercy on us and is giving us a holy house. In this we will pray for the nations."

"Dec. 10, 1841.

"The last two Sabbaths we have assembled in our new chapel. Only one half is completed, though husband and Mr. Pettijohn have been very diligent and successful. You can scarcely imagine what a task building is in a land where there is such a scarcity of materials and men. During the summer great exertions were made to prepare lumber, and two men were employed about two months in sawing it with a whip-saw. The woods were searched and researched for two or three miles for suitable timber, and the result was about 3,200 feet—which is not enough—at an expense of $150. I might mention other hindrances, but notwithstanding them all, the Lord has evidently prospered the work, and our expectations have been fully realized, if our wishes have not."

Besides Simon Anawangmane, two or three other young men were won over to the religion of Christ before 1842. One of these was Paul Mazakootaymane. Paul was a man of different stamp from Simon. He was a native orator. But he was innately lazy. Still he has always been loyal to the white people, and has done much good work on their behalf.

There was, at this time, an elderly man who sought admission to the church at Lac-qui-parle, *Left Hand* by name. This man was Mr. Renville's brother-in-law. We could not say he was not a true believer—he seemed to be one. But he had two wives, and they both had been received into church fellowship. They had been admitted on the ground, partly, that it could not be decided which, if either, was the lawful wife, and partly on the ground that Dakota women heretofore could not be held responsible for polygamy. And now Left Hand claimed for himself that he had lived with these women for a quarter of a century, and had a family by each; that he had entered into this relation in the days of ignorance, and that the Bible recognized the rightfulness of such relations under certain circumstances, since David and Jacob had more than one wife. Mr. Renville, who was a ruling elder in the church, took this position, and the members of the mission were not a unit against it. So the question was referred to the Ripley Presbytery. The result was that our native church was saved from sanctioning polygamy. We had the two wives of Left Hand, and two women also in another case. But the husbands' dying has long since left them widows, and some of them also have gone to the eternal world. The loose condition of the marriage relation is still that, in the social state of the Dakotas, which gives us the most trouble.

The fifth winter in our "little chamber" was one full of work. In the early part of it, Mary was still in the school. In the latter part, our third child was born. She was named "Martha Taylor," for the grandmother in Massachusetts. During the years previous, I had undertaken to translate a good portion of the New Testament, the Acts, and Paul's Epistles and the Revelation. This winter the corrected copy had to be made. Of necessity, I learned to do my best work surrounded by children. My study and work-shop was our sitting-room, and dining-room, and kitchen, and nursery, and ladies' parlor. It was often half filled with Indians. Besides my own translations, I copied for the press the Gospel of John and some of the Psalms. A part of the latter were my own translation, and a part were secured as the Gospel was, through Mr. Renville. There was also a hymn-book to edit, and some school-books to be prepared. So the winter was filled with work and service. The remembrance of it is only pleasant. Doubtless the ordinary family trials were experienced. The bucket of water was spilled and leaking down on Mrs. Williamson's bed—or one of the children fell down the stairs, or our little Bella crawled out of the window and sat on the little shelf where the milk was set to cool in the morning, giving us a good scare.

MARY TO HER BROTHER ALFRED:

"LAC-QUI-PARLE, April 28, 1841.

"Your letter presented to my 'mind's eye' our mountain home. I entered the lower gate, passed up the lane between the elms, maples and cherries, and saw once more our mountain home embowered by the fir-trees and shrubbery I loved so well. How many times have I watched the first buddings of those rose bushes and lilacs, and with what care and delight have I nursed those snowballs, half dreaming they were sister spirits, telling by their delicate purity of that Eden where flowers never fade, and leaves never wither. Perhaps I was too passionately fond of flowers; if so, that fondness is sufficiently blunted, if not subdued. Not a solitary shrub, tree or flower rears its head near our dwelling, excepting those of nature's planting at no great distance on the opposite side of the St. Peter's, and a copse of plums in a dell on the left, and of scrub-oak on the right. Back of us is the river hill which shelters us from the furious wind of the high prairie beyond. Until last season we have had no enclosure, and now we have but a poor defense against the depredations of beasts, and still more lawless and savage men. On reading descriptions of the situation of our missionary brethren and sisters in Beirut, Jerusalem and elsewhere, the thought has arisen, 'That is such a place as I should like to call home.' But the remembrance of earthquakes, war and the plague, by which those countries are so often scourged, hushed each murmuring thought. When I also recollected the mysterious providences which have written the Persian missionaries *childless*, how could I long or wish to possess more earthly comforts, while my husband and our two 'olive plants' are spared to sit around our table. Little Bella already creeps to her father, and if granted a seat on his knee, folds her little hands, although, as Alfred says, 'she does not wait till papa says amen.' While we are surrounded by so many blessings, I would not, like God's ancient people, provoke him by murmuring, as I fear I have done, and if he should deprive us of any of the comforts we now possess, may he give us grace to feel as did Habakkuk, 'Although the fig-tree shall not blossom, neither shall fruit be in the vine, etc., yet I will rejoice in the Lord and joy in the God of my Salvation.'

"I suppose you have hardly yet found how much of romance is mingled with your ideas of a married state. You will find real life much the same that you have ever found, and with additional joys, additional cares and sorrows. I have realized as much happiness as I anticipated, though many of my bright visions have not been realized, and others have been much changed in outline and finishing. For instance, our still winter evenings are seldom enlivened by reading, while I am engaged lulling our little ones or plying my needle. Although I should greatly enjoy such a treat *occasionally*, I cannot in our situation expect it, while it is often almost the only time husband can secure for close and uninterrupted study You know the time of a missionary is *not his own*."

"Thursday, May 19, 1841.

"Perhaps the scene that would amuse you most would be 'the babies' morning ride.' The little wagon in which Isabella and my namesake, Mary Ann Huggins, are drawn by the older children, even Alfred ambitious to assist, would be in complete contrast with 'the royal princess' cradle;' yet I doubt not it affords them as much pleasure as a more elegant one would. Alfred's was made by his father, and Hetta, an Indian girl living at Mr. Huggins, constructed a canopy, which gives it a tasteful, though somewhat rude appearance. Mrs. Williamson's son John draws his sister in a wagon of his own, so that the whole troop of ten little ones with their carriages form a miniature pleasure party."

"Lac-qui-parle, Feb. 26, 1842.

"We are grateful for the expression of kindness for us and for our children, and we hope that our duty to those whom God has committed to our care will be made plain. Before your letter reached us, containing the remark of 'Mother Clark' about taking the little girl, we had another little daughter added to our family, and had concluded to leave Isabella with Miss Fanny Huggins, as it is probable we shall return to this region, instead of ascending the Missouri. Our little Martha we shall of course not leave behind if our lives are spared and we are permitted to go East; and Alfred we intend taking with us as far as Ohio."

Of the next year, from the spring of 1842, little need be said in this connection. The preparations were all made. Mary and I took with us the little boy, now in his fifth year, and the baby, while the little girl between was left in the care of Miss Fanny Huggins. It was a year of enjoyment. Mary visited the old home on Hawley hills. The old grandfather was still there, and the younger members of the family had grown up. Here during the summer, the little boy born in Dakota land gathered strawberries, in the meadows of Massachusetts. Our school-books and hymn-book were printed in Boston; and in the autumn we came to Ohio. During the winter months the Bible printing was done in Cincinnati.

When we were ready to start back, in the spring of 1843, we had secured as fellow-laborers, at the new station which we were instructed to form, Robert Hopkins and his young wife Agnes, and Miss Julia Kephart, all from Ripley, Ohio. The intercourse with so many sympathising Christian hearts, which had been much interested in the Dakota mission from its commencement, was refreshing. We found, too, that we had both been forgetting our mother tongue somewhat, in the efforts made to learn Dakota. This must be guarded against in the future. In our desire to be Dakotas we must not cease to be English

The bottoms of the Lower Minnesota were putting on their richest robes of green, and the great, wild rose gardens were coming into full perfection of beauty, when in the month of June, our barge, laden with mission supplies, was making its way up to Traverse des Sioux. At what was known as "The Little Rapids," was a village of Wahpaton Dakotas, the old home of the people at Lac-qui-parle. There were certain reasons why we thought that might be the point for the new station. We made a halt there of half a day, and called the chief men. But they were found to be too much under the influence of the Treaty Indians below, to give us any encouragement In fact, they did not want missionaries.

We passed by, and landed our boats at the Traverse. The day before reaching this point, Mrs. Hopkins and Mary had made arrangements to have some light bread— they were tired eating the heavy cakes of the voyage. They succeeded to their satisfaction, and placed the warm bread away, in a safe place, as they supposed, within the tent, ready for the morning. But when the breakfast was ready, the bread was not there. During the night, an Indian hand had taken it.

The Dakotas were accustomed to do such things. While at Lac-qui-parle we were constantly annoyed by thefts. An ax or a hoe could not be left out of doors, but it would be taken. And in our houses we were continually missing little things. A towel hanging on the wall would be tucked under the blanket of a woman, or a girl would sidle up to a stand and take a pair of scissors. Any thing that could be easily concealed was sure to be missing, if we gave them an opportunity. And these people at the Traverse, (Sissetons they were) we found quite equal to those at Lac-qui-parle. Stealing, even among themselves, was not considered very dishonorable. The men said they did not steal, but the women were all *wamanonsa*.

We had decided to make this our new station. We should consult the Indians, but our staying would not depend upon their giving us an invitation to stay. And so the first thing to be done was to start off the train to Lac-qui-parle. In the early part of June, 1842, after Mary and I left, there had come frosts which cut off the Indian corn. The prospect was that the village would be abandoned, pretty much during the year. This led Dr. Williamson to come down to Fort Snelling, as Mr. S. W. Pond and wife had already gone up to take our place.

This spring of 1843, Mr. Pond had left, and Dr. Williamson could not return until the autumn, as he had engaged temporarily to fill the place of surgeon in the garrison. In these circumstances, it was deemed advisable for Mr. and Mrs. Hopkins to go on to Lac-qui-parle for a year. Mary took her baby, Martha Taylor, now fifteen months old, and went up with them to bring down Isabella.

Thomas Longley, a young man of 22 years, and rejoicing in a young man's strength, had joined us at Fort Snelling. He was a part of our boat's company up the Minnesota; and now he and I and the little boy, Zitkadan Washtay, remained to make a beginning. Immediately I called the Indians and had a talk with them, at Mr. Le Bland's trading-post. I told them we had come to live with them, and to teach them. Some said *yes* and some said *no*. But they all asked, What have you to give us?

It was at a time of year when they were badly off for food, and so I gave them two barrels of flour. Before the council was over, some of the principal men became so stupid from the influence of whisky which they had been drinking, that they did not know what they were saying. Old Sleepy Eyes and Tankamane were the chief men present. They were favorable to our stopping, and remained friends of the mission as long as it was continued there. But some of the younger men were opposed. One especially, who had a keg of whisky that he was taking to the Upper Minnesota, was reported as saying, that when he had disposed of his whisky, he would come back and stop Tamakoche's building. But he never came back—only a few days after this he was killed in a drunken frolic.

We expected to meet with opposition, and so were not disappointed. Thomas and I pitched our tents under some scrub-oaks, on a little elevation, in the lower river bottom, a half a mile away from the Trader's. Immediately we commenced to cut and haul logs for our cabin. In the mean time the party going to Lac-qui-parle were nearing their destination. With them there were three young men who had accompanied us to Ohio, and spent the year .Their baptized names were *Simon, Henok* and *Lorenzo*. Each was about twenty years old. While on their way down, we had cut off their hair and dressed them up as white men. They had all learned much in their absence ; while two of them had added their names to the rolls of Christian churches in Ohio. Thus, they were returning. The party spent the Sabbath a day's travel from Lac-qui-parle. On Monday, before noon, these young men had seen, on some far-off prairie elevation, what seemed to be Indians lying down. But their suspicions of a war party were not very pronounced.

Five miles from the mission, the road crosses the *Mayawakan*—otherwise called the Chippewa River. It was a hot afternoon when the mission party approached it. They were thirsty, and the young men had started on to drink. Simon was ahead, and on horseback. Suddenly, as he neared the stream, there emerged from the wood a war party of Ojibwas, carrying two fresh scalps. Simon rode up and shook hands with them. He could do this safely, as he was dressed like a white man. They showed him the scalps, all gory with blood ; but he wot not that one of them was his own brother's. This brother and his wife and a young man were coming to meet their friends. As the two men came to the crossing, they were shot down by the Ojibwas, who lay concealed in the bushes. The woman, who was a little distance behind, heard the guns and fled, carrying the news back to the village. And so it happened, that by the time the mission teams had fairly crossed the river, they were met by almost the whole village of maddened Dakotas. They were in pursuit of the Ojibwas. But had not the missionaries taken these boys to Ohio? And had not these two young men been killed as they were coming to meet the boys? Were not the missionaries the cause of it all? So questioned and believed many of the frantic men. And one man raised his gun and shot one of the horses in the double team, which carried Mrs. Hopkins and Mary. This made it necessary for them to walk the remainder of the way in the broiling sun of summer. Mary found her little girl too heavy a load, and after awhile was kindly relieved of her burden by a Dakota woman, whom she had taught to wash. The excitement and trouble were a terrible strain on her nervous system, and prematurely made the grey hairs come here and there among the black.

CHAPTER VI.

1843–1846.—Great Sorrow.—Thomas Drowned.—Mary's Letter.—The Indians' Thoughts.—Old Grey-Leaf.—Oxen Killed.—Hard Field.—Sleepy Eyes' Horse.—Indian in Prison.—The Lord keeps us.—Simon's Shame.—Mary's Letter.—Robert Hopkins and Agnes.—Le Bland.—White Man Ghost.—Bennett.—Sleepy Eyes' Camp.—Drunken Indians.—Making Sugar.—Military Company.—Dakota Prisoners.—Stealing Melons.—Preaching and School.—A Canoe Voyage.—Red Wing.

Suddenly, at the very commencement of our new station, we were called to meet a great sorrow. Mary had come back from Lac-qui-parle with the two little girls, and our family were all together once more. Mr. Huggins and his sister, Miss Fanny Huggins, and Mr. Isaac Pettijohn had come down along. Mr. Pettijohn helped us much to forward the log-cabin. Saturday came, the 15th of July—and the roof was nearly finished. We should move into its shelter very soon. No one was rejoicing in the prospect more than the young brother, Thomas Lawrence Longley. He sang as he worked that morning.

Mr. Huggins had the toothache, and about 10 o'clock, said he would go and bathe, as that sometimes helped his teeth. Brother T. proposed that we should go also, to which I, at first, objected, and said we would go after dinner. He thought we should have something else to do then; and, remembering that once or twice I had prevented his bathing, by not going when he wished, I consented. We had been in the water but a moment, when, turning around, I saw T. throw up his hands and clap them over his head. My first thought was that he was drowning. The current was strong and setting out from the shore. I swam to him—he caught me by the hand, but did not appear to help himself in the least—probably had the cramp. I tried to get toward shore with him, but could not. He pulled me under once or twice, and I began to think I should be drowned with him. But when we came up again, he released his grasp, and, as I was coming into shallow water, with some difficulty, I reached the shore. But the dear boy Thomas appeared not again. The cruel waters rolled over him. In the meantime, Mr. Huggins had jumped into a canoe, and was coming to our relief But it was *too late*—TOO LATE!

Mary's first letter after the 15th of July, 1843 :—
"*Traverse des Sioux,* Friday noon : What shall I add my dear parents, to the sad tidings my husband has written? Will it console you in any measure, to know that one of our first, and most frequent, petitions, at the throne of grace, has been that God would prepare your hearts for the news, which we feared would be heart-breaking, unless 'the Comforter' comforted you, and the Almighty strengthened you? We hope—indeed some small measure of faith is given us to believe—that you will be comforted and sustained, under this chastening from the Lord. And oh,—like subdued, humbled and penitent children,—may we all kiss the rod, and earnestly pray that this sore chastisement may be for our spiritual good.

"I feel that this affliction, such as I have never before known, is intended to prepare us who are left for *life and death.* Perhaps some of us may soon follow him whom we all loved. When I stand by his grave, overshadowed by three small oaks, with room for another person by his side, I think that place may be for me.

"The last Sabbath he was with us was just after my return from Lac-qui-parle. I reached here on Saturday, and having passed through distressing scenes on our way to Lac-qui-parle, occasioned by an attack of the Chippewas on some Sioux who were coming to meet us, I felt uncommon forebodings lest something had befallen the dear ones I had left here. But I endeavored to cast my care upon the Lord, remembering that while we were homeless and houseless, we were more like our Saviour. And that if *He* was despised and rejected of men, *we* surely ought not to repine if we were treated as our Master. With such feelings as these, as we came in sight of husband's tent, I pointed it out to Isabella, when she asked, 'Where's papa's house,' and soon I saw Mr. Riggs and Brother Thomas and little Alfred coming to meet us.

"Not quite one week after that joyful hour, Mr. Riggs came home from the Saint Peter's, groaning, 'Oh, Mary, Thomas is drowned—Thomas is drowned!' I did not, I could not receive the full import. I still thought his body would be recovered and life restored; for your sakes I cried for mercy, but it came not in the way I then desired. Still I tried to flatter myself, even after search for the body had been given up for the day, that it had floated down upon a sand-bar, and he would yet live and return in the dusk of the evening. But when I lay down for the night, and the impossibility of my illusive hopes being realized burst upon me, oh—

"The hand of the Lord had touched us, and we were ready to sink; but the same kind hand sustained us. May the same Almighty Father strengthen you. One thought comforted me not a little. 'If Brother Thomas had gone home to our father's house in Massachusetts, I should not have grieved much; and now he had gone to his Father's and our Father's home in Heaven, why should I mourn so bitterly? I felt that God had a right to call him when He pleased, and I saw His mercy, in sparing my husband to me a little longer, when he was but a step from the eternal world. Still I felt that I had lost a brother, and *such a brother!*

"Before I went to Lac-qui-parle, I had confided Alfred to his special care. I knew that the rejection of our offer of stopping at the Little Rapids, by the Indians there, had been exceedingly painful and discouraging to Mr. Riggs, and the rumor that the Indians here would do likewise was no less so; and I should have felt very unpleasantly in going for Isabella at that time, but it seemed necessary, and I felt that Brother Thomas would be, what he was, 'a friend in need.' On my return, on recounting the scenes I had passed through, the killing by the Chippewas of the eldest brother of one of our young men, as he was coming to meet him—the shooting of one of our horses by a Sioux man, who pretended to be offended because we did not pursue the Chippewas, when we were more than three miles from the mission, and that I carried Martha there in my arms, one of the warmest afternoons we had— Thomas said, 'I see you have grown poor, but you will improve from this time.'

"On Saturday morning, as we were busily engaged near each other, he sang, 'Our cabin is small and coarse our fare, But love has spread our banquet here!' Soon afterward he went to bathe, and of course our roof and floor remained unfinished, but that evening we terminated in sadness, what had been to us a happy feast of tabernacles, by moving into our humble dwelling. For a little while on Sabbath, his remains found a resting place within the house his hands had reared. I kissed his cheek as he lay upon a plank resting on that large red chest and box which were sent from home, but, owing to the haste and excitement, I did not think to take a lock of hair. It curled as beautifully as ever, although dripping with water, and the countenance was natural I thought, but it has rather dimmed my recollections of him as he was when living. I felt so thankful that his body had been found before any great change had taken place, that gratitude to God supplanted my grief while we buried him. Mr. Huggins and Fanny sang an Indian hymn made from the 15th chapter of First Corinthians, and then, 'Unveil thy bosom faithful tomb.' We came *home* just after sunset. It is but a little distance from our dwelling, and in the same 'garden of roses,' as Thomas called it, where he now sleeps."

Only a few additional circumstances need to be noted. The sad story was carried speedily to the Indian tents, and those who were in the neighborhood came to look on and give what sympathy and help they could. That was not much. The deep hole was too deep to be reached by any means at our command. The waters rolled on, and to us, as we gazed on them, knowing that the dear brother Thomas was underneath them, they began more and more to assume a frightful appearance. For months and months after, they had that frightful look. I shuddered when I looked. The Indians said their water god, *Oonktehe*, was displeased with us for coming to build there. *He* had seized the young man. It did seem sometimes as though God was against us.

The Saturday's sun went down without giving success

to our efforts, and on Sabbath morning the Indians renewed the search somewhat, but with no better result. Toward evening the body was found to have risen and drifted to a sand-bar below. We took it up tenderly, washed and wrapped it in a clean linen sheet, and placed it in the new cabin, on which his hands had wrought. A grave was dug hastily under the scrub-oaks, where, with only some loose boards about it, we laid our brother to rest until the resurrection. That was our Allon-bachuth. We were dumb, because God did it. That was the first great shadow that came over our home. It was one of ourselves that had gone. The sorrow was too great to find expression in tears or lamentations. The Dakotas observed this. One day old *Black Eagle* came in and chided us for it. " The ducks and the geese and the deer " he said, "when one is killed, make an outcry about it, and the sorrow passes by. The Dakotas, too, like these wild animals, make a great wailing over a dead friend—they wail out their sorrow, and it becomes lighter; but you keep your sorrow—you brood over it, and it becomes heavier." There was truth in what the old man said. But we did not fail to cast our burden upon the Lord, and to obtain strength from a source which Black Eagle knew not of.

The old men frequently came to comfort us in this way, and it gave us an opportunity of telling them about Christ, who is the great Conqueror over death and the grave. Sometimes they came in and sat in silence, as old Sleepy Eyes and Tankamane often did, and that did us good. Old Grey Leaf had a gift of talking—he believed in talking. When he came in he made an excited speech, and at the close said, " I don't mean anything."

About this time Mary wrote : " A few days after T.

was drowned, some of the Indians here, entirely regardless of our affliction, came and demanded provisions, as pay for the logs in our cabin. Mr. Riggs had previously given them two barrels of flour, and it was out of our power to aid them any more then, although Mr. R. told them after their cruel speeches, that he would endeavor to purchase some corn, when the Fur Company's boat came up. They threatened killing our cattle and tearing down our cabin, and husband's proposition did not prevent their executing the first part of their threat. Just one week after dear T. was drowned, one ox was killed, and in eight days more the other shared the same fate. Then we *felt* that it was very probable our cabin would be demolished next."

The summer was wearing away. We were getting some access to the people. On the Sabbath, we could gather in a few, to be present while we sang Dakota hymns, and read the Bible and prayed. But there was a good deal of opposition. As our oxen had been killed and eaten, and we were approaching the winter, it was necessary that we have some means of drawing our fire wood. So I bought *one* ox, and harnessed him as the Red River people do. He was a faithful servant to us during that winter, but the next summer he too was killed and eaten. This time they came boldly, and broke open our stable, and killed and carried away the animal. It seemed as if they were determined that we should not stay. Did the Lord mean to have us give up our work there? We did not want to decide that question hastily.

In the meantime the field was proving to be a very unpromising as well as difficult one, because of the great quantities of whisky brought in. Saint Paul was then made up of a few grog shops, which relied chiefly on the trade with the Indians. They took pelts, or guns, or blankets, or horses—whatever the Indian had to give for his keg of whisky. The trade was a good one. The Lower Sioux bought for the Upper ones, and helped them to buy; and those at the Traverse and other points engaged in the carrying trade. When a keg was brought up, a general *drunk* was the result; but there was enough left to fill with water, and carry up farther and sell for a pony. This made our work very discouraging. Besides, we were often annoyed by the visits of drunken Indians. Sometimes they came with guns and knives. So that we all felt the strain of those years, and we often asked one another, " What good is to come of this ?"

One winter night, Sleepy Eyes had come in from Swan Lake, and placed his horse at our haystack, while he himself went to the trader's to spend the night. Just before we retired to rest, we heard voices and feet hurrying past our door. I went out and found that two men and a woman were at the stable—the men were shooting arrows into Sleepy Eyes' horse. One of the men said, " I asked uncle for this horse, and he did not give it to me—I am killing it." They had done their work. Perhaps I had interfered unnecessarily—certainly unsuccessfully. As they returned and passed by our cabin, I was behind them, and as I was stepping in at the door, an arrow whizzed by. Was it intended to hit?

The next morning that Indian started off for whisky, but a white man passed down the country also, and told the story at Fort Snelling. The result was, that the man who killed his uncle's horse was put in the guard house. Not for that, but for shooting at a white man, he was to be taken down into Iowa, to be tried for assault. The commandant of the post at Snelling doubted whether good would come of it, and I fully agreed with him. And so, in the month of March, Tankamane (Big Walker), and I went down to the Fort and procured his release. He promised well—he would drink no whisky while he lived—he would always be the white man's friend. He signed the pledge and went back with Big Walker and myself. A captain's wife asked how I dared to go in company with that man. I said, "Madam, that man will be my best friend." And so he was. He went up to the Blue Earth hunting grounds, and brought us in some fine venison hams.

But still intemperance increased. A drunken man went to the mission singing, and asked for food. They gave him a plate of rice and a spoon, but he did not feel like eating then. After slobbering over it awhile, he compelled the white women to eat it. They were too much afraid to refuse. One time Mr. Hopkins and I were both away until midnight, when my friend, Tankamane, while drunk, visited the house and threatened to break in the door. But we reached home soon afterward, and the women slept. Thus we had the "terror and the arrow," but the Lord shielded us.

These were very trying years of missionary work. It was at this time our good friend and brother, Simon Anawangmane, who had come from Lac-qui-parle, gave way to the temptation of strong drink. We were grieved and he was ashamed. We prayed for him and with him, and besought him to touch it not again. He promised, but did not keep his promise. He soon developed a passion for "fire water." It was not long before he put off his white-man's clothes, and, dressed like an Indian, he, too, was on his way to the western plains, to buy a horse with a keg of whisky. There were times of repenting and attempted reformation, but they were followed by sinning again and again. Shame took possession of the man, and shame among the Dakotas holds with a terrible grip. He will not let go, and is not easily shaken off. *Shame* is a shameless fellow; it instigates to many crimes. So eight years passed with Simon. Sometimes he was almost persuaded to attempt a new life. Sometimes he came to church and sat down on the door step, not venturing to go in, he was afraid of himself, as well he might be.

"TRAVERSE DES SIOUX, July 13, 1844.

"* * * The Indians and the babies, the chickens and the mice seem leagued to destroy the flowers, and they have well nigh succeeded. Perhaps you will wonder why I should bestow any of my precious time on flowers, when their cultivation is attended with so many difficulties. The principal reason is, that I find my mind needs some such cheering relaxation. In leaving my childhood's home for this Indian land, you know, my dear mother, I left almost everything I held dear, and gave up almost every innocent pleasure I once enjoyed. Much as I may have failed in many respects, I am persuaded there was a firmness of purpose, to count no necessary sacrifice *too great* to be made. I do not think I have made what should be called *great sacrifices*, but I am using the phrase as it is often used, and I am conscious that, in some respects, I have tasked myself too hard. I feel that I have grown old beyond my years. Even the last year has added greatly to my gray hairs. I have been spending my strength too rapidly, and I have often neglected to apply to Him for strength, of whom Isaiah says, 'He giveth power to the faint, and to them that have no might He increaseth strength.' How beautiful and precious is the promise to those who wait upon the Lord! When 'even the youths shall faint and be weary, and the young men shall utterly fall;' 'they that wait upon the Lord shall renew their strength, they shall mount up with wings, as eagles, they shall run and not be weary, they shall walk and not faint.' Oh, if we could *live by faith*, the difficulties and the trials of the way would not greatly trouble or distress us."

In the spring of 1844, Robert and Agnes Hopkins came down from Lac-qui-parle, and, for the next seven years, were identified with the missionary work at Traverse des Sioux. The opposition to our remaining gradually died away and was lived down. Louis Provencalle, the trader, alias Le Bland, had probably tried to carry water on both shoulders, but he was thoroughly converted to our friendship by an accident which happened to himself. The old gentleman was carrying corn, in strings, into his upper chamber by an outside ladder. With a load of this corn on his back, he fell and caught on his picket fence, the sharp pointed wood making a terrible hole in his flesh. For months I visited him almost daily and dressed his wound. He recovered, and although he was not the less a Romanist, he and his family often came to our meetings, and were our fast friends. Perhaps some seeds of truth were then sown, which bore fruit in the family a score of years afterward.

Thus we had, occasionally, an opportunity to help a fellow white man in trouble. It was one Saturday in the early part of September, while we were at work on our school-house, that an Indian runner came in from Swan Lake, to tell us that a "ghost" had come to their camp. A white man had come in in the most forlorn and destitute condition. The story is well told by Mary in her letters home.

"TRAVERSE DES SIOUX, Oct. 10, 1844.

" We have just returned in safety, after spending a week very pleasantly and profitably at Lac-qui-parle. An armed force, from Forts Snelling and Atkinson, have recently passed up to Lake Traverse, to obtain the murderers of an American killed by a Sisseton war party, this summer.

The circumstances of the murder were very aggravating, as communicated to us by the only known survivor. A gentleman from the State of Missouri, Turner by name, with three men were on their way to Fort Snelling with a drove of cattle for the Indians. Being unacquainted with the country, they wandered to the north-west, when they were met by a war party of Sisseton Sioux, returning from an unsuccessful raid upon the Ojibwas. Finding them where they did, on their way apparently to the Red River of the North, they supposed they belonged to that settlement, with whom they had recently had a quarrel about hunting Buffalo. And so they commenced to treat these white men roughly, demanding their horses, guns, and clothes. One man resisted and was killed, the others were robbed. Shirts, drawers, hats and vests were all that were left them. Some of the cattle were killed, and the rest fled. One of the Americans, with some Indians, was sent after them, but he made his escape, and was never heard of again. The next morning, the other two were permitted to leave, but the only requests they made for their coats, a knife, and a life preserver, were not granted.

"The second and third day after this escape, they saw

the cattle, and if only a knife had been spared them, they might have supplied themselves with provisions, but as they were, it was safest, they thought, to hasten on. On the fourth day, they came to a stream too deep to ford, and Turner could not swim. Poor Bennett attempted to swim with him, but was drawn under several times, and, to save his own life, was obliged to disengage himself from Turner, who was drowned. Bennett came on alone five days, finding nothing to eat but hazel-nuts, when at length he came in sight of the Sioux Lodges at Swan Lake. He lay awake that night deliberating whether he should go to them or not. 'If I went,' he said, 'I expected they would kill me; if I did not go, I knew I must die, and I concluded to go, for I could but die.'

"The next morning he tottered toward the Sioux camp. Ever and anon he stopped and hid in the grass. The Dakotas watched his movements. Some young men went out to meet him, but Bennett was afraid of them, and tried to crawl away. When the old man Sleepy Eyes himself came in sight, his benevolent, honest countenance assured the young white man, and he staggered toward the Dakota chief. His confidence was not misplaced. Sleepy Eyes took the *wanage, ghost*, as they called him, to his tent, and his daughter made bread for him of flour, which the old man had bought of us a few days before ; and Bennett, declared he never ate such good bread in his life. Mr. Riggs brought him home, for which he said he was willing to be his servant forever. We furnished him with such clothing as we had, and after three weeks recruiting, we sent him home. At Fort Snelling, he was furnished with money to go to his parents, whom he had left without their consent.

"Since our return from Lac-qui-parle, the Indians

have been drunk less than for some time before. At one time quite a number of men came in a body and demanded powder, which Mr. Riggs intended giving them. I buttoned the door to prevent their entrance, as Mr. R. was not in at the moment, but the button flew into pieces as the sinewy arm of Tankamane pressed the latch. Some of the party were but slightly intoxicated. Those Mr. R. told positively that he should not listen to a request made by drunken men, notwithstanding their threatening "to soldier kill" him—that is, to kill his horse. Tankamane was so drunk that he would not be silent enough to hear, until Mr. R. covered his mouth with his hand and commanded him to be still, and then assured them that he was not ready to give them the powder, and that they had better go home, which they did soon.

"I am not usually much alarmed, though often considerably excited. Some Sabbaths since, a party of Indians brought a keg of whisky, and proposed drinking it in our new building, which is intended for a chapel and school-room. But the Lord did not permit this desecration. One of their number objected to the plan, and they drank it outside the door."

When our school-house was erected and partly finished, our efforts at teaching took on more of regularity. It was a more convenient room to hold our Sabbath service in. In religious teaching, as well as in the school, Mr. Hopkins was an indefatigable worker. He learned the language slowly but well. Often he made visits to the Indian camps miles away. When the Dakotas of that neighborhood abstained for awhile from drinking, we became encouraged to think that some good impressions were being made upon them. But there would come a new flooding of *spirit water*, and a revival of drinking. Thus our hopes were blasted.

"TRAVERSE DES SIOUX, March 15, 1845.

"At the present time our Indian neighbors are absent, some at their sugar camps, and others hunting muskrats. Thus far the season has not been favorable for making sugar, and we have purchased but a few pounds, giving in return flour or corn, of which we have but little to spare. Last spring we procured our year's supply from the Indians, and for the most of it we gave calico in exchange. Not for our sakes, but for the sake of our ragged and hungry neighbors, I should rejoice in their having an abundant supply. They eat sugar, during the season, as freely as we eat bread, and what they do not need for food they can exchange for clothing. But they will have but little for either, unless the weather is more favorable the last half than it has been the first part of this month. And they are so superstitious, that some, I presume, will attribute the unpropitious sky and wind to our influence. Mr. Hopkins visited several camps about ten miles distant, soon after the first, and, thus far, the only good sugar weather. One woman said to him, "You visited us last winter; before you came there were a great many deer, but afterward, none; and now we have made some sugar, but you have come, and perhaps we shall make no more."

"June 23, 1845.

"*My Dear Mother*,—

"Having put our missionary cabin in order for the reception of Captains Sumner and Allen, and Doctor Nichols, of the army, I am reminded of home. I have not made half the preparation which you used to make to receive military company, and I could not if I would, neither would I if

I could. I do, however, sometimes wish it afforded me more pleasure to receive such guests, when they occasionally pass through the country. We have so many uncivilized and so few civilized, and our circumstances are such that I almost shrink from trying to entertain company. I sometimes think that even mother, with all her hospitality, would become a little selfish, if her kitchen, parlor, and dining-room were all *one*."

This was the second military expedition made to secure the offenders of the Sisseton war party. The one made in the fall of 1844 secured five Indians, but not the ones considered most guilty. But they made their escape on the way down to Traverse des Sioux. The expedition, to which reference is made above, was more successful. The Indians pledged themselves to deliver up the guilty men. They did so. Four men were delivered up and taken down to Dubuque, Iowa, where they were kept in confinement until winter. Then they were permitted to escape, and, strange to say, *three* of them died while making their way back, and one lived to reach his friends. It was very remarkable, that *three Indians* should be placed over against *three white men*, in the outcome of Providence.

"August 15, 1845.

"Our garden enclosure extends around the backside and both ends of our mission house, while in front is a double log cabin, with a porch between. Back of the porch we have a *very small* bed-room, which our children now occupy, and back of our cabin, as it was first erected, we have a larger bed-room, which, by way of distinction, we call the *nursery*. The door from this room opens into the garden. The room does not extend *half* the length of the double log cabin, so that Mr. Hopkins has a room corresponding with our nursery, and then between the two wings, we have two small windows, one in the children's bed-room, and the other in our family-room. Shading the latter are Alfred's morning-glories and a rose bush. A shoot from this wild rose has often attracted my attention, as day after day it has continued its upward course. It is now *seven feet high*—the growth of a single season—and is still aspiring to be higher. Bowed beneath it is a sister stalk laden with rose-buds. Last year it was trampled upon by drunken Indians, but now our fence affords us some protection, and we flattered ourselves that our pumpkins and squashes would be unmolested. But we found, to our surprise one day, that our garden had been stripped of the larger pumpkins the night previous. Our situation here, at a point where the roving sons of the prairie congregate, exposes us to annoyances of this kind more frequently than at other stations among the Sioux. I can sympathize very fully with Moffat in like grievances, which he mentions in his 'Southern Africa.'"

"January 29, 1846.

" For several Sabbaths past we have had a *small* congregation. It encourages us somewhat to see even a few, induced to listen for a short time to the truths of the gospel. But our chief encouragement is in God's unfailing promises. The Indians here usually sit during the whole service, and sometimes smoke several times.

"For some weeks I have been teaching the female part of our school. Some days half a dozen black-eyed girls come, and then again, only one or two. Their parents tell them that we ought to pay them for coming to school, and although there have been no threats of cutting up the blankets of those who read, as there was last winter, they are still ridiculed and reproached. We have, in various ways, endeavored to reward them for regular attendance, in such a manner as not to favor the idea that we were hiring them."

In the spring of 1846, Mary wanted to get away, for a little rest. We fitted up a canoe, and, with a young man of the fur trade, we started down the Minnesota. Mary had her baby, our fourth child, whose name was Anna Jane. We had scarcely well started, when we met drunken Indians. Their canoe was laden with kegs of whisky, and they were on shore cooking. They called to us to come over and give them some food; but we passed by on the other side. One man raised his gun and poured into us a volley of buck-shot. Fortunately, Mary and the baby were not touched. The canoe and the rest of us were somewhat sprinkled, but not seriously hurt.

That canoe voyage was continued down the Mississippi River as far as Red Wing. At Mr. Pond's station we took in Jane Lamonte, afterward Mrs. Titus. Where the city of St. Paul now is we made a short stop, and I hunted up one of our Dakota church members, the wife of a Frenchman. A half a dozen log houses, one here and one there, made up the St. Paul of that day. At Pine Bend, Mr. Brown left us. After that the rowing was heavy and the muscles were light. Just above the mouth of the St. Croix we found a house, where we spent the night comfortably. The next day, we reached Red Wing, a Dakota village, or Hay-minne-chan, with much difficulty. We had to row against a strong head wind, and I, who was the principal oarsman, fell sick. But as Providence would have it, we came upon a woodman, who took us to the village.

Red Wing was the station of the Swiss mission, occupied by the Dentans. Mrs. Dentan had been a teacher in the Mackinaw mission school. Here we found good Christian friends, and spent two weeks in helping them to do missionary work. While we were there, I went to see a young man whom the medicine men were conjuring. The Dakota doctor claimed that the spirit, which caused the disease, was greatly enraged at my presence. And so, at their earnest request, I retired. That sick young man is now one of our excellent native pastors. We have since talked over the event with much interest.

CHAPTER VII.

1846–1851.—Returning to Lac-qui-parle.—Reasons Therefor.—Mary's Story.—"Give me my Old Seat, Mother."—At Lac-qui-parle.—New Arrangements.—Better Understanding.—Buffalo Plenty.—Mary's Story.—Little Samuel Died.—Going on the Hunt.—Vision of Home.—Building House.—Dakota Camp.—Soldier's Lodge.—Wakanmane's Village.—Making a Presbytery—New Recruits.—Meeting at Kaposia.—Mary's Story.—Varied Trials.—Sabbath Worship.—"What is to Die?"—New Stations.—Making a Treaty.—Mr. Hopkins Drowned.—Personal Experience.

The time came when it was decided that Mary and I should go back to Lac-qui-parle. The four years since we left had brought many changes. They had been years of discouragement and hardship all along the line. The brothers Pond had built among the people of their first love—the old Lake Calhoun band, now located a short distance up from the mouth of the Minnesota. There they had a few who came regularly to worship and to learn the way of Life. But the mass of the people of Cloud Man's village were either indifferent or opposed to the gospel of Christ.

At Lac-qui-parle, where had been the best seed-sowing and harvesting for the first seven years, the work had gone backward. Bad corn years had driven some of the native Christians to take refuge among the annuity Indians of the Mississippi. Temptations of various kinds had drawn away others—they had stumbled and fallen.

Persecutions from the heathen party had deterred others, and some had fallen asleep in Christ. Among these last was Mr. Joseph Renville, who had stood by the work from the beginning. He had passed away in the month of March; and thus the Lac-qui-parle church was reduced to less than half its members of four years ago.

Out of this church there had gone a half a dozen or so, chiefly women, down to Kaposia, or Little Crow's village, which was on the Mississippi, a few miles below the site of St. Paul. Through them, more than any other influence perhaps, there came an invitation from Little Crow and the head men of the village, to Dr. Williamson, through the Indian agent at Fort Snelling, to come down and open a school and a mission. This application was considered at the meeting of the Dakota mission held at the Traverse, and the voices were in favor of acceptance. But if Dr. Williamson left Lac-qui-parle, that involved the necessity of our returning thither. This proposition Mary could not entertain willingly. True, the work at the Traverse had been full of hardships and suffering, but the very sufferings and sorrows, and especially that great first sorrow, had strongly wedded her affections to the place and the people. It was hard to leave those Oaks of Weeping. She could not see that it was right, still she would not refuse to obey orders.

And so the month of September, 1846, found us traveling over the same road that we had gone on our first journey, just nine years before. Then we two had gone; now we had with us our four little ones, but it was a sad journey. The mother's heart was not convinced, nor was it satisfied we had done right, until some time after we reached Lac-qui-parle.

MARY'S STORY.

"TRAVERSE DES SIOUX, Sept. 17, 1846.

"This is probably the last letter I shall write you from this spot so dear to us. If I could see that it was duty to go, it would cheer me in the preparations for our departure, but I cannot feel that the interests of the mission required such a sacrifice as leaving this home is to me.

"These are some of the thoughts that darken the prospect, when I think of leaving the comforts and conveniences which we have only enjoyed one or two short summers—such as the enclosure for our children—our rude back porch which has served for a kitchen, the door into which I helped Mr. Riggs saw with a cross-cut saw, because he could get no one to help him. We located here in the midst of opposition and danger, yet God made our enemies to be at peace with us. Sad will be the hour when I take the last look of our low log cabins, our neat white chapel, and dear Thomas' grave."

"LAC-QUI-PARLE, Dec. 10, 1846.

"How pleasant it would be, dear mother, to join your little circle around home's hearth; but it is vain to wish, and so I take my pen, that this transcript of my heart may enter where I cannot. In one of the late New York *Observer's*, I found a gem of poetry, which seemed so much like the gushings of my affection for my mother, that I must send you the verse which pleased me best:

"'Give me my old seat, mother,
  With my head upon thy knee;
I've passed through many a changing scene,
  Since thus I sat by thee.
Oh, let me look into thine eyes—
  Their meek, soft, loving light
Falls like a gleam of holiness,
  Upon my heart, to-night!'

"How very often have I found myself half wishing for my old seat, with my head upon thy knee, that I might impart to you my joys and my sorrows, and listen to your own. In times of difficulty and distress, how I have longed for your counsel and cheering sympathy. After leaving our home at Traverse des Sioux and reaching this place, my heart yearned to embrace you. My associates could not comprehend why it should be so trying to me to leave that place so dear to us. I had hoped to live and die and be buried there by the loved grave of Thomas. I had laid plans for usefulness there, and the change that came over us in one short week, during which we packed all our effects and prepared for the journey, was so sudden and so great, that it often seemed I should sink under it. Had I been able to see it clearly our duty, the case would have been different. I hope it will prove for the best. Doubtless I was too much attached to that burial spot and that garden of roses. Henceforth, may I more fully realize that 'we have no abiding city here,' and, like a pilgrim, press onward to that eternal haven—that unchanging home—little mindful where I pass the few brief nights that may intervene."

"Dec. 16.

"You will, I think, feel gratified to know that there are some things pleasant and encouraging here, notwithstanding the discouragements. The sound of the church-going bell is heard here—the bell which we purchased with the avails of moccasins donated by the church members. Some of those contributors are dead, and others have backslidden or removed, still there are more hearers of the word here than at Traverse des Sioux, although the large majority in both places turn a deaf ear to the calls and entreaties of the gospel. Quite a number of the women who attend the Sabbath services can read, but some of them cannot find the hymns, and I enjoy very much finding the places for them."

Our place at the Traverse was filled by Mr. A. G Huggins' family, who thenceforward became associated with Mr. Hopkins until they closed their connection with the mission work. Fanny Huggins had married Jonas Pettijohn, and they were our helpers at Lac-qui-parle for the next five years.

The time seemed to have come when our relations to the Indians should, if possible, be placed upon a better basis. From the time that the chief men came to understand that the religion of Christ was an exclusive religion, that it would require the giving up of their ancestral faith, they set themselves in opposition to it. Sometimes this was shown in their persecution of the native Christians, forbidding them to attend our meetings, and cutting up the blankets of those who came. Sometimes it was exhibited in the order that the children should not attend school. But the organized determination to drive us from the country showed itself most decidedly in killing our cattle. We could not continue in the country, and make ourselves comfortable, without a team of some kind. This then was to be their policy. They would kill our cattle. They would steal our horses. And they had so persistently held to this line of treatment, during the last four years, that Dr. Williamson and his associates had, with difficulty, kept a team of any kind. Once they were obliged to hitch up milch cows to haul fire-wood.

The Indians said we were trespassers in their country, and they had a right to take reprisals. We used their wood and their water, and pastured our animals on their grass, and gave them no adequate pay. We had helped them get larger corn patches by ploughing for them, we had furnished food and medicines to their sick ones, we had often clothed their naked ones, we had spent and been spent in their service, but all this was, in their estimation, no compensation for the field we planted, and the fuel we used, and the grass we cut, and the water we drank. They were worth a thousand dollars a year!

And so it seemed to me the time had come when some better understanding should be reached in regard to these things. I called the principal men of the village—Oo-pe-ya-hdaya, Inyangmane and Wakanmane, and others, and told them that, as Dr. Williamson was called away by the Lower Indians, my wife and I had been sent back to Lac-qui-parle, but we would stay only on certain conditions. We knew them and they knew us. If we could stay with them as friends, and be treated as friends, we would stay. We came to teach them and their children. But if then, or at any time afterward, we learned that the whole village did not want us to stay, we would go home to our friends. For the help we gave them, the water we used must be free, the wood to keep us warm must be free, the grass our cattle ate must be free, and the field we planted must be free; but when we wanted their best timber to build houses with, which we should do, I would pay them liberally for it. This arrangement they said was satisfactory, and soon afterward, we bought from them the timber we used in erecting two frame houses.

From this time onward we did not suffer so much from cattle killing, though it has always been an incident attaching to mission life among the Indians. For the years that followed we were generally treated as friends. Sometimes there was a breeze of opposition, some wanted us to go away, but we always had friends who stood by us. And they were not always of the same party. The results of mission work began to be seen in the young men who grew up, many of them desirous of adopting, in part at least, the habits and the dress of the whites.

There was another reason for a cessation of hostilities on their part; viz., that starvation did not so much stare them in the face. They had better corn crops than for some years previous. And besides this, for two seasons the buffalo range was extended down the Minnesota far below Lac-qui-parle. For many years they had been far away, west of Lake Traverse. Now they came back, and for two winters our Indians reveled in fresh buffalo meat, their children and dogs even growing fat. And the buffalo robes gave them the means of clothing their families comfortably.

Sometimes the herds of bison came into the immediate neighborhood of the village. One morning it was found that a large drove had slept on the prairie but a little distance back of our mission houses. Mr. Martin McLeod, the trader, and a few others organized a hunt on horseback. There was snow on the ground, I hitched our ponies to a rude sled, and we went to the show. As the hunters came into the herd and began to shoot them, the excitement increased in our sled—the ponies could not go fast enough for the lady.

We now addressed ourselves afresh to the work of teaching and preaching. The day-school filled up. We took some children into our families. The young men who had learned to read and write when they were boys, came and wanted to learn something of arithmetic and geography. In the work of preaching, I began to feel more freedom and joy. There had been times when the Dakota language seemed to be barren and meaningless

The words for Salvation and Life, and even Death and Sin, did not mean what they did in English. It was not to me a heart-language. But this passed away. A Dakota word began to *thrill* as an English word. Christ came into the language. The Holy Spirit began to pour sweetness and power into it. Then it was not exhausting, as it sometimes had been—it became a joy to preach.

MARY'S STORY.

"LAC-QUI-PARLE, May 17, 1847.

"Since Mr. Riggs left home, two weeks to-day, I have had a double share of wants to supply. I could almost wish he had locked up the medicine case and taken the key with him, for I have not so much confidence in my skill as to suppose the Indians would have suffered, if it had been out of my power to satisfy their wants. I purposed only giving rhubarb and a few other simples, but I have been besieged until I have yielded, and have no relief to hope for until Mr. Riggs returns.

"In addition to the medicines, there has been a great demand for garden seeds, to say nothing of the common wants of a little thread, or soap, or patches for a ragged short-gown, or a strip of white cloth for the head to enable them to kill ducks or buffalo, as the case may be. There is scarcely any view of God's character that gives me so clear an apprehension of his infinite goodness and power, as that of his kind care of his sinful creatures. He listens to their requests, and giving doth not impoverish, neither doth withholding enrich Him."

"May 26.

"This afternoon twenty-six armed Indian men paraded before the door and discharged their guns. I was a little startled at first, but soon learned that they had been in search of Chippewas, that were supposed to be concealed near by, and that they had returned unsuccessful, and were merely indulging in a little military exercise."

"January 11, 1848.

"The last Sabbath in December, Mr. Riggs spent at an Indian encampment about sixteen miles from this place. When he left home, baby *Samuel*, Mr. and Mrs. Pettijohn's only child, was ill, but we did not apprehend dangerously so; when he returned on Monday noon, little Samuel was dead. This has been a severe affliction to them. Why was this first born and only son taken, and our five children spared, is a query that often arises.

"Some weeks ago, an elderly woman with a young babe, begged me for clothing for the little one. I asked her if it was her child. She replied that it was her grandchild, that its mother died last summer, and that she had nursed it ever since. At first she had no milk, but she continued nursing it, until the milk flowed for the little orphan. This, thought I, is an evidence of a grandmother's love not often witnessed. I felt very compassionate for the baby, and gave the grandmother some old clothing. After she left, a knife was missing, which seemed rather like a gypsy's compensation for the kindness received. But perhaps she was not the thief, as our house was then thronged with visitors from morning till night. We endeavor to keep such things as they will be tempted to steal, out of their reach, but a mother cannot watch three or four children, and perform necessary household duties at the same time, without sometimes affording an opportunity for a cunning hand to slip away a pair of scissors or a knife unnoticed.

"The buffalo are about us in large herds. I have just taken a ride of four or five miles to see these natives of the prairie. Before the herd perceived our approach they were quietly standing together, but, on perceiving us, they waited a moment for consultation, and then started bounding away. Those who were prepared for the chase entered their ranks, and then the herd separated into three or four parts, and scampered for life in as many different directions. Several were killed and dressed, and we brought home the huge head of one for the children to see, besides the tongue and some meat, which were given us as our share of the spoils."

"May 25, 1848.

"How very quiet and green I think those lanes are— no noise except the whispering winds in those beautiful elms and maples; and those still rooms, where rang the merry shout of children returned from school. I could almost fancy they would look as sober and somber as those dark firs under which we played when we and they were small. *They* still are young and vigorous, for aught I know, but *we*, alas! are young no longer. Do the lilacs, and roses, and snowballs still bloom as brightly as ever? But the thought of those bright and beautiful scenes makes me sad, and I wish to write a cheering letter, so good-by to the visions of departed joys.

"We are building, this summer, a plain, snug, one-story house, with a sitting-room, kitchen and two bed-rooms on the lower floor, and two rooms above, if ever they should be completed. We have been hoping to have a young lady to assist in teaching, etc., for an occupant of one of our bed-rooms, but the prospect is rather discouraging. And yet, I feel that it is no more so than we deserve, for I have not exercised faith in this respect. I have, however some hope that He, 'Who is able to do exceeding abundantly above all that we ask or think,' will send us such fellow laborers as we need."

During these two buffalo winters, almost the whole village removed up to the Pomme de Terre, or *Owobaptay* River, as the Dakotas called it. That was a better point to hunt from. For the regulation of the hunt, and to prevent the buffalo from being driven off, they organized a *Soldiers' Lodge*. This was a large tent pitched in the center of the camp, where the symbols of power were kept in two bundles of *red* and *black* sticks. These represented the soldiers—those who had killed enemies and those who had not. To this tent the women brought offerings of wood and meat; and here the young and old men often gathered to feast, and from these headquarters went forth, through an *Eyanpaha* (cryer), the edicts of the wise men.

For these two winters, I arranged to spend every alternate Sabbath at the camp, going up on Saturday and returning on Monday. This soldiers' tent was, from the first, placed at my disposal for Sabbath meetings. It was an evidence of a great change in the general feeling of the village toward Christianity. It was a public recognition of it. All were not Christians by any means; but the *following* was honorable and honored, and we usually had a crowded tent. Our evening meetings were held in the tent of one of our church members. So the Word of God grew in Dakota soil.

Where the village of Lac-qui-parle now stands, is the site of Wakanmane's planting-place and village of those days. In one of the summer bark houses, we were accustomed to hold a week-day meeting. Our mission was three miles from there, and on the other side of the Minnesota; but it was only a pleasant walk of a summer day, and I was sure to find a little company, chiefly women, of from half a dozen to a dozen present. After two-years' absence, Dr. Williamson returned to Lac-qui-parle on a visit, and remarked that he had found no meetings among the Dakotas so stimulating and encouraging as that weekly prayer-meeting. I have since spent a Sabbath, and worshiped with white people on the same spot. It seemed like Jacob coming back to Bethel, where the angels of God had been.

There were still few things to encourage, and many to discourage, all through the Dakota field; but it began to appear to us, that if our forces could be doubled, the work, with God's blessing, might be pushed forward successfully. And so the Dakota Presbytery, which was organized in 1845, proceeded to license and ordain Gideon H. Pond and Robert Hopkins as ministers of the gospel. They had both been working in this line for years, and it was fit that they should now be properly recognized as fellow laborers in the vineyard of the Lord.

The American Board was ready also to respond to our call for more help. In the spring of 1848, Rev. M. N. Adams and Rev. John F. Aiton were sent up from Ohio and Illinois; and later in the season, Rev. Joshua Potter came from the Cherokee country. Our annual meeting was held that year with Dr. Williamson, at his new station, Kaposia, a few miles below St. Paul. It was a meeting of more than ordinary interest; not only on account of our own reinforcements, but because we met there two lady teachers, (Gov. Slade's girls), the first sent out to the white settlements of Minnesota. The toilers of fourteen years among the Dakotas now shook hands with the first toilers among the white people.

The boy Thomas had been added to our little group of

children. With a part of the family, Mary now made the trip back to the Traverse, with a much gladder heart than she had when coming up two years before.

MARY'S STORY.

"LAC-QUI-PARLE, Oct. 16, 1848.

"This year the annual meeting of our mission was at Kaposia, the station occupied by Dr. Williamson and family. I accompanied Mr. Riggs with three of our children. From the Traverse, Mr. Hopkins had arranged that we should proceed through the Big Woods, by means of ox carts. There was no road cut yet, and hundreds of large logs lay across the path; but the patient animals worried over them, and drivers and riders were very weary, when, late at night, we came into camp. At Prairieville, as *Tintatonwe* signifies, where Mr. S. W. Pond is located, we spent the Sabbath, and reached Dr. Williamson's on Monday, *only eight days* from Lac-qui-parle, not a little fatigued, but greatly prospered in our journey. More truly than did the Gibeonites, could we say, 'This our bread we took hot for our provision, out of our houses, on the day we came forth to go unto you, but now behold it is dry, and it is moldy.'

"At Kaposia we found the Messrs. Pond, also Mr. and Mrs. Aiton, and Mr. and Mrs. Adams, who have recently joined the Sioux mission. Mr. and Mrs. Hopkins with their three children, who were of our party from the Traverse, and ourselves in addition to Dr. Williamson's family, made such a company as I had not seen for a long time. The warm reception we met with from so many kindred in Christ excited me almost as much as did the greeting at home after five-years' absence. It reminded me of that happy meeting, and, as at that time, I was overpowered with joyful emotions.

"We passed nearly a week at Kaposia, and then set our faces homeward, spending a night at Mr. G. H. Pond's, at Oak Grove, and one also at Mr. Samuel W. Pond's, at Tintatonwe. Two nights we camped out, and reached Traverse on Friday afternoon. While there I often went to brother Thomas' grave. The turf which I assisted in setting was very green, and the rose bushes were flourishing. The cedar we planted withered, but a beautiful one, placed by Mr. Hopkins near the grave, is fresh and verdant. Mr. and Mrs. Adams returned with us to Lac-qui-parle."

"LAC-QUI-PARLE, Jan. 6, 1849.

"The Spirit has seemed near us, and we hope A. is listening to his teachings. Some of the Indians also have manifested an inquiring state of mind, but Satan is very busy, and unless the Lord rescues his rebellious subjects from the thralldom of the devil, I fear the Holy Spirit will depart from us.

"The same foolish yet trying accusations are made—such as that we are to receive pay according to the number of scholars in the school here when the land is sold—that we are using up their grass and timber and land, and making then no requital. A few days ago the old chief and his brother-in-law came and rehearsed their supposed claims, and said that the Indians were tired eating corn, and wanted one of our remaining cattle. Truly we can say that this earth is not our *rest*, and rejoice that we shall not live here always.

"We have had faith to expect that the Lord was about to 'make bare His arm,' for the salvation of these degraded Indians; and although the heathen rage, we know that 'He who sitteth on the circle of the earth, and the inhabitants thereof are as grasshoppers,' can turn the hearts of this people ' as the rivers of water are turned."

" May 31, 1849.

"During Mr. Riggs' absence, our worship on the Sabbath, both in Sioux and English, has consisted of reading the Scriptures, singing and prayer. I have been gratified that so many attended the Sioux service—about thirty each Sabbath. Anna Jane remarked the Saturday after her father left home, ' We can't have any Sabbath because two men and one woman are gone,' referring to her papa and Mr. and Mrs. Adams. Still these Sabbaths have brought to us privileges, even though the preached Word and the great congregation have been wanting."

" June 15.

" Mr. Riggs reached home two weeks ago, and last Monday he left again for Big Stone Lake, accompanied by Mr. Hopkins, of Traverse des Sioux. They have gone hoping for opportunities to proclaim the Word of God to the Sioux in that region."

"Sept. 2, 1850.

" Last evening, hearing Thomas cry after he had gone to rest, I went to the chamber. Alfred was teaching him to say, ' Now I lay me,' and the sentence, ' If I should die,' distressed him very much. I soothed him by asking God to keep him through the night. He has never seen a corpse, but, a few weeks ago, he saw Mrs. Antoine Renville buried, and he has seen dead birds and chickens. He said, ' What is to die, mamma?' and evidently felt that it was something very incomprehensible and dreadful. I felt a difficulty in explaining it, and I wished to soothe the animal excitement, and not lessen the serious state of mind he manifested. I think I will tell him more about Jesus' death—his burial and resurrection. It is this that has illumined the grave. It is faith in Him who has conquered 'him that had the power of death,' which will give us the victory over every fear."

With an increased missionary force, we hoped to see large results within the next few years. There *was* progress made, but not so much as we hoped for. In fact, it was chiefly apparent in "strengthening the things that remain." Just before this enlargement, Mr. S. W. Pond had separated from his brother, and formed a station at Shakopee, or Six's Village, which he called *Prairieville*. After awhile, little churches were organized at Kaposia, Oak Grove, Prairieville, and Traverse des Sioux. At Lac-qui-parle the numbers in the church were somewhat increased. We began to have more young men in the church, and they began to separate themselves more and more from the village, and to build cabins and make fields for themselves. Thus the religion of Christ worked to disintegrate heathenism.

The summer of 1851 came, which brought great changes, and prepared the way for others. It was one of the very wet summers in Minnesota, when the streams were flooded all the summer through. In making our trip for provisions in the spring, we were detained at the crossing of one stream for almost a whole week. In the latter part of June, the Indians from all along the upper part of the Minnesota were called down to Traverse des Sioux, to meet commissioners of the government. They were obliged to swim at many places. The Minnesota was very high, spreading its waters over all the low bottom contiguous to the mission premises. Governor Ramsay and Commissioner Lea were there for the government.

Gen Sibley and the fur traders generally were present, with a large number of the Wahpaton and Sisseton Sioux.

The Fourth of July was to be celebrated grandly, and Mr. Hopkins had consented to take a part in the celebration, but the Lord disposed otherwise. In the early morning, Mr. Hopkins went to bathe in the overflow of the river. When the family breakfast was ready he had not returned. He was sought for, and his clothes alone were found. He had gone up through the flood of water. It was supposed that, unintentionally, he had waded in beyond his depth, and as he could not swim, was unable again to reach the land.

This was the second great sorrow that came, in the same way, to the mission band of Traverse des Sioux. It threw a pall over the festivities of the day. The Indians said again the Oonktehe—their Neptune—was angry and had taken the *wechasta wakan*. But the mission families were enabled to say, "It is the Lord." When the body floated it was caught in fishing nets, and carefully taken up and buried by the "Oaks of Weeping." Mr. Hopkins did not live to see much matured fruit of his labors, but he had put in eight years of good, honest work for the Master, among the Dakotas, and he has his reward.

The Treaty was made, which, with one consummated immediately after, at Mendota, with the Lower Sioux, conveyed to the white people, all their land in Minnesota, except a reserve on the upper part of the river. These treaties had an important bearing on our mission work, and on all the eastern Dakotas.

The messenger who brought word to us at Lac-qui-parle, of the sudden death of our brother, Robert Hopkins, brought also to me a pressing invitation from the commission to attend the making of the Treaty. I at once mounted a pony and rode down. It gave me an opportunity of seeing the inside of Indian treaties. On my return, I was in advance of the Indians, and, coming to the Chippewa alone, I found no way of crossing its swollen tide but by swimming. In the middle of the stream, my horse turned over backward, and we went down to the bottom together. He soon, however, righted himself, and I came up by his side, with one hand holding his mane. I remember well the feeling I had when in the deep waters, that my horse would take me out. And I was not disappointed. This event has ever since been to me a lesson of trust. "Though I walk through the valley of the shadow of death, I will fear no evil: for Thou art with me; Thy rod and Thy staff they comfort me."

CHAPTER VIII.

1851-1854.—Grammar and Dictionary.—How it grew.—Publication.—Minnesota Historical Society.—Smithsonian Institution.—Going East.—Mission Meeting at Traverse de Sioux.—Mrs. Hopkins.—Death's Doings.—Changes in the Mode of Writing Dakota.—Completed Book.—Growth of the Language.—In Brooklyn and Philadelphia.—The Misses Spooner.—Changes in the Mission.—The Ponds and Others Retire.—Dr. Williamson at Pay-zhe-hoo-ta-ze.—Winter Storms.—Andrew Hunter.—Two Families Left.—Children Learning Dakota.—Our House Burned.—The Lord Provides.

A grammar and dictionary of the Dakota language had been going through the process of growth, in all these years. It was incidental to our missionary work, and in the line of it. The materials came to us naturally, in our acquisition of the language, and we simply arranged them. The work of arrangement involved a good deal of labor, but it brought its reward, in the better insight it gave one of their forms of thought and expression.

To begin with, we had the advantage of what had been gathered by the Messrs. Pond and Stevens and Dr. Williamson, in the three years before we came. Perhaps an effort made still earlier, by some officers of the army at Fort Snelling, in collecting a vocabulary of a few hundred words of the Sioux language, should not be overlooked. Thus, entering into other men's labors, when we had been a year or more in the country, and were somewhat prepared to reap on our own account, the vocabulary which I had gathered from all sources, amounted to about three thousand words.

From that time onward, it continued to increase rapidly, as by means of translations and otherwise, we were gathering new words. In a couple of years more, the whole needed revision and rewriting, when it was found to have more than doubled. So it grew. Mr. S. W. Pond also entered into the work of arranging the words and noting the principles of the Dakota language. He gave me the free use of his collections, and he had the free use of mine. This will be sufficient to indicate the way in which the work was carried on, from year to year. How many dictionaries I made I cannot now remember. When the collection reached ten thousand words and upward, it began to be quite a chore to make a new copy. By and by we had reason to believe that we had gathered pretty much the whole language, and our definitions were measurably correct.

It was about the beginning of the year 1851, when the question of publication was first discussed. Certain gentlemen in the Legislature of Minnesota, and connected with the Historical Society of Minnesota, became interested in the matter. Under the auspicies of this society, a circular was printed setting forth the condition of the manuscript, and the probable expense of publication, and asking the co-operation of all who were interested in giving the language of the Dakotas to the literary world in a tangible and permanent form. The subscription thus started by the Historical Society, and headed by such names as Alexander Ramsay then governor of the Territory, Rev. E. D. Neill the secretary of the society, H. H. Sibley, H. M. Rice and Martin McLeod, the chiefs of the fur trade, in the course of the summer, amounted to about eight hundred dollars. With this sum pledged, it was considered quite safe to commence the publication. The American Board of Commissioners for Foreign Missions very cheerfully consented to pay my expenses while carrying the work through the press, besides making a donation to it directly from their Treasury.

From these sources we had $1,000; and with this sum the book might have been published in a cheap form, relying upon after sales to meet any deficiency. But, after considering the matter, and taking the advice of friends who were interested in the highest success of the undertaking, it was decided to offer it to the Smithsonian Institution, to be brought out as one of their series of contributions to knowledge. Prof. Joseph Henry at once had it examined by Prof. C. C. Felton and Prof. W. W. Turner. It received their approval and was ordered to be printed.

In the meantime, Mary and I had undertaken our second trip to the East. Mr. and Mrs. Adams, who had been away awhile on account of Mrs. Adams' health, were now back at Lac-qui-parle, associated with Mr. and Mrs. Pettijohn. We commenced our journey across the prairie about the first of September. The waters were still high, and we found it necessary to make a boat which should serve as a bed for one of our wagons, and be easily transferred to the water.

Our children now numbered a round half dozen. The baby, Henry Martyn, about two years old, must be taken along of course. The boy, "Good Bird," now about fourteen, we would take down with us and send to school in Illinois. Isabella we concluded to take on to the mother's mountain home in Massachusetts. The two little girls were kindly cared for in the family of Rev. E. D. Neill, of St. Paul; and the little boy, Thomas, was to stay in Dr. Williamson's family, at Kaposia. Thus the distribution was finally made.

The mission meeting took place this year at Traverse des Sioux. Among other consultations it was adjudged wise for Mrs. Hopkins and her three children—the father and husband being gone—to accompany us on their return to her friends in Southern Ohio. The brothers Pond, and Rev. Joseph Hancock, who had joined the mission and was stationed at Red Wing, all had their horses, and the travel by land being difficult, they put them on board our good mission boat *Winona*, and so we had a full cargo down to St. Paul.

From there we had a steamer to Galena, where we took passage in freight wagons that were going to Elgin, the terminus of the railroad that was then being made west from Chicago. This trip across the country, we all greatly enjoyed, stopping at Freeport over the Sabbath, and listening to the somewhat celebrated revivalist, Elder Knapp. We crossed Lake Michigan, and by the Michigan Central to Detroit, and then took a lake boat to Cleveland. That night we encountered a lake storm; and while almost every one was sea-sick, Mary and I stood on the fore deck and enjoyed watching the mountain waves.

Reaching the land in safety, Mrs. Hopkins and her little family went to Southern Ohio, and we spent a few days in Medina, with Mary's brother, Rev. M. M. Longley. We found that the eight years which had passed since we were East before, had made a good many vacant chairs in our home circles. My own father had been called from earth very suddenly, in 1845. He was well and had done a hard day's work, but ere the evening shadows fell he had passed beyond the river. The angel of death and the angel of life had visited Mary's home again and again. First the grandfather, Col. Edmund Longley, had gone to his fathers, at the good old age of ninety-five. Then in 1848, the *pater familias*, Gen. Thomas Longley, had wrapped his cloak about him and laid him down to rest. The next to hear the summons was the little sister, Henrietta Arms. She had grown to be a woman, and Mary fondly hoped to have her companionship and aid in the Dakota field. But the Master called her up higher. And then, only a few months before we reached Ohio, the loving, cultured, and beloved brother, Alfred, had passed through months of weariness and pain, up to the new life and vigor of the heavenly world. He had been preaching for several years in Northeastern Ohio. So many had gone that when we reached the mountain home in Hawley, we found it desolate. Only Joseph and his mother remained. Mary soon persuaded her mother to go down to South Deerfield, that they might together spend the winter with the older sister, Mrs. Cooley. And I went to New York City, and was, the next seven months, engaged in getting through the press the grammar and dictionary of the Dakota language.

Of the various hindrances and delays, and of the burning of the printing office in which the work was in progress, and the loss of quite a number of pages of the book which had to be again made up, I need not speak. They are ordinary incidents. Early in the summer of 1852, the work was done—and done, I believe, to the satisfaction of all parties. It has obtained the commendation of literary men generally, and it was said that for no volume published by the Smithsonian Institution, up to that time, was the demand so great as for that. It is now out of print, and the book can only be bought at fancy prices.

The question of republication is sometimes talked of, but no steps have been taken yet to accomplish the object. While, as the years have gone by, and the book has been tested by Dakota scholars and found to be all that was ever claimed for it, yet, in case of a republication, some valuable additions can be made to the sixteen thousand words which it contains. The language itself is growing. Never probably, in its whole history, has it grown so much in any quarter of a century, as it has in the twenty-five years since the dictionary was published. Besides, we have recently been learning more of the Teeton dialect, which is spoken by more than half of the whole Sioux nation. And, as the translation of the Bible has progressed, thoughts and images have been brought in, which have given the language an unction and power unknown to it before.

While we were in the East, several offers were made in regard to taking one of our children. These offers came from the best families, where a child would have enjoyed all the comforts and many of the luxuries of life, more than could be had in our Indian home. It was a question that had often claimed our thought, and sometimes had been very favorably considered, but when the opportunity came, we decided to keep our children with us for the present. The circumstances of our home life had changed somewhat; home education could be carried on to better advantage, and with less drawbacks than in the first years of our missionary life.

And so in the month of June, when the Philadelphia market was red with its best strawberries, we started westward, bringing the two children with us. It had been a profitable year to Isabella. The mother and children had spent a couple of the last months with relatives and friends in Brooklyn; and now we made a little stop in the Quaker City, and visited Gerard College, Fairmount, and other places of interest. It was September, when we had gathered all our six children together, and were making the trip across the prairie to Lac-qui-parle. This time we had with us the Misses LUCY and MARY SPOONER, of Ky.— since, Mrs. Drake and Mrs. Worcester. They came out to spend two years in the mission. Miss Lucy's teaching in music, vocal and instrumental, as well as other branches, was of singular advantage to our own children, as well as to the Indians.

Miss Mary went into the family of Mr. Adams, who had gathered a little boarding-school of Dakota children. This might be called the first effort in this line made among the Dakotas. Before our return, Mr. and Mrs. Pettijohn had taken the pre-emption fever, and had left the mission and gone to the Traverse and made a claim. Mrs. Pettijohn had been connected with the mission work since 1839, and Mr. P. for a shorter period. Both had been conscientious workers and had done good service. They now wanted to make a home for their growing family. Mr. Huggins also, about the same time, left the mission work and made a home in the same neighborhood. Mr. Potter had left the Dakota field after only a year's trial, regarding it as a very difficult one, as compared with the one he had left in the Indian Territory South. Now, in the years 1852 and 1853, our numbers diminished very rapidly. The Indians were to be removed, according to the stipulations of their treaties, to their reserve on the Upper Minnesota. Both the brothers Pond elected to stay where they were and minister to the white people who were rapidly settling up the country. Both were successful in organizing churches, one at Shakopee and the other at Bloomington. Both still live, but have retired from the work of the ministry, and are waiting for the translation to the upper world.*

Likewise, for the same reasons, Mr. John F. Aiton retired from the service of the Board, about the same time, and Mr. Hancock also. Dr. Williamson elected to continue his work among the Dakotas, and so made arrangements, in advance of the removal of the Indians, to open a new station near the Yellow Medicine, which he called Pay-zhe-hoo-ta-ze—the Dakota name for that stream.

During the summer of 1852, Dr. Williamson had erected his dwelling house at this new place, but it was still in quite an unfinished state, when he removed his family up in the beginning of the cold weather. That fall the snows came early, and found the family without any sufficient supplies for the winter. In December, the storms were incessant, and the snow became very deep, at which time the doctor's men were toiling against odds, endeavoring to bring up provisions to the family on the Yellow Medicine. But they could not succeed When they were yet more than forty miles away, their teams gave out and were buried in the snow. The men, both frozen badly, Mr. Andrew Hunter much maimed, barely succeeded in reaching the mission. How the family were to winter through was not apparent, but the Lord provided. Unexpectedly, the Indians found fish in the river, and Mr.

---

* Since this chapter was written, Rev. G. H. Pond, the younger of the brothers, has gone to see the King in his Beauty, in the Land that is not very far off. He departed on the 20th of January 1878, leaving a family of *fifty*—twenty-two were grandchildren—and all, except the sixteen youngest, professing Christians.

Adams, with a young man, worked his way down from Lac-qui-parle, and carried them what provisions they could on a hand-sled. Thus they weathered the terrible winter. Thus they commenced mission work at this new place, where they continued for ten years, until the outbreak.

At Lac-qui-parle we were doing effective Christian work. Our own family were all together. The hard winter entailed a good deal of hard work. The snow would sift through our roofs and pack into the upper part of our houses, until, as we sometimes said, there was more inside than outside. Every day, also, our hay-stacks were covered up with snow, so as to make the labor of feeding the cattle very great. But still these were years of enjoyment and profit. A company of Dakota young men were growing up and preparing for work in the future.

The next year Mr. Adams received an invitation to take charge of the church of white people at Traverse des Sioux, which was the continuation of the mission church organized there. This invitation he accepted, and closed his connection with the special work for the Dakotas. It will occur to every reader of these memoirs to note how many men the foreign mission work among the Dakotas gave to the home mission work among the white people of Minnesota. The shepherds were here in advance of their flocks. The work is one—the world for Christ.

The Dakota mission was now reduced to its lowest terms; only Dr. Williamson's family and my own remained. If the Lord had not given us the victory when we were many, would He do it when we were few? We were sure He could do it. While it is true that the Lord is often on the side of the strong battalions, it is not always so. And spiritual forces are not measured by the same rules that measure material forces. So we toiled on with good hope, and when a year later, we were called to leave Lac-qui-parle, and commence our station elsewhere, Secretary Treat proposed that we call it *New Hope.*

In carrying on missionary labor among a heathen people, the question, What shall be the relation of the children of the mission family to the people? is often a difficult and perplexing one. The springs of the home life must be kept, as far as possible, from being contaminated. And yet the daily intercourse with those of impure thoughts and impure words is contaminating. Shall we make our family a *garden inclosed?* If so, the children when small must not learn the language of the natives. Mary and I adopted this principle and carried it out very successfully. Up to the time of our return in 1852, our children had hardly learned any Dakota. Now our boy Alfred was fifteen years old, and had assigned to him duties which made it necessary that he should understand the Indians somewhat, and make himself undertood by them. So he commenced to learn the language. John P. Williamson had commenced to talk it much earlier. Doubtless, the advantage in speaking a language is with those who learn in their very childhood, other things being equal. The reason for the exclusion had partly passed by, and the taking of Dakota children into our family, and being closely connected with a boarding-school of Dakota children, made it impossible, if it had been desirable, longer to keep up the bars.

By and by came along the THIRD of March, 1854. The spring had opened early, the ground was bare of snow, and every thing was dry. Our cellars had been in the habit of freezing, and to protect our potatoes and other vegetables we had been in the habit of stuffing hay under the floor all around, in the fall. This hay had not yet been removed, and was very dry. The cellar was dark, and a lighted candle was needed by those who went down for any purpose. The mother was preparing for the family dinner, and so had sent down the little boys Thomas and Henry, in their seventh and fifth years respectively, to bring her up potatoes. Through carelessness, and without thought, perhaps, they held the lighted candle too near the dried hay. It took fire immediately, and in a few seconds of time so filled the cellar with smoke, that the boys with some difficulty made their escape.

There was no supply of water nearer than the river and spring run, down quite a hill. But every boy and girl were soon carrying water. The difficulty was to reach the fire with the water. The floor was flooded and a hole was cut through, but the fire had taken such a hold of the whole interior, that our little pails full of water were laughed at by the flames. The effort was now made to save something from the burning house. Some articles were carried into the other house which stood near by. But that also took fire, and both houses were soon consumed, with almost all they had contained. A few books were saved, and the chief part of Miss Spooner's wardrobe and bedding, her room being on the corner away from where the fire commenced. Before noon the fire-fiend had done his work, and our mission houses were a mass of coals and ashes. Very little had been saved. The potatoes in the cellars were much burned and cooked, but underneath, a portion of them were found to be in a good state of preservation.

The adobe church, that stood partly under the hill, was the only building that escaped. Thither we removed what few things we had saved, and our Dakota neighbors were very kind, bringing us what they could; while Mr. Martin McLeod, the trader, sent us blankets and other things to meet the present necessity, partly as a gift, and partly to be paid for. In a few days Dr. Williamson came up from Pay-zhe-hoo-ta-ze with further supplies. And all along through the spring and summer, as our friends in the East heard of our loss, the boxes and barrels were sent for our relief. It did us good to know that we had so many true-hearted friends.

CHAPTER IX.

1854–1856.—Simon Anawangmane.—Rebuilding after the Fire. —Visit of Secretary Treat.—Change of Plan.—Hazelwood Station.—Circular Saw-Mill.—Mission Buildings.—Chapel. —Civilized Community.—Making Citizens.—Boarding School.—Educating our own Children.—Financial Difficulties.—The Lord Provides.—A Great Affliction.—Smith Burgess Williamson.—"Aunt Jane."—Bunyan's Pilgrim in Dakota.

When, after the fire, we were somewhat comfortably domiciled in the adobe church, the time came for our regular communion. The disaster had made all our hearts tender, and the opportunity for helpfulness on the part of our native church members, which had been improved by many of them, had drawn us toward them. It was an appropriate time to remember what Christ had done for us. And just then we were made very glad by the return of Simon Anawangmane from his long wanderings. Some years before, he had broken away from strong drink, but he was so overcome with remorse and shame, that he could not get up courage enough to come back, and take again upon him the oath of fealty to the wounded Lord. He edged his way back. He had often come and sat on the door-step, not daring to venture in. Then he came in and sat down in a corner. By and by he took more courage. He had talked with Dr. Williamson at Yellow Medicine, who gave him a letter, saying, "I think Simon should now be restored to the Church." We did reinstate him. And for more than a score of years since his restoration, Simon has lived, so far as we can see, a true Christian life. For nearly all that time he has been a ruling elder in the church, and for ten years past a licensed exhorter.

We decided almost immediately to rebuild our burnt houses, and as soon as we had taken care of the potatoes in the cellars, that were not too much injured, we set about getting out timbers. It was a slow process to saw boards and timbers with the whip-saw, but up to this time this had been our only way of making material for building. This work had been pushed on so well that, when, by the first of June, Secretary S. B. Treat, of the mission house in Boston, made us a visit, we had gotten out material for the frame of our house. His visit, at this time, was exceedingly gratifying and helpful to us all. It was good to counsel with such a sagacious, true, thoughtful, Christian counsellor as Mr. Treat.

The whole line of mission work was carefully reviewed. The result was, that we gave up our plan of rebuilding at Lac-qui-parle and sought a new place. The reasons for this were; First, We had from the beginning been widely separated in our work, spreading out our labors and attempting to cultivate as much of the field as possible. This had obviously had its disadvantages. We were too far apart to cheer and help each other. Now, when we were reduced to two families, Mr. Treat advised concentrating our forces. That was in accordance with our own inclinations. And, Secondly, The Yellow Medicine had been made the head quarters of the Indian Agency for the four thousand upper Indians. The drift was down toward that point. It was found that we could take with us almost all the Christian part of our community. The idea was to commence a settlement of the civilized and Christianized Dakotas, at some point within convenient distance from the Agency, to receive the help which the government had by treaty pledged itself to give. And so we got on our horses and rode down to Dr. Williamson's, twenty-five or thirty miles; and Mr. Treat and Dr. Williamson, and Miss Spooner, and Mary and I, rode over the country above Pay-zhe-hoote-ze, which was selected as the site for the new station, afterward called Hazlewood. At Dr. Williamson's, we had a memorable meeting, at which Mr. Treat told our Dakota church members of a visit he had made to the Choctaws, and Cherokees. We also had consultations on various matters; among which was that of getting out a new Dakota hymn-book, which should contain the music as well as the hymns. A new departure was thus inaugurated in our mission work, and in after years, TIME was often counted from this visit of Secretary Treat.

The building materials we had prepared at Lac-qui-parle were partly hauled by land, and partly floated down the river; and by the month of September, our house was so far finished that we removed the family down. Also we had erected a small frame which served for various purposes, as school-room and dwelling. But while the work was progressing, Mary had quite a sudden and severe attack of sickness. It was nearly sundown when the messenger arrived, and Dr. Williamson and I had a night ride over the prairie. The shadows looked weird and ghostly—perhaps tinged by the mental state of the beholder. At midnight we reached the sufferer, who was, by wise, doctoring and skillful nursing restored in a week.

The Dakotas entered at once into the idea of the new

settlement, and no sooner had we selected the spot for our building and set a breaking-plow to work in making a mission field, than they were at work in the same line. The desirable places were soon selected and log cabins went up, the most of which were replaced by frame buildings or brick within a year or two. The frames were put up by themselves, with the assistance we could give them;—the brick houses were built by the government.

We had been long enough schooling ourselves in the use of the whip-saw. That was one of the processes of labor that, years before, I had determined not to learn. I had acquired some skill in the use of the broad ax, and rather liked it. I had applied my knowledge of mathematics in various ways to the work of framing houses, and it became a pleasure. But I thought I should avoid the whip-saw. The time however came when I needed a sawyer greatly, and could obtain none, and so took hold myself.

But now we decided that it would be more economical to make boards by horse and ox power than by man-power alone; and so the committee at Boston authorized the purchase of a small circular saw-mill. This proved quite a help in our civilized community. It enabled us to put up, in the next season, a house for a small boarding-school, and also a neat church building. This latter was erected and finished at a cost of about $700, only $200 of which was mission funds. At this time the Indians were receiving money annuities. It was paid them in gold, about $10 for each individual. So that the men received from thirty to fifty dollars. At a propitious time I made a tea-party, which was attended by our civilized men largely, and the result was, that with some assistance from white people, they were able to raise about five hundred dollars. It was a success beyond my most sanguine expectations.

We had now such a respectable community of young men, who had cut off their hair and exchanged the dress of the Dakotas for that of the white man, and whose wants now were very different from the annuity Dakotas generally, that we took measures to organize them into a separate band, which we called the Hazelwood Republic. They elected their President for two years, and other needed officers, and were without any difficulty recognized by the agent as a separate band. A number of these men were half breeds, who were, by the organic law of Minnesota, citizens. The constitution of the State provided that Indians also might become citizens by satisfying a court of their progress in civilization.

A few years after the organization of this civilized community, I took eight or ten of the men to meet the court at Mankato, but the court deciding that a knowledge of English was necessary to comply with the laws of the State, only one of my men was passed into citizenship.

A part of the plan of our new community was a mission boarding-school. Almost from the beginning we had been making trial of educating Dakota children in our own families. Mary had a little girl given her the first fall after we came to Lac-qui-parle; she was the daughter of Eagle Help, my Bible reader; but after she had washed and dressed her up, she staid only a month, and then ran away. The Mr. Ponds raised one or two in their families. Dr. Williamson had several Dakota children when at Kaposia, and afterward at Pay-zhe-hoo-ta-ze. Mr. Adams had at one time a boarding-school of a half dozen, at

Lac-qui-parle, and we had two or three in our family. Now the work was to be attempted on a larger scale.

The Hazelwood boarding-school was for awhile cared for by Miss Ruth Pettijohn, and afterward by Mr. and Mrs. H. D. Cunningham. Counting those in Dr. Williamson's family and our own, the boarding scholars amounted to twenty. This was the extent of our ambition in that line at that time. A large boarding-school demands a large outlay for buildings, as well as for its continual support. The necessities of our mission work did not then demand the outlay, nor could it have been easily obtained from the funds of the Board. Connected with this school, as teachers, were Mrs. Annie B. Ackly, and Miss Eliza Huggins and Isabella B. Riggs.

We had reached the time in 1854, when it became necessary to enter upon some plan to educate our children, beyond what we could give them in our Indian home. Three years before this, Alfred had been at school in Illinois, but that was only a temporary arrangement; now he was seventeen years old and prepared to enter college. Mary and I often discussed the question of ways and means. It was our desire to give our children as good an education as we possessed ourselves—at least to give them a chance of obtaining such an education. We did not feel that our position as missionaries should make this impossible, and yet how it was to be accomplished we could not see. We had neither of us any patrimony. In this respect we were on an equality. She received $100 from her father's estate, and I but a little more than that, and we did not know of any rich friends to whom we could apply for aid. Our salary had been small from the beginning. We entered the mission work at a time when the Board was cutting down everywhere. So that we started on a salary or allowance of about $250, and for the first quarter of a century it did not materially differ from the basis of a Methodist circuit rider in the West, of olden times; that is, $100 apiece, and $50 for each child. At this time when our family numbered eight, we had an allowance of $500. We were both close calculators, and we never ran in debt. We could live comfortably with our children at home, each doing something to carry the burdens of life. But how could we support one or more away at school. A third of the whole family allowance would not suffice to pay the expenses of one, at the most economical of our colleges or schools. To begin the work required faith. We determined to begin, by sending Alfred to Knox College, at Galesburg, Illinois. From year to year we were able to keep him there until he finished the course. Two years after sending Alfred, we sent Isabella to the Western Female Seminary, at Oxford, Ohio. This, however, we were enabled to do by the help which Mrs. Blaisdell and other christian friends of the Second Presbyterian Church, of Cincinnati, gave.

With two away at the same time, " the barrel of meal did not waste nor the cruse of oil fail." In various ways the Lord helped us. One year our garden produced a large surplus of excellent potatoes, which the Indian agent bought at a very remunerative price. From year to year our faith was strengthened. "Jehovah Jireh" became our motto. He stood by us and helped us in the work of education all through the *twenty-three* years that have followed, until the last of Mary's eight children has finished at the Beloit high-school. We have redeemed our promise and pledge made to each other. We have given, by the Lord's help, each and all of our children a chance to become as good, or better scholars than their father and mother were.

The third of March was associated in our minds with calamity, from the burning of our houses at Lac-qui-parle. But two years later, or in the spring of 1856, the third of March brought a great shadow over Dr. Williamson's household. Smith Burgess Williamson was just coming up to young manhood. He was large of his age, a very manly boy. On this third of March he was engaged in hauling up fire-wood with an ox team. He probably attempted to get on his loaded sled while the oxen were in motion, and missing his step, fell under the runner. He was dragged home a distance of some rods, and his young life was entirely crushed out. We were immediately summoned over from Hazelwood. Human sympathy could go but a little way toward reaching the bottom of such a trouble. It was like other sorrows that had come upon us, and we were prepared to sit down in silence with our afflicted friends, and help them think out, "It is the Lord." "I was dumb because thou didst it." The family had been already schooled in affliction, and this helped to prepare them better for the Master's work.

During these passing years, the educational work among the Dakotas was progressing beyond what it had done previously. Our boarding-school at Hazelwood, in charge of H. D. Cunningham, was full and doing good service. Our civilized and Christian community had come to desire and appreciate somewhat the education of their children. At Dr. Williamson's, also, several were taken into the family, and the day-school prospered. Miss Jane S. Williamson, a maiden sister of the doctor, had come to the land of the Dakotas when Mary and I returned in 1843. From the association and connection of her father's family with slavery in South Carolina, she had grown up with a great interest in the colored people. She had taught colored schools in Ohio, when it was very unpopular, even in a free state, to educate the blacks. When she came to the Dakotas, her enthusiasam in the work of lifting up the colored race was at once transferred to the red men, and she became an indefatigable worker in their education.

She often carried cakes and nuts in her pocket, and had something to give to this and that one, to draw them to her school. The present race of Dakotas remember AUNT JANE, as we called her, or Dowan Dootawin, *Red Song Woman*, as they called her, with tender interest, and many of them owe more to her than they can understand.

At this time, a translation of the first part of John Bunyan's Pilgrim, which I had prepared, was printed by the American Tract Society, and at once became a popular and profitable reading book for the Dakotas.

CHAPTER X.

1857-1862.—Spirit Lake.—Massacres by Inkpadoota.—The Captives.—Delivery of Mr. Marble and Miss Gardner.—Excitement.—Inkpadoota's Son Killed.—U. S. Soldiers.—Maj. Sherman.—Indian Councils.—Great Scare.—Going Away.—Indians Sent after Scarlet End.—Quiet Restored.—Children at School.—Quarter-Century Meeting.—John P. Williamson at Red Wood.—Dedication of Chapel.

By the northern line of Iowa, where the head waters of the Des Moines come out of Minnesota, is a lake, or group of lakes, called "Minne Wakan," *Mysterious Water*, or, as the name goes, SPIRIT LAKE. Sometime in 1855, this beautiful spot of earth was found and occupied by seven or eight white families, far in advance of other white settlements. In the spring of 1857, there were, in this neighborhood and at Springfield, ten or fifteen miles above, on the Des Moines, and in Minnesota, nearly fifty white persons. During the latter part of that winter the snows in Western Iowa and Minnesota were very deep, so that traveling on the prairies was attended with great difficulty.

It appears that during the winter, a few families of annuity Sioux, belonging to the somewhat roving band of Leaf Shooters, had, according to their habit, made a hunting expedition down into Iowa, on the Little Sioux. *Inkpadoota*, or Scarlet End, and his sons were the principal men. The deep snows made game scarce and hunting difficult, so that when, in the month of March, this party of Dakotas came into the Spirit Lake settlement, they were in a bad humor from hunger, and attempted at once to levy blackmail upon the inhabitants. Their wishes not being readily complied with, the Indians proceeded to help themselves, which at once brought on a conflict with the white people, and the result was that the Indians massacred almost the entire settlement, killing about forty persons and taking four women captive.

Some one carried the news to Fort Ridgely, and a company of soldiers was sent out to that part of the country, but with small prospect of finding and punishing the Indians. The deep snows prevented rapid marching, and the party of Scarlet End, who were still in the Spirit Lake country, managed to see the white soldiers, albeit the soldiers could not discover them.

Soon after this event, we, at the Yellow Medicine, heard of it by a courier who came up the Minnesota. It proved to be quite as bad as represented. But nothing could be done at that season of the year, either to obtain the captives or punish the perpetrators. So the spring passed. When the snows had melted away, and the month of May had come, there came a messenger from Lac-qui-parle to Dr. Williamson and myself, saying that *Sounding Heavens* and *Grey Foot*, two sons of our f.iend *Spirit Walker*, had brought in one of the captive women taken by Scarlet End's party, and asking us to come up and get her that she might be restored to her friends.

We lost no time in going up to Lac-qui-parle. At the trader's establishment, then in the keeping of *Weeyooha*, the father of *Nawangmane win*, who was the wife of *Sounding Heavens*, we found MRS. MARBLE, rather a small but good-looking white woman, apparently not more than twenty-five years old. She was busily engaged with the aforesaid Mrs. Sounding Heavens, in making a calico dress for herself. When I spoke to her in English, she was at first quite reserved. I asked if she wanted to return to her friends. She replied, "I am among my friends."

She had indeed found friends in the two young men who had purchased her from her captors. They took her to their mother's tent, who had, many years before, become a member of the Lac-qui-parle church, and been baptized with the Christian name of *Rebekah*. They clothed her up in the best style of Dakota women. They gave her the best they had to eat. They brought her to their planting place, and furnished her with materials with which to dress again like a white woman. It was no wonder she said, "I am among my friends." But after talking awhile, she concluded it would be best for her to find her white friends. She did not before understand that these Dakota young men had bought her, and carefully brought her in, with the hope of being properly rewarded. *They* were not prepared to keep her as a white woman, and really, with her six or seven weeks' experience as an Indian, she would hardly care to choose that kind of life.

Mrs. Marble's husband had been killed with those who were slain at Spirit Lake. Her story was, that four white women were reserved as captives. They were made to carry burdens and walk through the melting snow and water. When they came to the Big Sioux, it was very full. The Indians cut down a tree, and the white women were expected to walk across on that. One of the women fell off, and her captor shot her in the water. Her fellow captives thought she was better off dead than alive. When Mrs. Marble was rescued from her captors, two others still lived, Mrs. Nobles and Miss Abbie Gardner. The Indians were then west of the Big Sioux, in the valley of the James or Dakota River.

We took Mrs. Marble down, accompanied by *Sounding Heavens, Grey Foot* and their father, *Wakanmane*. She remained a few days at our mission home at Hazelwood, and in the mean time Maj. Flandreau, who was then Indian agent, paid the young men $500 in gold, and gave them a promissory note for the like amount. This was a very creditable reward.

But what was most important to be done just then, was to rescue the other two women, if possible. We had Dakota men whom we could trust on such a mission better than we could trust ourselves. There was PAUL MAZAKOOTAMANE, the president of the Hazelwood Republic. White people said he was lazy. There was truth in that. He did not like to work. But he was a real diplomatist. He could talk well, and he was skilled in managing Indians. For such a work there was no better man than he. Then there was JOHN OTHERDAY, the white man's friend. He could not talk like Paul; but he had rare executive ability, and he was a fearless fellow. There was no better second man than he. For the third man we secured *Mr. Grass*. These three we selected, and the agent sent them to treat for Miss Gardner and Mrs. Nobles. They took with them an extra horse and a lot of goods. In about three weeks they returned, but only brought Miss Gardner. Mrs. Nobles had been killed before they reached Scarlet End's camp.

As a consequence of this Spirit Lake trouble, we lived in a state of excitement all the summer. At one time the report came that Inkpadoota's sons, one or more of them, had ventured into the Yellow Medicine settlement. News was at once taken to Agent Flandreau, who came up with a squad of soldiers from Fort Ridgely, and, with the help of John Otherday and Enos Good Hail, and others, this son of a murderer was killed, and his wife taken prisoner. The excitement was very great, for Scarlet End's family had friends among White Lodge's people at the Yellow Medicine.

Then came up Maj. T. W. Sherman with his battery. The Spirit Lake murderers must be punished, but the orders from Washington were that the annuity Indians must do it. To persuade them to undertake this was not an easy task. It is very doubtful whether the plan was a wise one. There were too many Dakotas who sympathized with Inkpadoota. This appeared in the daring of a young Dakota, who went into Maj. Sherman's camp and stabbed a soldier. He was immediately taken up and placed under guard, but it was a new element in the complication.

Council after council was held. Little Crow, and the chiefs and people generally of Red Wood, were at the Yellow Medicine. The Indians said to Superintendent Cullen, and Maj. Sherman, "We want you to punish Inkpadoota, we can't do it." But they were told that the Great Father required *them* to do it, as a condition of receiving their annuities. In the mean time, several hundred Yanktonais Sioux came over from the James River who had complaints of their own against the government. One day there was a grand council in progress, just outside of Maj. Sherman's camp. The Dakota who stabbed the white soldier managed to get his manacles partly off, and ran for the council. The guard fired, and wounded him in the feet and ankles, some shots passing into the council circle. From the Indian side guns were fired, and the white people fled to the soldier's camp, the Dakota prisoner being taken into the keeping of his friends.

For a while it was uncertain whether we were to have war or peace. The hundreds of Sioux teepees, which covered the prairie between Dr. Williamson's place and the agency, were suddenly taken down, and the whole camp was in motion. This looked like war. Dr. Williamson asked for a guard of soldiers. The request could not be granted. The doctor and his folks, they said, could come to the soldiers' camp. But in an hour or two, when the good doctor saw the teepees going up again, a couple of miles off, he was content to remain without a guard—there would not be war just then. The Dakota prisoner could have been reclaimed, but it was thought best to let him go, as the white soldier was getting well.

That evening when I returned home from the council, I found Aunt Ruth Pettijohn and our children in a state of alarm. Mary had gone down below on a visit. The Sioux camp was all around us, and we were five miles away from the soldiers' camp. What might take place within a few days we could not tell. It seemed as if the nervous strain would be less if they could go away for awhile. And so the next morning we put our house in the charge of Simon, and we all started down to the Lower Sioux Agency. We had no settled plan, and when we learned that matters were being arranged, we were at once ready to return, having met Mary with a company of friends, who were on their way up to the mission. Alfred was coming home to spend his vacation, and had brought with him a college friend; and Mrs. Wilson, a sister of Dr. Williamson, and her daughter,

Sophronia, and Miss Maggie Voris were come to make a visit.

When we reached home, the Yanktonais had departed, and Little Crow with a hundred Dakota braves were starting out to seek Inkpadoota and his band. They came upon them by a lake, and the attack was reported as made in the night, in the reeds and water. Afterward, when in Washington, Little Crow claimed to have killed a dozen or more, but the claim was regarded by the Indians as untrue. The campaign being over, the Indians returned and received their annuities, and thus was the Spirit Lake affair passed over. There was no sufficient punishment inflicted. There was no fear of the white soldiers imparted; perhaps rather a contempt for the power of the government was the result, in the minds of White Lodge and other sympathizers with Inkpadoota. And even Little Crow and the Lower Sioux were educated thereby for the outbreak of five years later.

Isabella Burgess had been two years in the Western Female Seminary, at Oxford, Ohio, and *Alfred Longley* was completing his academical course at Knox College. Isabella came to see him graduate, and then, together, they started for their Indian home, in Minnesota. It was about the first of July, 1858, and at midnight, when the steamboat on which they were traveling, having landed at Red Wing and discharged some freight, and pushed out again into the river, was found to be on fire. The alarm was given, and the passengers waked up, and the boat immediately turned again to the landing; but the fire having caught in some cotton bales on the front deck, spread so rapidly, that it was with difficulty the passengers made their escape, the greater part of them only in their night dress. Their baggage was all lost. But the good people of Red Wing cared for the sufferers, and started them homeward, with such clothing as could be furnished. Of the catastrophe we knew nothing, until I met the children at Saint Peter, whither they came by steamboat. This, and what had gone before, gave us something of a reputation of being a *fiery* family, and the impression was increased somewhat, when, nearly two years later, *Martha Taylor*, in her second year at Oxford, escaped by night, from the burning Seminary building.

After Alfred's return, in the summer of 1858, he spent a year at Hazelwood, in teaching a government school, and then joined the Theological Seminary at Chicago. In the summer of 1860, the absent ones were all at home. During the six years we had been at Hazelwood, two other children had been given us, *Robert Baird* and *Mary Cornelia Octavia*, which made a very respectable little flock of *eight*. This, I think, was the last time that the whole family were together.

Twenty-five years had passed since Dr. Williamson came to the Dakotas. Many changes had taken place. It was fitting that the two families which remained should, in some proper way, put up a quarter century milestone. And so we arranged an out-door gathering, at which we had food for the body and food for the mind. Among other papers read at this time was one which I prepared with some care, giving a short biographical sketch of all the persons, who, up to that time, had been connected with the Dakota mission; a copy of which was afterward placed in the library of the Historical Society of Minnesota.

Ever since the removal of the Lower Indians up to their reservation, there had been several members of Dr. Williamson's church at Kaposia, living near the Red Wood

Agency. They would form a very good nucleus of a church, and make a good beginning for a new station. This had been in our thought for several years, but only, when in 1861, John P. Williamson finished his Theological studies at Lane Seminary, had we the ability to take possession of that part of the field. While we waited, Bishop Whipple came up and opened a mission, placing there S. D. Hinman. Still it was thought advisable to carry out our original plan, and accordingly young Mr. Williamson took up his abode there, organized a church of ten or twelve members, and proceeded to erect a chapel. In the last days of the year 1861, I went down, by invitation, to assist in the dedication of the new church.

That journey, both going and returning, was in my sorest experience of winter travel, but it helped to start forward this new church organization, which was commencing very auspiciously. Mr. Williamson had his arrangements all made to erect a dwelling house early in the next season. And when the outbreak took place in August, 1862, as Providence would have it, he had gone to Ohio, as we all supposed, to consummate an engagement which he had made while in the seminary.

CHAPTER XI.

1861-1862.—Republican Administration.—Its Mistakes.—Changing Annuities.—Results.—Returning from General Assembly. —A Marriage in St. Paul.—D. Wilson Moore and Wife.— Delayed Payment.—Difficulty with the Sissetons.—Peace Again.—Recruiting for the Southern War.—Seventeenth of August, 1862.—The Outbreak.—Remembering Christ's Death. —Massacres Commenced.—Capt. Marsh's Company.—Our Flight.—Reasons Therefor.—Escape to an Island.—Final Leaving.—A Wounded Man.—Traveling on the Prairie.— Wet Night.—Taking a Picture.—Change of Plan.—Night Travel.—Going around Fort Ridgely.—Night Scares.—Safe Passage.—Four Men Killed.—The Lord Leads Us.—Sabbath.—Reaching the Settlements.—Mary at St. Anthony.

When President Lincoln's administration commenced we were glad to welcome a change of Indian agents. But after a little trial, we found that a Republican administration was quite as likely to make mistakes, in the management of Indians, as a Democratic one. Hardly had the new order of things been inaugurated in 1861, when Superintendent Clark W. Thompson announced to the Sioux gathered at Yellow Medicine, that the Great Father was going to make them all very glad. They had received their annuities for that year, but were told that the government would give them a further bounty in the autumn. At one of Thompson's councils, Paul made one of his most telling speeches. He presented many grievances, which the new administration promised to redress. But when the superintendent was asked where this additional gift came from, he could not tell—only it was to be great, and would make them very glad.

By such words, the four thousand Upper Sioux were encouraged to expect great things. Accordingly, the Sissetons from Lake Traverse came down in the autumn, when the promised goods should have been there, but low water in the Minnesota and Mississippi delayed their arrival. The Indians waited, and had to be fed by Agent Galbraith. And when the goods came the deep snows had come also, and the season for hunting was past. Moreover, the great gift was only $10,000 worth of goods, or $2.50 apiece! While they had waited, many of the men could have earned from $50 to $100, by hunting. It was a terrible mistake of the government at Washington. The result was, that of the Upper Sioux, the agent was obliged to feed more than a thousand persons all winter.

The Lower Sioux were suspicious of the matter, and refused to receive their ten thousand dollars worth of goods, until they could know whence it came. By and by the Democrats in the country learned that the administration had determined on changing the money annuity into goods, and had actually commenced the operation, sending on the year before $20,000 of the $70,000 which would be due next summer. The knowledge of this planning of bad faith in the government greatly exasperated the annuity Indians, and was undoubtedly the primal cause which brought on the outbreak of the next summer. Men who were opposed to the Republican administration and the Southern war had now a grand opportunity to work upon the fears and the hopes of the Indians, and make them badly affected toward the government. And they seemed to have carried it a little too far, so that when the conflict came, it was most disastrous for them.

As the summer of 1862 came on, the Washington government recognized their mistake, and sought to rectify it, by replacing the $20,000 which had been taken from the money of the July payment. But to do this, they were obliged to await a new appropriation, and this delayed the bringing on of the money full six weeks beyond the regular time of payment. If the money had been on hand the first of July, instead of reaching Fort Ridgely after the outbreak commenced, one cannot say but that the Sioux war would have been prevented.

About the first of July, I returned from Ohio, whither I had been to attend the General Assembly in Cincinnati, and to bring home Martha Taylor, who had just completed the course at College Hill. After the fire at Oxford, she had accepted Rev. F. Y. Vail's invitation to go to his institution near Cincinnati. There she remained until the end of the year. Then Isabella and Anna went on—the latter going to Mr. Vail's seminary, and the former attending the senior class of the Western Female Seminary, under a special arrangement before the seminary was rebuilt. So that now, both the older girls had completed the course.

On our return this time, we had with us Marion Robertson, a young woman with a little Dakota blood, who had been spending some time in Ohio, and who was affianced to a Mr. Hunter, a government carpenter at the Lower Sioux agency. By arrangement, Mr. Hunter met us in Saint Paul, and I married them one evening, in the parlors of the Merchant's Hotel. Six or seven weeks after this, Mr. Hunter was killed in the outbreak.

At that marriage in the hotel, were present D. Wilson Moore and his bride from Fisslerville, New Jersey, near Philadelphia. Mr. Moore was of the firm of Moore Brothers (engaged extensively in glass manufacturing), had just married a young bride, and they had come to Minnesota on their wedding trip. We had reached home only a few days before, when, to our surprise, Mr. Moore and his wife drove up to our mission. They had heard that the Indian payment was soon to be made, and so had come up; but, not finding accommodations at the agency, they came on to see if we would not take them in. We had a large family, but if they would be satisfied with our fare, and take care of themselves, Mary would do the best she could for them. This will account for the way in which Mrs. Moore lost all her silk dresses.

The whole four thousand Indians were now gathered at the Yellow Medicine. The Sissetons of Lake Traverse had hoed their corn and come down. It was the regular time for receiving their annuities, before the corn needed watching. But the annuity money had not come. The agent did not know when it would come. He had not sent for them and he could not feed them—he had barely enough provisions to keep them while the payment was being made. The truth was, he had used up the provisions on them, in the previous winter. So he told them he would give them some flour and pork, and then they must go home, and wait until he called them. They took the provisions, but about going home they could not see it in that way. It was a hundred miles up to their planting place, and to trudge up there and back, with little or nothing to eat, and carry their tents and baggage and children on horse-back and on dog-back and on woman-back, was more than they cared to do. Besides, there was nothing for them to eat at home. They must go out on the buffalo hunt, and then they might miss their money. And so they preferred to stay, and beg and steal, or starve.

But stealing and begging furnished but a very scanty fare, and starving was not pleasant. The young men talked the matter over, and concluded that the flour and pork in the warehouse belonged to them, and there could not be much wrong in their taking it. And so one day, they marched up to the storehouse with axes in hand, and battered down the door. They had commenced to carry out the flour, when the lieutenant with ten soldiers turned the howitzer upon them. This led them to desist, for the Dakotas were unarmed. But they were greatly enraged, and threatened to bring their guns and kill the little squad of white soldiers. And what made this seem more likely, the Sioux tents were at once struck and the camp removed off several miles. Agent Galbraith sent up word that he wanted help. And when Mr. Moore and I drove down, he said, "If there is anything between the lids of the Bible that will meet this case, I wish you would use it." I told him I thought there was; and advised him to call a council of the principal men and talk the thing over. Whereupon I went to the tent of Standing Buffalo, the head chief of the Sissetons, and arranged for a council that afternoon.

The chiefs and braves gathered. The young men who had broken the door down were there. The Indians argued that they were starving, and that the flour and pork in the warehouse had been purchased with their money. It was wrong to break in the door, but now they would authorize the agent to take of their money and repair the door. Whereupon ᐧthe agent agreed to give them some provisions, and insisted on their going home, which they promised to do. The Sissetons left on the morrow, and so far as they were concerned the difficulty was over; for, on reaching home, they started on a buffalo hunt. Peace and quiet now reigned at the Yellow Medicine. Mr. Moore occupied himself in shooting pigeons, and we all became quite attached to Mrs. Moore and himself.

In the meantime, an effort was made at the agencies, among half-breeds and employes, to enlist soldiers for the Southern war. Quite a number were enlisted, and when the trouble came, Agent Galbraith was below with these recruits. Several strangers were in the country. It was afterward claimed that there were men here in the interests of the South. I did not see any of that class. But some photographers were there. Adrian J. Ebell, a student of Yale College, was taking stereoscopic views, and a gentleman from St. Paul also.

The seventeeth of August was the Sabbath. It was sacramental Sabbath at Hazelwood. As our custom was, both churches came together to celebrate the Lord's death. Our house was well filled, and we have always remembered that Sabbath as one of precious interest, for it was the last time we were to meet in that beautiful little mission chapel. A great trial of our faith and patience was coming upon us, and we knew it not. But the dear Christ knew that both we and the native Christians needed just such a quiet rest with Him, before the trials came.

While we, at Hazelwood and Pay-zhe-hoo-ta-ze, were thus engaged on that Sabbath of August seventeenth, the outbreak was commenced in the border white settlements at Acton, Minnesota. As usual the difficulty was commenced at a grog shop. Some four or five Indians made demands which were not complied with, whereat they began to kill the whites. That night they reached the villages at the Lower Sioux Agency, and a council of war was called.

Something of this kind had been meditated, and talked of, and prepared for undoubtedly. Sometime before this, they had formed the *Tee-yo-tee-pe*, or Soldiers' Lodge, which is only organized on special occasions, for the hunt or for war. Some negotiations were probably going on with the Winnebagoes and Ojibwas. But they were not perfected. Several Winnebagoes were at this time at the Lower Agency, but they do not appear to have been there for the purpose of the outbreak. In the council held that night, Little Crow is reported to have expressed his regret that the matter was precipitated upon them, but he yielded to the argument that their hands were now *bloody*.

The attack was commenced in the early morning at the stores, Mr. James W. Lynd at Myrick's store being the first white man shot down. So the ball rolled. Many were killed and some escaped. Word of the rising was carried to Fort Ridgely, and Capt. Marsh was sent up to quell it. The Indians met his company of fifty men at the Ferry, and killed half of them there, the rest making their escape with difficulty. These things had been going on during the day, forty miles from us, but we knew it not. Five miles below, at the Yellow Medicine, they had heard of it by noon. The Indians gathered to consult what they would do. Some, we learned, gave their voice for killing the white people, but more were in favor of only taking the goods and property. The physician at the Yellow Medicine was absent, and a young man started down that day with the doctor's wife and children in a buggy. Before they reached Red Wood, they were met by two Dakota men—the white man was killed and the woman and children taken captive.

The sun was getting low Monday evening, when we at Hazelwood heard of what was going on. Mr. Antoine Renville, one of the elders of my church, came running in much excited, and said the Indians were killing white people. We thought it must be only a drinking quarrel. The statement needed to be repeated and particularized somewhat before we could believe it. Soon others came in and told more. Blackness seemed to be gathering upon all faces. The parents came to the boarding-school and took away their children. For several years Mary had kept Angelique and Agnes Renville. At this time, the older one was in Ohio, and the younger one went home with her mother.

Jonas Pettijohn, an old associate in mission work at Lac-qui-parle, had been for some years a government teacher at Red Iron's village, about fifteen miles above us. He had now been released, and was removing his family. Mrs. Pettijohn and the children had reached our house. Mr. Pettijohn came in the dusk of the evening with his last load, which he was bringing with my horse team. The Indian men, who had brought down his goods, when they heard of the *emeute*, started back immediately, and meeting Mr. Pettijohn, took the horses. They justified themselves by saying that somebody would take them.

Thus, as the darkness came on, we became sure that our Dakota friends believed the reports. In the gloaming, strange men appeared at our stables, and others of our horses were taken. A dozen of our neighbor men came, and said they would stand guard with their guns. As the evening progressed we sent a messenger down to the Yellow Medicine, who brought word that the stores were surrounded by Indians, and would be broken in soon. Mr. Givens, the sub-agent, sent up a note asking me to come down very early in the morning. Some of the Christian Dakota women gathered into our house, and we prayed, and sang "God is the refuge of his saints."

It was after midnight before we thought of leaving. The young folks had lain down and slept awhile. By and by Paul came, and asked me to give him some blue cloth I had on hand—he must dress like an Indian to be safe. And they evidently began to feel that *we* might not be safe, and that our staying would endanger them. This was made the more serious because of Mrs. Moore and our three grown daughters. Indian men would kill us to get possession of them. Thus the case was stated by our neighbors. Afterward we had good reason to know that they reasoned rightly.

And so we waked up the children and made preparations to depart. But it was only to be temporary. The plan was to go down to an island in the Minnesota River, and remain until the danger was overpast. Mr. Moore looked to his revolver, the only reliable weapon among us. Thomas and Henry got their double barrel shot-gun. Mary put up a bag of provisions, but unfortunately we forgot it when we departed. Fortunately again, it was brought to us in the morning by Zoe, a Dakota woman. Each one had a little baggage, but there was not enough extra clothing in the company to make them comfortable at night. When the daylight came, we were all over on the island, but our team was left, and was stolen, with the exception of one horse. So we were in rather a helpless condition as regards further escape.

On this little island we were away from the excitement and present danger; but how long it would be safe for us to remain there was quite uncertain. We could trust our own Indians that we should not be personally injured, but how soon strange Indians would find our hiding place, we could not tell. During the forenoon I crossed back and went to the village, to learn the progress of events. They did not seem to be encouraging. The stores at the Yellow Medicine had been sacked. The white people had all left in the early morning, being convoyed by John Otherday. The only safe course open to us appeared to be in getting away also. It was after midday, when we learned that Andrew Hunter and Dr. Williamson's young folks had succeeded in coming away with both a horse team and an ox team. They had some flour and other provisions with them, and had driven along the doctor's cattle. Moreover, they had succeeded in crossing the Minnesota at a point a mile or two below where we then were. From the island we could wade over to the north side. This we proceeded to do, leaving the only trunk that had been brought this far, by Mr. Cunningham's sister.

Andrew Hunter drove one of his wagons around on the prairie to meet our party as we emerged from the ravine, each carrying a little bundle. The women and children who could not walk were arranged with the bundles in the wagon. Mr. Cunningham was successful in getting one of his horses—the other had been appropriated by an Indian together with mine. His one horse he attached to my buggy and brought it over the river, and we proceeded to join the rest of Mr. Hunter's party.

Two or three families of government employes from the saw-mill had found their way to our missionary company. Thus constituted, we started for the old crossing of Hawk River, some six or eight miles distant.

While we were still in sight of the river bluffs, we discovered a man coming after us. He was evidently a white man, and hobbled along with difficulty, as though he were wounded. We stopped until he overtook us. It proved to be a man by the name of Orr, whose comrades had been killed up near the mouth of the Chippewa, and he escaped in a crippled condition. Our wagons were more than full, but we could make room for a wounded white man. About this time a rain shower came upon us, which was a God-send in many ways, although it made camping that night rather unpleasant.

When night overtook us, we were across the stream—Hawk River—and we lay down to rest and to consider what should be our course on the morrow. In the morning, we had decided to cross the country, or endeavor to do so, toward Hutchinson or Glencoe. But the country was not familiar to us. We frequently found ourselves stopped in our course by a slough which was not easy to cross. Still we kept on our way during Wednesday, and in the afternoon there fell to us four men from Otherday's party. These men all had guns which were not of much account. They belonged at New Ulm, and did not want to go to Hutchinson. But they continued with us that day.

The evening came with a slow continued rain. The first night we were out, the smaller children had cried for home. The second night some of the older children would have cried if it had been of any use. We had no shelter. The wagons were no protection against the continued rain, but it was rather natural to crawl under them. The drop, *drop*, DROP, all night long from the wagon beds, on the women and children, who had not more than half covering in that cold August rain, was not promotive of cheerfulness. Mrs. Moore looked sad and disheartened, and to my question as to how she did, she replied that one might as well die as live under such circumstances.

Thursday morning found us cold and wet, and entirely out of cooked food. Since the first night we had not been where we could obtain wood. And then, and since, we should have been afraid to kindle a fire lest the smoke should betray us. But now it was necessary that we should find wood as soon as possible. And so our course was taken toward a clump of trees which were in sight. When we came into their neighborhood about noon, we found them entirely surrounded by water. But the men waded in and brought wood enough for the purposes of camping. There we spent the afternoon and night. There we killed one of the cows. And there we baked bread and roasted meat on the coals, having neither pot nor kettle nor pan to do it in. And while we were eating, Mr. Ebell fixed up his apparatus and took a very good stereoscopic picture of the party.

We had discovered from surveyor's stakes that we were making slow progress, and so we decided, as we started Friday morning, to abandon our plan of going to Hutchinson, and turn down to the old Lac-qui-parle road, which would lead us to Fort Ridgely. This road we reached in time to take our noon rest at Birch Coolie, nearly opposite the Lower Sioux Agency, where the massacres had commenced. We were not much posted in what had taken place there. Mr. Hunter rode over to see his house only a couple of miles distant. There he met Tatemema

—Round Wind—an old Indian whom he knew, who told him to hurry on to the Fort, as all the white people had been killed or had fled. Just as we were starting from this place a team came in sight, which proved to be Dr. and Mrs. Williamson and Aunt Jane with an ox team. They had remained until Wednesday morning, and thought to stay through the trouble, but finally concluded it was best to leave and follow us. Our company now numbered over forty, but it was a very defenceless one.

We were sixteen miles from Fort Ridgely, and our thought was to go in there under cover of the night. The darkness came on us when we were still seven or eight miles away; and then in the gloaming there appeared, on a little hill-top, two Indians on horseback. They might bring a war party upon us. And so we put ourselves in the best position for defense. Martha and Anna had generally walked with the boys. Now they piled on the wagons, and the men and boys, with such weapons as we had, marched by their side. As the night came on we began to observe lights as of burning buildings, and rockets thrown up from the garrison. What could the latter mean? We afterward learned they were signals of distress!

In our one-horse buggy, Mr. and Mrs. Hunter drove ahead of the party, and he crawled into the garrison. He found that the Indians had beleaguered them, had set fire to all the out-buildings of the Fort, appropriated all their stock, had been fighting all day, and had retired to the ravine as the night came on. The Fort was already crowded with women and children, and scantily manned by soldiers. We could come in, they said, but our teams would be taken by the Indians. They expected the attack would be renewed the next day.

When Mr. Hunter returned we stopped in the road and held a *hasty* consultation, as we were in a good deal of fear that we were even now followed. We had just passed a house where the dogs alone remained to bark, which they did furiously. And just then some of the party, walking by the side of our wagons, stumbled over the dead body of a man. There was no time to lose. We decided not to go in, but to turn out and go around the Fort and its beleaguering forces, if possible. The four men who had fallen to our company—three Germans and an Irishman—dissented. But we told them no one should leave us until we were past the danger. And to prevent any desertion in this our hour of trial, Mr. Moore cocked his revolver, and would shoot down the man who attempted to leave.

It was ten o'clock, and the night was dark. We turned square off the road, and went up northward to seek an old ford over the little stream that runs down by the Fort. The Lord guided us to the right place, but while we were hunting in the willows for the old unused road, there was a cry heard so much like a human cry, that we were all quite startled. We thought it was the signal of an attack by the Indians. Probably it was only the cry of a fox. Just then Dr. Williamson came to me and said perhaps he had counseled wrongly, and that if it was thought best, he was quite willing to go back to the Fort. But I replied that we were now almost around it, and it would be unwise to go back. And so we traveled on over the ravine and up on the broad prairie beyond, and received no harm. Our pulses began to beat less furiously as we traveled on toward three o'clock in the morning, and felt that we were out of sight and hearing of the Sioux warriors. So we stopped to rest our weary cattle. Some slept for an hour, but the greater part kept watch.

As we were around the Fort, and around the danger so far as we knew, it was understood that the four men who wanted to leave in the night, might leave us in the morning. And as it was possible they might have an opportunity to send a letter to Gov. Ramsey before we should, Dr. Williamson and I attempted to write something by starlight. But nothing came of that letter. When the light began to dawn in the east, our party was aroused and moving forward. We had been guided aright in the night travel, for here we were at the old Lac-qui-parle crossing of Mud River. Here the four men left us, and as the sun arose we saw the sheen of their guns as they were entering a little wood two or three miles away. And only a little while after that we heard the report of guns; the poor fellows had fallen in with the Sioux army, which in that early morning were on their march to attack New Ulm. We did not know their fate until afterward.

Our party now fell into the road that leads to Henderson, and traveled all that Saturday in safety. But on the Saint Peter road, five or six miles to our right, we saw the burning stacks and houses, and afterward knew that the Sioux were on that road killing white people all that day. It was the middle of the afternoon when we came to a deserted house. The dishes were on the table. We found cream and butter in the cellar, and potatoes and corn in the garden. We stopped and cooked and ate a good square meal, of which we were greatly in need. Then we pushed on and came to another house sometime after nightfall, which was deserted by the humans, but the cattle were there. Here we spent the night, and would have been glad to rest the Sabbath, but as yet there was too much uncertainty. Three or four hours' travel, however, brought us to a cross-roads, where the whole settlement seemed to have gathered. We there learned that a company of troops had passed up, and had turned across to Saint Peter. This seemed to be a guarantee of safety, and so we rested the remainder of the day, gathering in the afternoon to worship Him, who had been, and was, our deliverer and guide.

All the events of the week past appeared so strange. We had hardly found any time to consider them. But often the thought came to us, What will become of our quarter-century's work among the Dakotas? It seemed to be lost. *We* could see no good way out of the difficulties. As we came into the settlements we began to learn something of the terribleness of the *emeute*, how the Indians had spread terror and death all along the frontier. And still their deadly work was going on. In the dusk of the Sabbath evening we talked over matters a little, as we planned to separate in the morning. Some pecuniary adjustments were made, D. Wilson Moore being the only one who had any money. But all the party exchanged promises.

In the morning of Monday, Dr. Williamson and his part of the company started across to Saint Peter. There remained only Mr. Moore and wife and Adrian J. Ebell and my family, and we had the use of an ox team to take us to Shakopee. It was twelve miles to Henderson. When we came to the brow of the hill above the town, we were met by several women who were strangers to us. They rushed up and grasped our hands. I asked what they knew of us. They said, "We have white hearts, and we heard you were all killed." Our young folks had worn out their shoes, and their feet also, by walking through the sharp grass, and needed something to wear. When these wants were attended to, and we all had partaken of a good dinner at the hotel, we started on—Mr. and Mrs. Moore taking the little steamboat to Saint Paul. When they arrived there, Mr. Shaw, of the Merchants Hotel, telegraphed back to Mr. John Moore, of Philadelphia, of their arrival. He had just before received an urgent telegram, "Get the bodies at any cost."

On our way to Shakopee we were met by our old friend S. W. Pond, who had been trying for days to ascertain whether the report of our being killed was true or not. He gave Mary and the children a cordial welcome to his home. They remained there a few days, and then went on to G. H. Pond's, and from thence to Saint Anthony, where Mary found an old personal friend in Mrs. McKee, the wife of the pastor of the Presbyterian church. They also found friends in all the good families, and soon rented a house and commenced living by themselves, the neighbors helping them to many articles which they needed.

On hearing of the outbreak, Alfred, who had been preaching a few months at Lockport, Ill., furnished himself with a revolver, and hastened up to see what could be done. But meeting the family at Shakopee, he returned to Illinois without making any demonstration of prowess, taking with him Anna, and, after she was somewhat recruited, sending her to Rockford Female Seminary.

CHAPTER XII.

1862.—Gen. Sibley's Expedition.—I Go as Chaplain.—At Fort Ridgely.—The Burial Party.—Birch Coolie Defeat.—Simon and Lorenzo Bring in Captives.—March to Yellow Medicine.—Battle of Wood Lake.—Indians Flee.—Camp Release.—A Hundred Captives Rescued.—Amos W. Huggins Killed.—We Send for His Wife and Children.—Spirit Walker has Protected Them.—Martha's Letter.

When Mary and the children had safely reached friends and civilization at Mr. Pond's, I was pressed in spirit with the thought that I might have some duty to perform in the Indian country. At Lac-qui-parle, twenty-five miles beyond our station at Hazelwood, were Amos W. Huggins with wife and children, and Miss Julia La Framboise. They had been in the employ of the government as teachers, at Wakanmane's village. What had befallen them we knew not, but we knew that white men had been killed between our place and Lac-qui-parle. Then our native church members—they might need help. And so I took a boat at Shakopee, and went down to Saint Paul, and offered my services to Governor Ramsey, in whatever capacity he chose to put me. He immediately commissioned me as chaplain to Gen. Sibley's expedition. The last day of August I was at Saint Peter, where I learned from Mr. Huggins' friends the story that he had been killed, and that his wife and children were captives. In regard to them I received a special charge from Mrs. Holtsclaw, and I conceived a plan of immediately sending for Mrs. Huggins. But circumstances made it impossible to carry out that plan for several weeks.

The next day, Sabbath though it was, I rode up with Col. Marshall and others to Fort Ridgely, where Gen. Sibley's command was encamped. He was waiting for reinforcements and ammunition supplies. At the first news of the massacres, a large number of citizens had impressed their neighbors' horses, and had started for the Indian country. Many of them were poor riders, and they were all poorly armed. They were without military organization and drill, and were felt to be an element of weakness rather than strength. A night or two before I reached the camp, a couple of shots had been fired, supposed to have been by Indians. The drum beat the "long roll," and the men that formed this "string-bean cavalry," as they were called, crawled under the wagons. The next morning many of them had had a clairvoyant communication with their families at home, and learned that their wives were sick. They were permitted to depart.

Three days before, a detachment of cavalry and infantry had been sent up as far as the Lower Sioux Agency, to find and bury the dead. They had done their work, as they supposed, and crossed back to the north side of the Minnesota, without seeing any Indians. As the sun was setting on that Sabbath evening, they ascended the hill and made their camp on the top of the Birch Coolie bluff. But the Sioux had discovered them, and that night they were surrounded by twice their own number of the enemy. In the early morning the attack was made and kept up all day. The report of the musketry was heard at Gen. Sibley's camp, eighteen miles away, but the reverberation made by the Minnesota hills placed the conflict apparently within six or eight miles. A detachment sent to their relief soon returned, because after they had gone a short distance, they could hear nothing. But the firing still continued, and another detachment with a howitzer was sent, with orders to go on until the absent ones were found.

The sun was low when a messenger came from the troops last sent. The Indians were in such large force that they did not dare risk a conflict, and so had retired to the prairie. Gen. Sibley's whole force was then put in readiness, and we had a night march up to Birch Coolie. The relief detachment was reached, and an hour or two of rest obtained before the morning light.

When our camp was in motion the Indians came against us and surrounded us; but soon perceiving that the force was not what they had seen the night before, they commenced making their escape, and we marched on to the original camp. It was a sad sight—dead men and dead horses lying in the hastily-dug breastworks. Twelve men were found dead whom we buried in one grave. Thirty or forty were wounded, and nearly the whole of the ninety horses were lying dead. The camp had suffered greatly for want of water, as the Indians had cut them off entirely from the stream.

This defeat showed more clearly than before the necessity of being well prepared, before an advance was made upon the hostile Sioux. It also served to arouse Minnesota thoroughly—a number of the killed and wounded in this battle were St. Paul men. But the middle of September had come and gone before Gen. Sibley felt ready to move up the river. In the meantime, while we were still at Ridgely, Simon Anawangmane came down by land, and brought Mrs. Newman and her children to our camp. And Lorenzo Lawrence brought in canoes Mrs. De Camp and children and others.

Mrs. Newman had been taken captive by the Lower Sioux, and when they reached the Yellow Medicine, she was apparently allowed by those who had her to go where she pleased. One day she came to Simon's tent, and hearing them sing and pray, she felt like trusting herself and children rather to Simon than to the others. When the camp started to go farther north, Simon stayed behind, and then placing Mrs. N. and her children in his one-horse wagon, and hitching to his horse, he and his son brought them down. Mrs. De Camp's husband had been severely wounded in the battle of Birch Coolie, and had died only a couple of days before she and the children were brought in. Lorenzo also brought with him a large English church Bible, and my own personal copy of Dakota Grammar and Dictionary, which I prized very highly.

The 21st of September, or five weeks after the outbreak commenced, we were marching by the Lower Sioux Agency and Red Wood, and getting an impression of what the *emeute* had been, in occasionally finding a dead body, and seeing the ruins of the buildings. The Sioux were now watching our movements closely. Indeed, they had kept themselves informed of our motions all along. It was this day, at the Red Wood, John Otherday went into a plum-orchard and left his horse a little ways out. One of the hostiles who had been hid there jumped on it and rode off. This made Otherday greatly ashamed. The night of the 22d we camped on the margin of Wood Lake, within three miles of the Yellow Medicine. Here we were to rest the next day and wait for a train that was behind.

At the Yellow Medicine were fields of corn and potatoes, and some of our men were anxious to add to their store of provisions. Accordingly, before our breakfast was over at Gen. Sibley's tent, some soldiers in a wagon were fired upon and two of them killed by Sioux concealed in a little ravine about a half a mile from our camp. This brought on the battle. Almost immediately the hills around were seen to be covered with Indians on foot and on horseback. The battle lasted for two or three hours. The Sioux had compelled every man in their camp, which was twenty miles above, to come down, except John B. Renville. They were playing their last card, and they lost. When it was over we gathered up and buried sixteen *dead* and *scalped* Indians, and four of our own men. Besides, we had a large number of wounded soldiers. This battle made H. H. Sibley a brigadier-general.

Thus the Indians were beaten and retired. During the fight John Otherday captured a Dakota pony, and so made good the loss of his stolen horse. Simon Anawangmane was wounded in the foot in passing out to the hostile Sioux and back to our camp; and the younger Simon was brought in wounded, and died some days afterward. The day following this battle, our camp was removed to a point beyond the mission station at Hazelwood. As I rode down to see the ruins of our buildings, some of our soldiers were emptying a *cache* near where our house had stood. The books they threw out, I found, were from my own library. A part of these, and some other things, which were in good condition, I secured. They had been buried by our friends.

The next day was the 26th of September, when we pushed on to Camp Release, where the friendly Dakotas were encamped. The hostiles, and such as feared to remain, had fled to the British Possessions. The friendly Indians had by some means come into the possession of almost all the captive white women and children. One of our chief objects in pursuing the campaign had been to prevent the killing of these captives. Little Crow had written to General Sibley that he had many captives; and General Sibley had replied, " I want the captives."

Now they came into our hands, nearly a hundred, besides half-breeds, many of whom had been in a kind of captivity. The white women had dressed up as well as they could for the occasion, but many of them only showed their white relationship by the face and hands and hair—they were dressed like Indians. It was a time of gladness for us. White men stood and cried for joy. We took them all to our camp, and wrapped them up as well as we could. Some of the women complained because we did not furnish women's clothing; but that was unreasonable. This was *Camp Release.*

Mr. Amos W. Huggins was the eldest child of Alexander G. Huggins, who had accompanied Dr. Williamson to the Sioux country in 1835. Amos was born in Ohio, and was at this time over thirty years old. He was married, and two children blessed their home, which, for sometime before the outbreak, had been at Lac-qui-parle, near where the town of that name now stands. It was then an Indian village and planting place, the principal man being Wakanmane—Spirit Walker, or Walking Spirit. If the people of the village had been at home, Mr. Huggins and his family, which included Miss Julia La Framboise, who was also a teacher in the employ of the government, would have been safe. But in the absence of Spirit Walker's people, three Indian men came—two of them from the Lower Sioux Agency—and killed Mr. Huggins and took from the house such things as they wanted.

The women and children were left uninjured. But after they had, in a hasty manner, buried the father and husband, whither should they go for protection? At first they thought to find safety with a French and half-breed family living across the Minnesota, where our old mission house had been. But there, for some reason, they were coldly received. Soon the brother of Julia La Framboise came up from Little Crow's camp and took her down. Spirit Walker had now returned, and Mrs. Huggins took refuge in his friendly teepee, where she found a welcome, and as good a home as they could make for her and her fatherless children.

Spirit Walker would probably have attempted to take them to the white soldiers' camp, if she had been decided that that was the wisest course. But Mrs. Huggins was timid, and preferred rather that her Dakota protector should decide which was the best way. And so it happened, that when the flight took place, Spirit Walker's folks generally were drawn into the swirl, and Mrs. H. found herself on the journey to Manitoba.

Immediately after we had reached Camp Release, and had learned the state of things, I presented the matter to Gen. Sibley, whereupon, the same night, he authorized the selection of four Dakota young men to be sent after Mrs. Huggins. ROBERT HOPKINS, DANIEL RENVILLE, ENOS GOOD HAIL, and MAKES HIMSELF RED were sent on this mission, which they fulfilled as expeditiously as possible. In a few days we were gladdened by the sight of Mrs. Huggins and her two children, and a child of a German woman, which they also brought in. The mother was with us, and was overjoyed to find her little girl.

While these things were taking place on the Upper Minnesota, MARTHA, now Mrs. Morris, still under the inspiration of the events, was in St. Anthony, writing the following letter to the "Cincinnati Christian Herald:"

In fancied security we had dwelt under our own vine and fig-tree, knowing naught of the evil which was to come upon us, until the very night of the 18th of August, 1862. Friendly Indians, who knew something of the evil intent of chiefs and braves, had given Miss Jane Williamson hints concerning it, during that day. More than that they *dared* not tell. But few of our own Indians had known much more respecting the coming storm than ourselves. When intelligence came of the bloody work which that morning's sun had looked upon, at the Lower Sioux Agency, thirty-five miles below, our good friends came to us, and in an agony of fear for our lives and for theirs, besought us to flee. We would certainly be killed, and they would be in danger on account of our presence. Some believed, but more doubted. We had heard Indian stories before; by morning light we were confident this too would prove nothing but a drunken frolic, and we would only lose our worldly possessions if we should depart. The believing ones made ready a little clothing and provision in case of need. The principal men gathered in council. *Could* they protect us? They would *try*, at least until the morning. We sang "God is the refuge of his saints," commended ourselves to our Father's safe-keeping, and most of us retired to rest. An hour or two passed in peaceful slumber by some—in nervous anxiety by others.

One o'clock had passed—a heavy knock at the door. Our friends had learned more of the extent of the outbreak, and felt that their protection would be worse than useless. "If you regard your own lives or ours, you must go." To their entreaties we yielded, and made hasty preparations to depart. In a quarter of an hour we had left our homes forever. Our company consisted of my father's family, Mr. Cunningham's, and Mr. Pettijohn's, and a Mr. and Mrs. Moore from New Jersey, in all twenty-one persons. Mr. Cunningham had charge of the Hazelwood Boarding School, and Mr. Pettijohn, a former missionary under the American Board, had been recently a Government teacher, twelve miles farther up the river. He had been moving his family down that day, on their way to St Peter. As he drove my father's team along, with the last of his goods, early in the evening, he was met by two Indians, who took the horses from him, and set him on an inveterately lazy horse belonging to another Indian. Consequently our family had but a light buggy and one horse left, which was to aid Mr Cunningham's two-horse team in carrying the *all* of the party. Room was found in the conveyances for the smaller children and all the women, except my sister Anna and myself. We walked with the men and boys. Our Indian friends guided us through the woods, the thick and tangled underbrush, the tall, rank grass drenched with dew, to the river side, where we were quickly and carefully conveyed to a wooded island, and then our guides left us. One of them, Enos Good-Voice-Hail, was in the East some three or four years since—a brave, handsome man, whose eye you could not but *trust*. Our teams could not cross at that place, so they were kept for us until the morning. All the rest of that weary night we sat on the damp grass, cold and dreary, wondering what the day dawn would bring. At length the morning came. My father and Mr. Cunningham paddled across the river to learn the state of affairs. We found we had neglected to bring the most of the provisions prepared, and wondered what we should do, even if permitted to go back home after a day or so spent on that island. While still talking, a woman hailed us from the opposite bank, who, as we found shortly, had brought several loaves of bread and some meat on her back, all the way from our houses. We received it as a Godsend—and soon after, my father returning, brought some more provision, which another friend had secured for us. A longer, drearier day was never passed—its every hour seemed a day. The rain came down and drenched us. My father went back and forth from the island to a village where the friendly Indians were mostly gathered, to find out what had been, and what could be done. We learned that Dr. Williamson had sent away the most of his family, considering it his duty still to remain; that his wife and sister were with him; but the others, with a number of cattle for future need, were secreted in the woods, a mile or two below us.

By noon our houses had been rifled, and gradually the idea

fixed itself upon us that we *must* leave if possible. We made arrangements to join Dr. Williamson's family, and about three o'clock took up our line of march, each carrying some bundles, having left on the island the only trunk belonging to the party. For more than a mile we walked along, with difficulty keeping our footing on the side-hills, which we chose for safety. When fairly out on the bluffs, we came up with one of the two teams, in charge of Mr. Hunter, Dr. Williamson's son-in-law. The baggage being transferred from our shoulders to the wagon, the feebler ones were provided with seats, while the stronger marched on. Soon we came up with the remainder of the party—Dr. Williamson's family, and half a dozen persons from one of the Government mills, who had cast in their lot with them. We struck out on the prairie to save ourselves if there was any chance. Our march was shortly rendered unpleasant by a fiercely-driving rain-storm, from the soaking effects of which we did not recover until the next day, though it had the good effect of obliterating our path. Our company was increased by the arrival of a Mr. Orr, who had been engaged in trading among the Indians, near the place Mr. Pettijohn had resided, and who had been shot and stabbed that morning. It seemed a marvel that he should ever have been able to walk that far, and room was immediately made for him in a wagon, though it curtailed that of others. Toward night we were overtaken by Mr. Cunningham, bringing one of his horses and our buggy, which he had succeeded in getting hold of, and which was the only vehicle belonging to twenty-one out of the thirty-eight. Night came on, and we lay down on the hard earth, with bed and covering both scant and wet, to *rest*. In the morning dawn, after our usual remembrance of Him who ruleth earth and sea, we went on our way, having had but little food, as cooked provisions were scarce, and we dared not kindle a fire for fear of attracting attention.

Our day's march was slow but steady—only stopping when necessary to rest the teams; and although we considered ourselves in danger, we found it quite enjoyable, more particularly after *we* and the *grass* got dry, so that we could walk with ease. We had counted on having a fine night's rest in spite of our scant bed-clothing, as we were all *dry*, but we were disappointed. A slow, steady rain fell through all the long night, completely saturating almost every article of bed-clothing, and every person in the company. In that comfortless rain we drank some milk, ate a crust or two, and traveled on through the long, wet swamp grass, and the swamps themselves, in wading which two or three of us became quite accomplished. By noon of that day, which was Thursday, we came to a wood, fifteen or sixteen miles east from a settlement on the river, which was about twenty miles from home.

Our progress had been very slow—without any road, the grass so wet, and the teams so heavily loaded. Still we could not but feel that the God who had led us during these long days, would neither suffer us to perish in this prairie wilderness, nor be taken by savages. At this place we stopped for the remaining half day, killed a beef, and luxuriated on meat roasted on sticks held over the fire. We also baked bread in quite a primitive style. The dough being first mixed in a bag—flour, water and salt the only ingredients—and molded on a box, it was made into thin cakes about the size of a hand-breadth, placed on forked sticks over the fire, to bake if possible, and to be smoked most certainly.

Here our party was immortalized by a young artist—a Mr. Ebell—who had gone up into our region of country a few days previous to our flight, for the purpose of taking stereoscopic views. The next day we struck for the river, coming in not far from a settlement called Beaver, about six miles from the Lower Agency. Mr. Hunter had formerly resided at the place, and as we had not at the time the remotest idea of the extent of the massacres, he drove in to ascertain the whereabouts of the settlers. He saw no signs of any dead bodies, but two or three Indians employed in pillaging, informed him that all the people had gone to Fort Ridgely, and advised him to hasten there, or some other Indians would kill him When just starting on after our noon rest, some one spied a team in the distance, which soon proved to be Dr. Williamson's, containing himself, wife, and sister. Previously, some of us fancied that we might have been unwise in fleeing, but when we saw them, we *knew we had not started too soon.* They left on Tuesday evening, being assisted to depart by two of the Christian Indians, Simon Anawangmane and Robert Chaske, at the peril of their own lives. They said they would gladly protect them longer, but it was impossible.

After holding council, we pursued our journey with the intention of reaching Fort Ridgely that night; and when within nine or ten miles, Mr. Hunter drove on to ascertain how matters stood there. We felt ourselves in danger, but thought if we were only inside the Fort walls, we would be safe. The men shouldered their arms, the daylight faded, and we marched on. In the mysteriously dim twilight, every taller clump of grass, every blacker hillock, grew into a blood-thirsty Indian, just ready to leap on his foe. All at once, on the brow of the hill, appeared two horsemen gazing down upon us. *Indians!* Every pulse stopped, and then throbbed on more fiercely. Were those men, now galloping away, sent by a band of warriors to spy out the land, or had they seen us by accident? We could not tell. The twilight faded, and the stars shone out brightly and lovingly. As we passed along we came suddenly on a dead boy, some days cold and stiff. Death grew nearer, and as we marched on, we looked up to the clear heavens beyond which God dwells, and prayed Him to keep us. When within a mile and a half of the Fort, we met Mr. Hunter returning, who reported as follows: He left the buggy in his wife's charge, outside the barracks, and crawled in on his hands and knees. Lieut. Sheehan, commander of the post, informed him they had been fighting hard for five days; the Indians had withdrawn at seven that evening, it being then between nine and ten; that if not reinforced, they could not hold out much longer. Some of the buildings had been burnt; they had then five hundred women and children inside, and if we *could* go on—*go!* We *went*, striking away out on the prairie.

Several of us girls had been mostly walking for the ten miles back, but now, to give the least trouble, we climbed on the wagons wherever we might find room to hold on, and sat patiently with the rest. Ah! if night of fear and dread was ever spent, that was one. Every voice was hushed except to give necessary orders; every eye swept the hills and valleys around; every ear was intensely strained for the faintest noise, expecting momentarily to hear the unearthly war-whoop, and see dusky forms with gleaming tomahawks uplifted. How past actions came back as haunting ghosts; how one's hopes of life faded away, away, and the things of earth seemed so little and mean compared to the glorious heaven beyond! And yet life was so sweet, so dear, and though it be a glorious heaven, this was such a hard way to go to it, by the tomahawk and scalping-knife! Oh, God! *our* God! *must* it be? Then came something of resignation to death itself, but such a sore shrinking from the dishonor which is *worse* than death; and we could not but wonder whether it would be a greater sin to take one's life than thus to suffer. So the night wore on, until two hours past midnight, when compelled by exhaustion, we stopped. Some slept heavily, forgetful of the danger past and present, while others sat or stood, inwardly fiercely nervous and excited, but outwardly calm and still. Two hours passed; the weary sleepers were awakened by the weary watchers, and as quietly as possible the march was renewed. It was kept up until about nine in the day, when we struck the Fort Ridgely and Henderson road.

Having traveled thus far without being pursued, we felt ourselves comparatively safe. I am sure there was not one who did not in heart join in the song and prayer of thanksgiving which went up from that lone prairie land, however much we may have forgotten or murmured since. "Jehovah hath triumphed; his people are free, are *free*," seemed to ring through the air. As we pursued our journey, we noticed dense columns of smoke springing up along the river with about the same rapidity we traveled, which we afterward learned were grain stacks fired by Indians. We rested for the night near a house, some fifteen miles from Henderson, from which the people had fled. Here we felt safe; but subsequently learned that we were not more than five or six miles from the Norwegian grove, where that same day a party of warriors had done their bloody work. Surely *God led us and watched over us*.

The next day being the Sabbath, we went on only as far as we deemed necessary for perfect safety. Toward evening my father held divine service, which was almost the only outward reminder that it was the Lord's Day. People coming and going—bustle here, there and everywhere—so different from our last quiet Sabbath at home, the last time we and our dear Indians gathered together around the table of our Lord, and perhaps the last time we ever shall, until we meet in the kingdom. The next morning our party separated, our family, with Mr. and Mrs. Moore, Mrs.

Williamson and second daughter, and two or three others, continuing on the Henderson road, and the rest striking across to St. Peter, where Dr. Williamson has found abundant work in the hospitals. Near there his family expect to remain during the winter.

We arrived that afternoon in Henderson, a town a hundred miles from home, and we had been a week on the way. "Why, I thought you were all killed!" was the first greeting of every one. A shoe store was hunted up before we proceeded to Shakopee, having first bidden a God-speed to our friends, Mr. and Mrs. Moore. By this time some of us "young folks" had acquired such a liking for walking, that we consider it superior to any other mode of locomotion to this day; and if it had not been that we were so ragged, and dirty and foot-sore, we should have preferred to continue our journey. During that week our ideas of paradise grew very limited, being comprised in having an abundance of water, some clean clothes, plenty to eat, and a nice bed to sleep in.

Since our entering Shakopee we have visited among kind friends, until two weeks since, when we endeavored to set up house-keeping in this town of St. Anthony. Notwithstanding the kindness of friends and strangers, we, in common with others, find it difficult to do *something* with *nothing*, especially as my father is with the expedition against the Indians. It can not but be that we should look back lovingly to the homes we have left, which are all, even "our holy and beautiful house" wherein we have worshiped, destroyed by fire; but I trust that we all endeavor to "take joyfully the spoiling of our goods." "Through much tribulation we shall enter into the kingdom of heaven." Among our many causes for thankfulness, one is suggested by the verse, "Pray ye that your flight be not in winter." Another cause is that there was so little loss of life among those connected with the mission. We mourn for our dear friend, Mr. Amos Huggins, son of a former missionary, and government teacher at Lac-qui-parle. His young wife and two small children were at last accounts in the hands of the Indians, as also Miss Julia La Framboise, an assistant teacher who resided in their family. Because of the influential relatives Miss La Framboise has among the Dakotas, we hope for her, while for Mrs. Huggins we can only *pray.*

It was not my intention, when I began this article, to enter at all into the causes of this outbreak;' but what I have written will excite your indignation against all Dakotas, and I cannot bear that it should be so. It must be remembered that the *church members*, as a whole, have had *no hand in it.* One, John Otherday, guided a party of sixty-two across the prairies. Two others, Lorenzo Lawrence and Simon Anawangmane, have recently brought into Fort Ridgely three captive women and eleven children; and we doubt not that others will also "let *their* light shine"—*at the peril of their lives*, remember.

The Indians have not been without excuse for their evil deeds. Our own people have given them intoxicating drinks, taught them to swear, violated the rights of womanhood among them, robbed them of their dues, and then insulted them! What more would be necessary to cause one nation to rise against another? What *more*, I ask. And yet there are many who curse this people, and cry, "Exterminate the fiends." *Dare* we, as a nation, *thus* bring a curse upon ourselves and on future generations?

Yours truly, MARTHA T. RIGGS.

CHAPTER XIII.

1862–1863.—Military Commission.—Excited Community.—Dakotas Condemned.—Moving Camp.—The Campaign Closed.—Findings sent to the President.—Reaching my Home in St. Anthony.—Distributing Alms on the Frontier.—Recalled to Mankato.—The Executions.—Thirty-eight Hung.—Difficulty of Avoiding Mistakes.—Round Wind.—Confessions.—The next Sabbath's Service.—Dr. Williamson's Work.—Learning to Read.—The Spiritual Awakening.—The Way it Came.—Mr. Pond Invited up.—Baptisms in the Prison.—The Lord's Supper.—The Camp at Snelling.—A like Work of Grace.—John P. Williamson.—Scenes in the Garret.—One Hundred Adults Baptized.—Marvelous in our Eyes.

No sooner had the white captives been brought over to our camp, than, from various sources, we began to hear of Indian men who had maltreated these white women, or in some way had been engaged in the massacres of the border. On the morrow, Gen. Sibley requested me to act as the medium of communication between these women and himself, inviting them to make known any acts of cruelty or wrong which they had suffered at the hands of Dakota men, during their captivity. The result of this inquiry was the apprehension of several men who were still in the Sioux camp, and the organization of a military commission composed of officers, to try such cases. Naturally we supposed that men who knew themselves guilty, would have fled to Manitoba with Little Crow. The greater number of such men had undoubtedly gone. But some were found remaining who had participated in individual murders, some who had abused white women, and more who had been mixed up in the various raids made upon the white settlements.

When the wheels of this military commission were once put in motion they rolled on, as the victims were multiplied. Besides those who remained in the camp when the flight took place, and supposed that clemency would be meted out to them, several small parties of Sioux, who had fled, were pursued by our troops and " gobbled up," as the camp phrase was. In all such cases the grown men were placed in confinement to await the ordeal of a trial. The revelations of the white women caused great indignation among our soldiers, to which must be added the outside pressure coming to our camp in letters from all parts of Minnesota,—a wail and a howl,—in many cases demanding the execution of every Indian coming into our hands. The result of these combined influences was, that in a few weeks, instead of taking individuals for trial against whom some specific charge could be brought, the plan was adopted to subject all the grown men, with a few exceptions, to an investigation of the Commission, trusting that the innocent could make their innocency appear. This was a thing not possible in the case of the majority—especially as conviction was based upon an admission of being present at the battles of Fort Ridgely, New Ulm, Hutchinson and Birch Coolie. Almost all the Dakota men had been at one or more of those places, and had carried their guns and used them. So that of nearly four hundred cases, which came before the Commission, only about fifty were cleared, twenty were sentenced to imprisonment, and more than three hundred were condemned to be hung. The greater part of these were condemned on general principles, without any specific charges proved, such as under less exciting and excited conditions of society, would have been demanded. They were Sioux Indians, and belonged to the bands that had engaged in the rebellion. Among those who were condemned to be hung was a negro called *Gusso*. By the testimony of Indians, through fear or a liking to the business, he had rather signalized himself by the killing of white people. But he talked French, and could give what appeared to be accurate and reliable information in regard to a great many of the Dakotas who were brought before the Commission. In consequence of this service, the Commission recommended that his capital punishment be changed to imprisonment.

More than a month passed before the Court had finished its work. In the meantime, we had changed our camp to the Lower Sioux Agency. From this point the women and children of the imprisoned men, together with such men as had escaped suspicion, were sent down under a military guard to Fort Snelling, where they, being about fifteen hundred souls, were kept through the winter.

At the close of their work, the Military Commission turned over their Findings and condemnations to Gen. Sibley for his approval. During the few days in which these passed under review, the principles on which the condemnations were based were often under discussion. Many of them had no good foundation. And they were only justified by the considerations that they would be reviewed by a more disinterested authority, and that the condemnations were demanded by the people of Minnesota. Gen. Sibley pardoned one man, because he was a near relative of John Otherday, who had done so much for white people.

The campaign was now closed. The work of the Military Commission was completed. It remained now to go into winter quarters, to guard the prisoners, and to await such orders as should come from the President. It was November when the camp was removed from the Lower Sioux Agency to Mankato. On our way thither we must needs pass by or through New Ulm. As we approached that place, with 400 manacled Sioux, carried in wagons, and guarded by lines of infantry and cavalry, the people came out and made an insane attack upon the prisoners. Gen. Sibley thought it best to yield so far to the wishes of the Germans, as to pass outside of the town.

On our reaching Mankato, I was released from further service in the camp, and sent down to carry the condemnations to the military headquarters at Saint Paul. At midnight the stage reached Minneapolis. My own family were across the river, living in a hired house in St. Anthony. I had received very particular information as to how I should find the place, and went directly there; but as no answer was made to my knocking, I went back to the church, to see if I could have made a mistake. After trying in other directions, I aroused Rev. Mr. Sercombe, who insisted on going with me to the place where I had stood knocking.

Mary and the children were comfortably housed. Mrs. Sophronia McKee, the wife of the Presbyterian clergyman, had been a fellow townswoman and special friend of Mary in their younger years. This was a guarantee of help in this time of need. They found friends. Donations of little things to help them commence housekeeping came in from interested hearts. Friends farther away sent boxes of clothing and in some cases money; so that, after more than two months, I found them in comfortable circumstances.

All along the line of the frontier, where the Sioux raids had been made, were many families who had returned to desolated homes. Many persons all over the country took a deep interest in this class of sufferers, and money contributions were made for their relief. The Friends in Indiana and elsewhere had placed their contributions in the hands of Friend W. W. Wales, of Saint Anthony. Here was a service in which I could engage, and find relief from the strain of the campaign and the condemnations. Accordingly, I undertook to hunt up needy families in the neighborhood of Glencoe and Hutchinson, and to dispense a few hundred dollars of this benevolent fund. One day, as I was traveling in my one-horse buggy over the snow between Glencoe and Hutchinson, I was overtaken by a messenger from Gen. Sibley, asking me to report to Col. Miller, who was in command of the prison at Mankato, to be present and give assistance at the time of the executions.

As a matter of duty I obeyed. From my youth up it had been a determination of mine, never to go to see a fellow-being hung. No curiosity could have taken me. Rather would I have gone the other way. But, if I could be of service to Indian or white man, in preventing mistakes, and furthering the ends of justice and righteousness, my own feelings should be held in abeyance and made to work in the line of duty.

On receiving the papers transmitted from the Military Commission, President Lincoln had placed them in the hands of impartial men, with instructions to report the cases which, according to the testimony, were convicted of participation in individual murders, or in violating white women. Acting under these instructions, thirty-nine cases were reported, and these were ordered by the President to be executed. But among so many it was a matter of much difficulty to identify all the cases. Among the condemned there were several persons of the same name—three or four *Chaskays*, two or three *Washechoons*. In the findings of the Commission they were all numbered, and the order for the executions was given in accordance with these numbers. But no one could remember which number attached to which person. The only certain way of avoiding mistakes was by examining closely the individual charges. To Joseph R. Brown, who, better than any other one man, knew all these condemned men—and he did not recognize all perfectly—was mainly committed the work of selecting those who were named to be executed. Extraordinary care was meant to be used; but after it was all over, when we came to compare their own stories and confessions, made a day or two before their death, with the papers of condemnation, the conviction was forced upon us that two mistakes had occurred.

The separation was effected on Monday morning, the men to be executed being taken from the log jail, in which all were confined, to an adjoining stone building, where they were additionally secured by being chained to the floor. Col. Miller then informed them of the order of the President, that they should be hung on the Thursday following, and they were advised to prepare themselves for that event. They were at liberty to select such spiritual counsel as they desired. Dr. Williamson was there as a Protestant minister, and Father Ravaux, of Saint

Paul, as a Catholic priest. They were advised not to select me, as I was acting interpreter for the government. More than three-fourths of the whole number selected Mr. Ravaux. This was accounted for by the fact that one of the Campbells, a half-breed and a Roman Catholic, was of the number. Some days before this, Dr. Williamson had baptized *Round Wind*, who was reprieved by an order from the President, which came only a day or so before the executions, reducing the number to thirty-eight.

Of this man *Round Wind* it is sufficient to say, that he was condemned on the testimony of a German boy, who affirmed that he was the man who killed his mother. But it was afterward shown by abundance of testimony, that *Round Wind* was not there.

As the time of their death approached, they manifested a desire, each one, to say some things to their Dakota friends, and also to the white people. I acceded to their request, and spent a whole day with them, writing down such things as they wished to say. Many of them, the most of them, took occasion to affirm their innocence of the charges laid against them of killing individuals. But they admitted, and said of their own accord, that so many white people had been killed by the Dakotas, that public and general justice required the death of some in return. This admission was in the line of their education. Perhaps it is not too much to call it an instinct of humanity.

The executions took place. Arrangements were made by which *thirty-eight* Dakota men were suspended in mid-air by the cutting of one rope. The other prisoners, through crevices in the walls of their log prison-house, saw them hung. And they were deeply affected by it; albeit they did not show their feelings as white men would have done, under like circumstances.

At the close of the week, Dr. Williamson, finding himself quite worn out with abundant labors, returned to St. Peter to rest in his family. The Sabbath morning came. The night before a fresh snow had fallen nearly a foot deep. Col. Miller thought it was only humane to let the prisoners go out into the yard on that day, to breathe the fresh air. And so it was, we gathered in the middle of that inclosure, and all that company of chained men stood, while we sang hymns and prayed and talked of God's plan of saving men from death. To say that they listened with attention and interest would not convey the whole truth. Evidently, their fears were thoroughly aroused, and they were eager to find out some way by which the death they apprehended could be averted. This was their attitude. It was a good time to talk to them of sin—to tell them of their sins. It was a good time to unfold to them God's plan of saving from sin—to tell them God's own son, Jesus Christ our Lord, died to save them from their sins, if they would only believe. A marvelous work of grace was already commencing in the prison.

The next day after the Sabbath I left Mankato, and returned to my family in Saint Anthony, where I spent the remaining part of the winter, partly in preparing school-books, for which there arose a sudden demand, and all we had on hands were destroyed in the outbreak; and partly in helping on the spiritual and educational work in the camp at Fort Snelling. But Dr. Williamson, living as he did in St. Peter, gave his time during the winter to teaching and preaching to the men in the prison. Immediately on their reaching Mankato, he and his sister came up to visit them, and were glad to find them ready to listen.

The prisoners asked for books. Only two copies of the New Testament and two or three copies of the Dakota hymn book were found in prison. Some of each were obtained elsewhere, and afterward furnished them, but not nearly as many as they needed. Some slates and pencils and writing paper were provided for them. And still later in the winter some Dakota books were given them. From this time on the prison became a school, and continued to be such all through their imprisonment. They were all exceedingly anxious to learn. And the more their minds were turned toward God and His word, the more interested they became in learning to read and write. In their minds, books and the religion we preached went together.

Soon after this first visit of Dr. Williamson, they began to sing and pray publicly, every morning and evening; which they continued to do all the while they were in prison. This they commenced of their own accord. At first the prayers were made only by those who had been church members, and who were accustomed to pray; but others soon came forward and did the same.

Before the executions, Robert Hopkins, who was, at that time, the leader in all that pertained to worship, handed to Dr. Williamson the names of thirty men who had then led in public prayer. And not very long after, sixty more names were added to the list of praying ones. This was regarded by themselves very much in the light of making a profession of religion.

In a few weeks a deep and abiding concern for themselves was manifest. Here were hundreds of men who had all their life refused to listen to the gospel. They now wanted to hear it. There was a like number of men who had refused to learn to read. Now almost all were eager to learn. And along with this wonderful awakening on the subject of education, sprang up the more marvelous one of their seeking after God—some god. Their own gods had failed them signally, as was manifest by their present condition. Their conjurers, their medicine men, their makers of *wakan*, were nonplused. Even the women taunted them, by saying, "You boasted great power as *wakan* men, where is it now?" These barriers, which had been impregnable and impenetrable, in the past, were suddenly broken down. Their ancestral religion had departed. They were unwilling now, in their distresses, to be without God—without hope, without faith in something or some one. Their hearts were aching after some spiritual revelation.

Then, if human judgment resulted in what they had seen and realized, what would be the results of God's judgment? If sin against *white men* brought *such death*, what death might come to them by reason of sin, from the Great Wakan? There was such a thing as sin, and there was such a person as Christ, God's Son, who is a Savior from sin. These impressions were made by the preaching of the Word. These impressions became convictions. The work of God's spirit had now commenced among them, and it was continued all winter, "deep and powerful, but very quiet," as one wrote.

Some of these men, in their younger days, had heard the Mr. Ponds talk of the white man's religion. They were desirous now, in their trouble, to hear from their old friends, whose counsel they had so long rejected. To this request, Mr. G. H. Pond responded, and spent some days in the prison assisting Dr. Williamson. Rev. Mr. Hicks, pastor of the Presbyterian church in Mankato, was also taken into their counsels and gave them aid. For several weeks previous, many men had been wishing to be baptized, and thus recognized as believers in the Lord Jesus Christ. This number increased from day to day, until about three hundred—just how many could not afterward be ascertained—stood up and were baptized into the name of the Father, of the Son and of the Holy Ghost. The circumstances were peculiar, the whole movement was marvelous, it was like a "nation born in a day." The brethren desired to be divinely guided; and after many years of testing have elapsed, we all say that was a genuine work of God's Holy Spirit.

Several weeks after the events above described, in the month of March, I went up to Mankato and spent two Sabbaths with the men in prison; and while there labored to establish them in their new faith, and at the close of my visit, by the request of Dr. Williamson, I administered to these new converts the Lord's Supper. *Robert Hopkins* and *Peter Big Fire* had both been prominent members and elders in Dr. Williamson's church at Pay-zhe-hoo-ta-ze. Naturally they, with others who were soon brought to the front, became the leaders and exponents of Christian faith among the prisoners.

This first communion in the prison made a deep impression upon myself. It began to throw light upon the perplexing questions that had started in my own mind, as to the moral meaning of the outbreak. God's thought of it was not my thought. As the heavens were higher than the earth, so his thoughts were higher than mine. I accepted the present interpretation of the events, and thanked God and took courage. The Indians had not meant it so. In their thought and determination, the outbreak was the culmination of their hatred of Christianity. But God, who sits on the throne, had made it result in their submission to him. This was marvelous in our eyes.

While these events were transpiring in the prison at Mankato, a very similar work went on in the camp at Fort Snelling. The conditions in both places were a good deal alike. In the camp as well as in the prison, they were in trouble and perplexity. In their distresses they were disposed to call upon the Lord. Many of our church members, both men and women, were in the camp. There were *Paul*, and *Simon*, and *Antoine Renville*, the elders of the Hazelwood church, and *Joseph Napayshne* of the Lower Sioux Agency. But the outlook was as dark to them as it was to us. Mr. J. P. Williamson thus describes the state of the camp in the closing days of 1862:

"The *suspense* was terrible. The ignorant women had not seen much of the world, and didn't know anything about law. They, however, knew that their husbands and sons had been murdering the whites, and were now in prison therefor, and they themselves dependent for life on the mercy of the whites. The ever-present query was, What will become of us, and especially of the men? With inquisitive eyes they were always watching the soldiers and other whites who visited them, for an answer, but the curses and threats they received were little understood, except that they meant no good. With what imploring looks have we been besought to tell them their fate. Strange reports were constantly being whispered around the camp. Now the men were all to be executed, of whom the thirty-eight hung at Mankato was the first installment, and the women and children scattered and made slaves; now they were all to be taken to a rocky barren island, somewhere, and left with nothing but fish for a support; and again they were to be taken away down south, where it was so hot they would all die of fever and ague."

Rev. John P. Williamson, having been providentially absent in Ohio at the time of the outbreak, returned to accompany this camp of despised and hated Dakotas in their journey from the Lower Sioux Agency to Ft. Snelling, But it did not immediately appear what he could do for them. He and I were in much the same condition, looking around for other work. He says of himself, that at this time he "made some effort to secure a place as stated supply in the neighborhood of St. Paul or Minneapolis, but was unsuccessful; and then he felt such drawings toward the Indian camp, that he took the nearest available quarters, and spent the winter ministering temporally and spiritually to this afflicted people."

When, in the spring following, they were taken down the Mississippi and up the Missouri to Crow Creek, he did not forsake them, but staid by them in evil and in good report, with the devotion of a lover. Every where and at all times, his thoroughly honest, devoted and unselfish course commanded the respect and confidence of white men in and out of the army. And his self-abandonment, to the temporal and spiritual good of the families of the men in prison, begot in them such admiration and confidence, that scarcely a prayer was made by them, in all those four years of their imprisonment, without the petition that God would remember and bless "the one who is called John."

The camp at Snelling was on the low ground near the

river, where the steamboats were accustomed to land. A high board fence was made around two or three acres of ground, inside of which the Dakotas pitched their cloth tents. In them they cooked and ate and slept, and read the Bible and sang and prayed, and wrote letters to their friends in prison.

By gradual steps, but with overwhelming power, came the heavenly visitation. At first Mr. Williamson used to meet the former members in one of their own teepees. Presently there was an evident softening of hearts. Now news came of the awakening among the prisoners at Mankato. The teepee would not contain half the listeners, so for some time, in the middle of winter, the meetings were held in the campus, then in a great, dark garret over a warehouse, without other fire than spiritual. In that low garret, when hundreds were crouched down among the rafters, only the glistening eyes of some of them visible in the dark, we remember how the silence was sometimes such that the fall of a pin might be heard. Many were convicted; confessions and professions were made; idols treasured for many generations with the highest reverence, were thrown away by the score. They had faith no longer in their idols. They laid hold on Christ as their only hope. On this ground they were baptized, over a hundred adults, with their children.

It was my privilege to be present frequently, and to see how the good hand of the Lord was upon them, in giving them spiritual blessings in their distresses. There was ever a large and active sympathy between the camp and the prison, and frequent letters passed between them. When, at one time, I brought down several hundred letters from the prisoners, and told them of the wonderful work there in progress, it produced a powerful effect. In both camp and prison, both intellectually and spiritually, it was a winter of great advancement.

CHAPTER XIV.

1863-1866.—The Dakota Prisoners taken to Davenport.—Camp McClellan.—Their Treatment.—Great Mortality.—Education in Prison.—Worship.—Church Matters.—The Camp at Snelling Removed to Crow Creek.—John P. Williamson's Story.—Many Die.—Scouts Camp.—Visits to Them.—Family Threads.—Revising the New Testament.—Educating Our Children.—Removal to Beloit.—Family Matters.—Little Six and Medicine Bottle.—With the Prisoners at Davenport.

The course of the Mississippi forming the eastern line of the State of Iowa is from north to south; but its trend, as it passes the city of Davenport, is to the west; so that what is called "East Davenport" is a mile above the city. At this point, in the beginning of the civil war, barracks had been erected for the accommodation of the forming Iowa Regiments, to which was given the name of "Camp McClellan."

Thither were transported the condemned Sioux who had been kept at Mankato during the winter. On the opening of navigation in the spring of 1863, a steamboat ascended to Mankato, took on the prisoners, and, on reaching Fort Snelling, put off about fifty men who had not been condemned, to unite their fortunes with those in the camp. The men under condemnation were taken down to Davenport, where, at Camp McClellan, they were guarded by soldiers for the next three years.

After a little while their irons were all taken off, and they enjoyed comparative liberty, being often permitted

13

to go to the town to trade their bows and arrows and other trinkets, and sometimes into the country around to labor, without a guard. They never attempted to make their escape, though at one time it was meditated by some, but so strongly and wisely opposed by the more considerate ones, that the plan was at once abandoned. Generally the soldiers who guarded them treated them kindly. It was remarked that a new company, whether of the regular army or of volunteers, when assigned to this duty, at the first treated the prisoners with a good deal of severity and harshness. But a few weeks sufficed to change their feelings, and they were led to pity, and then to respect, those whom they had regarded as worse than wild beasts.

The camp was not a pleasant place, except in summer. The surroundings were rather beautiful. The oak groves of the hill-side which bordered the river were attractive. And the buildings occupied by the troops were comfortable. But within the stockade, where the prisoners were kept, the houses were of the most temporary kind, through the innumerable crevices of which blew the winter winds and storms. Only a limited amount of wood was furnished them, which, in the cold windy weather, was often consumed by noon. Then the Indians were under the necessity of keeping warm, if they could, in the straw and under their worn blankets.

In these circumstances, many would naturally fall sick, go into a decline—pulmonary consumption, for which their scrofulous bodies had a liking—and die. The hospital was generally well filled with such cases. The death rate was very large—more than ten per cent. each year, making about 120 deaths while they were confined at that place. About one hundred men, women and children, who came afterward into the hands of the military, were added to those who were first brought down. These latter were uncondemned. As some women had been permitted to come with the prisoners at the first, and now more were added, a good many children were born there. And thus it came to pass, that all who were released, and returned to their people from this prison, numbered only about two hundred and four score.

For the first two years of their abode at Davenport, Dr. Williamson had the chief care of the educational and church work among them. During this time I only visited them twice, once when a difficulty and misunderstanding had arisen between Dr. Williamson and a Gen. Roberts, who at one time commanded that department, the doctor was obliged to return to his home in St. Peter. On learning the fact, I counseled with Gen. Sibley, who gave me a letter to Gen. Roberts. Before I reached there, however, Roberts had become ashamed of his conduct, as I judged, and so I found it quite easy to restore amicable relations. No such difficulties occurred thereafter.

For the prisoners these were educational years. They were better supplied with books than they could be at Mankato. A new edition of our Dakota hymn-book was gotten out, and in 1865, an edition of the Dakota Bible so far as translated, besides other books. The avails of their work in mussel shells and bows gave them the means of purchasing paper and books.

With only a few exceptions, all in the prison who were adults, professed to be Christians. A few had been baptized by Rev. S. D. Hinman, of the Episcopal church, who visited them once while at Davenport. But while a number were recognized as members of that church, they worshiped all together. Morning and night they had their singing and praying; but especially at night, when they were not likely to be disturbed by any order from the officer in command.

In church matters they naturally fell into classes according to their former clans or villages. In each of these classes one—or more than one—Hoonkayape was ordained. He was the elder and class leader. This arrangement was made by Dr. Williamson. It was one step toward raising up for them pastors from themselves. On our part it was a felt necessity, for *we* could not properly watch over and care for these people, as *they* could watch over and care for each other. So the work of education and establishment in the faith of the gospel was carried on.

Let us now return to follow for a little, the fortunes of those in the camp at Fort Snelling. The winter of suspense had worn away, and in the month of April, soon after the Mankato prisoners passed down into Iowa, those at Snelling were placed on a steamboat, and floated down to St. Louis, and up the Missouri to Crow Creek, where they were told to make homes. Mr. J. P. Williamson *went* with them, and *remained* with them, during those terrible years of suffering and death. Who can tell the story better than he?

"As they look on their native hills for the last time, a dark cloud is crushing their hearts. Down they go to St. Louis, thence up the Missouri to Crow Creek. But this brings little relief, for what of the men; and can the women and children ever live in this parched land, where neither rain nor dew was seen for many weeks?

"The *mortality* was fearful. The shock, the anxiety, the confinement, the pitiable diet, were naturally followed by sickness. Many died at Fort Snelling. The steamboat trip of over one month, under some circumstances, might have been a benefit to their health, but when 1,300 Indians were crowded like slaves on the boiler and hurricane decks of a single boat, and fed on musty hard tack and briny pork, which they had not half a chance to cook, diseases were bred which made fearful havoc during the hot months, and the 1,300 souls that were landed at Crow Creek June 1, 1863, decreased to one thousand. For a time a teepee where no one was sick could scarcely be found, and it was a rare day when there was no funeral. So were the hills soon covered with graves. The very memory of Crow Creek became horrible to the Santees, who still hush their voices at the mention of the name.

"Meetings, always an important means of grace, were greatly multiplied. Daily meetings were commenced at Fort Snelling; the steamboat was made a Bethel for daily praise, and the Crow Creek daily prayer-meetings were held each summer under booths, which plan was continued the first summer at Niobrara. Women's prayer-meetings were commenced at Crow Creek, deaconesses being appointed to have charge of them. The children also had meetings, conducted by themselves. All these means were blessed of the Holy Spirit to the breaking of the herculean chains of Paganism."

Soon after reaching Crow Creek, Mr. Williamson called to his assistance Mr. Edward R. Pond and his wife Mrs. Mary Frances Pond—born Hopkins—both children of the old missionaries, who continued with these people until the year 1870.

For the security of the Minnesota frontier, and to further chastise the Sioux, Military Expeditions were organized in the spring and summer of 1863. The one that went from Minnesota was in command of Gen. H. H. Sibley. Attached to this expedition was a corps of scouts, forty or fifty of them being Dakota men, who had in some way, and to some extent, showed themselves to be on the side of the white people, at the time of the outbreak. In this expedition I had the position of interpreter.

The families of these Sioux scouts were sent out to the frontier, and maintained by the government, not only during that summer, but for several years. This was known as the "Scout's Camp," and the church among them was called by the same name, until 1869, when several churches were formed out of this one, as they began to scatter and settle down on the new Sisseton Reservation.

In the summer of 1864, I visited their camp at the head of the Red Wood. The next summer I was with them for a short time at the Yellow Medicine. At each of these visits quite a number of additions was made to the roll of church members—infants and grown persons were baptized, marriages were solmnized, and ruling elders were ordained. During these years we had licensed and ordained as an evangelist, John B. Renville, who accompanied me on each of the visits mentioned.

Let me now gather up, and weave in, some threads of our home-life. For three years Mary and the children made their home in St. Anthony, now East Minneapolis, in a hired house. Our three boys, at the commencement of this period, being fifteen and thirteen and seven respectively, were at a good age to be profited by the schools of the town. Thomas and Henry soon commenced the rudiments of the Latin in Mr. Butterfield's school. While, to add to the family finances, Isabella and Martha, in turn, and sometimes both, engaged in teaching.

Mary's health, always tenacious but never vigorous, had received a severe shock by the outbreak and what followed. But she did not at once succumb. Her willpower was very strong, which often proved sufficient to keep her up, when some others would have placed themselves in the hands of a physician. But the house she lived in became more frail and worn in the summer and autumn of 1864, and she was obliged to take some special steps toward upbuilding. For some weeks at the close of the year, when I was absent, she was prevailed upon to try a residence at a water cure, but without any permanent benefit.

Returning from the military campaign in the fall of 1863, when there seemed to be no special call for my services with the Indians, I addressed myself, for the next six months, to a revision and completion of the New Testament in the Dakota language. It was a winter of very hard and confining work, and right glad was I when the spring came, and I could find some recreation in the garden.

The next autumn I went to New York and spent three months in the Bible House, reading the proof of our new Dakota Bible, and having some other printing done. To the New Testament above mentioned, Dr. Williamson had added a revised Genesis and Proverbs. It was at this time, the Bible Society commenced making electrotype plates of our Dakota Scriptures. At this writing— 1878—the Bible is nearly completed.

As yet, the Dakota work, while it had given each one of us plenty to do, did not assume any thing like a permanent shape. Things were still in a chaotic state. What would be the outcome, no one could tell in the year 1865. There was a time when I seriously asked the question, "What shall I do? Shall I seek some other work, or still wait to see what the months will bring forth?" I had even made it a subject of correspondence with Secretary Treat, whether I might not turn my attention *partly* to preaching to white people, and do a kind of half and half work. That plan was at once discouraged by Mr. Treat; and then Mr. G. H. Pond came to my relief, giving it as his decided conviction that I should hold on to the Dakota work. So that question was settled.

But where this work would be located did not then appear. There did not seem to be any great reason why we should remain in St. Anthony. The immediate family business was the education of our children. In the autumn previous, I had taken Thomas to Beloit, where, after making up some studies, he had entered the Freshman class. Could we not better accomplish this part of our *God-given-trust* by removing thither, and for a while making that our home? By so doing I might be farther away from any permanent place of work among the Dakotas. But on the other hand, I would be nearer to the prisoners at Davenport, and could relieve Dr. Williamson for the winter, which was desired. In this state of doubt, it often seemed that it would have been so comforting and satisfying if we could have heard the Lord say, "This is the way, walk ye in it." But no such voice came. However, as Mary recruited in the summer, and it seemed quite probable she would be able to remove, our judgment trended to Beloit, and I made arrangements for a family home by the purchase of a small cottage and garden, which have been a comfort to us in all these years.

And so, in the month of September, we came to the

southern line of Wisconsin. Anna had just completed the course at Rockford Female Seminary, and was ready to do duty in our new home. Martha accepted a call to teach at Mankato. Isabella accompanied us to Beloit, having under consideration the question of going to China with Rev. Mark W. Williams. This decision was not fully reached until the meeting of the American Board in Chicago, in the fall of 1865. One day she and I walked down Washington street together, and talked over the subject, and she gave in her answer.

In the early days of that year, two of the leaders in the out-break of 1862 were captured from beyond the British line, and after a trial by a Military Commission, were condemned to be hung. These men were commonly known as LITTLE SIX and MEDICINE BOTTLE. While in Chicago at the meeting of the Board, I received a note from Col. McLaren, commanding at Ft. Snelling, asking me to attend these men before their execution. The invitation was sent at their request. I obeyed the summons, and spent a couple of days with the condemned. But while I was there, a telegram came from Washington giving them a reprieve. This relieved me from being present when they were hung, one month afterward.

The winter that followed, I gave to the prisoners at Davenport. They had passed through the small-pox with considerable loss of life; and that winter, only the ordinary cases of sickness, and the ordinary number of deaths occurred. These were numerous enough. The confinement of nearly four years, and the uncertainty, which had always rested upon them like a night-mare, had all along produced many cases of decline. And even when the time of their deliverance drew nigh, and hope should have made them buoyant, they were too much afraid to hope—the promise was too good to be believed.

Before their release, I was called home to attend, on the 21st of February, the marriage of Isabella and Mr. Williams, and to bid them God-speed on their long journey by sailing vessel to China.

CHAPTER XV.

1866-1869.—Prisoners meet their Families at the Niobrara.—Our Summer's Visitation.—At the Scouts' Camp.—Crossing the Prairie.—Killing Buffalo.—At Niobrara —Religious Meetings.—Licensing Natives.—Visiting the Omahas.—Scripture Translating.—Sisseton Treaty at Washington.—Second visit to the Santees.—Artemas and Titus Ordained.—Crossing to the Head of the Coteau.—Organizing Churches and Licensing Dakotas.—Solomon, Robert, Louis, Daniel.—On Horseback in 1868.—Visit to the Santees, Yanktons, and Brules.—Gathering at Dry Wood.—Solomon Ordained.—Writing "Takoo Wakan."—Mary's Sickness.—Grand Hymns.—Going through the Valley of the Shadow.—Death!

The spring of 1866 saw the prisoners at Davenport released by order of the President; and their families, which had remained at Crow Creek for three dry and parched years, were permitted to join their husbands and brothers and fathers, at Niobrara, in the northeast angle of Nebraska. That was a glad and a sad meeting; but the gladness prevailed over the sadness. And now all the Dakotas with whom we had been laboring, were again in a somewhat normal condition. All had passed through strange trials and tribulations, and God had brought them out into a large place. The prisoners had prayed that their chains might be removed. God heard them, and the chains were now a thing of the past. They had prayed that they might again have a country, and now they were in the way of receiving that at the hand of the Lord.

And so, as Rev. John P. Williamson was with the united church of camp and prison on the Missouri, Dr. T. S. Williamson and I took with us John B. Renville and started on a tour of summer visitation. After a week's travel from St. Peter, in Minnesota, we reached the Scout's camp, which, in the month of June, 1866, we found partly on the margin of Lake Traverse, and partly at Buffalo Lake, in the country which was afterward set apart for their especial use.

At both of these places we administered the Lord's Supper, ordained *Daniel Renville* as a ruling elder, and licensed *Peter Big-fire* and *Simon Anawangmane* to preach the gospel. Neither of these men developed into preachers, but they have been useful as exhorters from that day to this. On the Fourth of July, we added *Peter* to our little company, and started across from Fort Wadsworth, which had only recently been established, to Crow Creek on the Missouri. From that point we passed down to the mouth of the Niobrara.

On this journey across the prairie we encountered many herds of buffalo. Sometimes they were far to one side of us, and we could pass by without molesting them. Once, on the first day from Wadsworth, we came suddenly upon a herd of a hundred or more, lying down. When we discovered them, they were only about half a mile in front of us. Peter said it was too good a chance not to be improved, he must shoot one. We gave him leave to try, and he crawled around over some low ground and killed a very fine cow. We could only take a little of the meat, leaving the rest to be devoured by prairie wolves. This episode in the day's travel frightened our horses, delayed us somewhat, and made us late getting into camp at the "Buzzard's Nest." The result was, that in the gloaming, our horses all broke away, and gave us four hours of hunting for them the next morning. Then we had a long, hot ride, without water, over the burning prairie to James River.

As I have said, the prisoners released from Davenport and their families from Crow Creek had met at Niobrara. This point had been selected for a town site, and a company had erected a large shell of a frame house intended for a hotel. Their plans had failed, and now the thought probably was to reimburse themselves out of the government.

We found the Indians living in tents, while the families of Mr. Williamson and Mr. Pond and others were accommodated with shelter in the big house. For their religious mass-meetings, they had erected a large booth, which served well in the dry weather of summer. Every day, morning and evening, they gathered there for prayer and praise, reading the Bible and telling what God had done for them. They had come too late to plant, and there was but little employment for them, and so the weeks we spent there were weeks of worship, given to the strengthening the things that remain, and arranging for future educational and Christian work. The churches of the prison and the camp were consolidated, and we selected and licensed *Artemas Ehnamane* and *Titus Ichadooze* as probationers for the gospel ministry. When we had remained as long as seemed desirable, Dr. Williamson and I left them, and came down to the Omaha Reserve, where we visited the new agency among the Winnebagoes and the Presbyterian Boarding-School among the Omahas. The latter was flourishing, but having been conducted in English alone, its spiritual results were very unsatisfactory.

The multiplication of Dakota readers, during the past few years, gave a new impulse to our work of translating the Scriptures, and made larger demands for other books. This furnished a great amount of winter work for both Dr. Williamson and myself. In five years we added the Psalms, Ecclesiastes, the Song and Isaiah, together with the other four books of Moses, to what we had printed in 1865.

The Wahpatons and Sissetons who constituted the Scouts Camp on the western border of Minnesota, and who had done good service in protecting the white settlements from the roving, horse-stealing Sioux, in the first months of 1867, sent a delegation to Washington to make a treaty, and obtain the guarantee of a home, and government help. While that delegation was in Washington, I took occasion to spend a month or more in lobbying in the interests of Indian civilization. To me this kind of work was always distasteful and unsatisfactory, and this time I came home to be taken down with inflammatory rheumatism. I had planned for an early summer campaign in the Dakota country, but it was July before I could get courage enough to start. And then it was with a great deal of pain that I endured the stage ride between Omaha and Sioux City. There I was met by Dr. Williamson, in his little wagon, and together we proceeded up to the settlement in Nebraska.

Since we had been there in the previous summer, these people had drifted down on to Bazille Creek, where Mr. Williamson and Mr. Pond had erected *shacks*—that is, log houses with dirt roofs—and between the two had made a room for assembly. The two men we had licensed the summer previous, were this season ordained and set over the native church, Mr. Williamson still retaining the oversight. At each visitation we endeavored to work the native church members up to a feeling of responsibility in the work of contributing to the support of their pastors, but it has been no easy undertaking.

This summer, with Robert Hopkins and Adam Paze for our companions in travel, the doctor and I crossed over directly from Niobrara to the head of the Coteau. Those Indians we now found considerably scattered on their new reservation. Some general lines began to appear in the settlement, and, during this, and our visit in the year following, several church organizations were effected; and *Solomon Toonkan-Shaecheya*, *Robert Hopkins*, *Louis Mazawakinyanna* and *Daniel Renville* were licensed to preach.

Louis was an elder in the prison and on the Niobrara, and, of his own motion, had gone over to Fort Wadsworth, and finding a community of Sioux scouts connected with the garrison, commenced religious work among them. In this he was supported and encouraged by the chaplain, Rev. G. D. Crocker. This year our camp-meeting was held on the border of the Coteau as it looks down on Lake Traverse.

The opening of the season of 1868 found me starting from Sioux City on a grey pony, which I rode across to Minnesota. But first I spent some weeks with the Santees. They had partly removed from Bazille Creek down to the bottom where the agency is now located. A long log house had been prepared for a church and schoolhouse. The Episcopalians were building extensively, and expensively, while our folks contented themselves with very humble abodes. The work of education had progressed very finely, Mr. Williamson and Mr. Pond giving much time to it, while Mrs. Pond and Mrs. Williamson greatly helped the women in their religious home-life.

This summer John P. Williamson and I took Artemas Ehnamane, the senior native minister of the Pilgrim Church, and crossed over to Fort Wadsworth, where Dr. Williamson and John B. Renville met us. On the way, we made a short stop at the Yankton Agency, which we had visited two years before. Now it was opening up as a field of promise to Mr. Williamson, and he proceeded to occupy it soon afterward. We made another stop, for preaching purposes, at Brule and Crow Creek, where the pastor of Santee showed himself able to gain the attention of the wild Sioux. Our ride across the desert land was enlivened by conversation on Dakota customs and Dakota songs. In both these departments of literature, this former hunter and warrior from Red Wing was an excellent teacher.

This annual gathering at the head of the Coteau was held at Dry Wood Lake, where Peter Big Fire had settled. It was the most remarkable of all those yearly camp-meetings. On this occasion about sixty persons were added to our church list. It was a sight to be remembered, when, on the open prairie, they and their children stood up to be baptized.

At the close of this meeting we held another at Buffalo Lake, in one of their summer houses, which was full of meaning. The recently organized church of Long Hollow, which then extended to Buffalo Lake, had selected SOLOMON to be their religious teacher. And this after meeting was held to ordain and install him as pastor of that church. He was a young man of Christian experience and blameless life, and has since proved himself to be a very reliable and useful native pastor.

Since the marvels of grace wrought among the Dakotas in the prison and camp, we had received numerous invitations to prepare some account thereof, for the Christian public. Several of these requests came from members of the Dakota Presbytery, which then covered the western part of Minnesota. Accordingly I had taken up the idea, and endeavored to work it out. Some chapters had been submitted, for examination, to a committee of the Presbytery, and commended by them for publication. In the autumn and winter of 1868, the manuscript began to assume a completed form. It was submitted to Secretary S. B. Treat for examination, who made valuable suggestions, and agreed to write an introduction to the book. This he did, in a manner highly satisfactory.

The manuscript I first offered to the Presbyterian Board of Publication. But the best that Dr. Dulles could do, was to offer me a hundred dollars for the copyright. Friends in Boston thought I could do better there. And so "Tahkoo Wakan," or, "The Gospel among the Dakotas," was brought out by the Congregational Publishing Society, in the summer of 1869. In the preparation of the book, Mary had taken the deepest interest, although not able to do much of the mental work. The preface bears date less than three weeks before her death.

Authors whose books do not sell very well, I suppose, generally marvel at the result. This little volume was, and is still, so intensely interesting to me, that I wonder why everybody does not buy and read it. But over against this stands the fact that hitherto less than two thousand copies have been disposed of. Pecuniarily, it has not been a success. But neither has it been an entire failure. And perhaps it has done some good in bringing a class of Christian workers into more intelligent sympathy and co-operation in the work of Indian evangelization; and so the labor is not lost.

Since we left Minnesota, Mary had apparently been slowly recovering from the invalidism of the past. She enjoyed life. She could occasionally attend religious meetings. The society of Beloit was very congenial. Sometimes she was able to attend the ministers' meetings, and enjoyed the literary and religious discussions and criticisms. The last winter—that of 1868–'69—she became exceedingly interested in a book called, "The Seven Great Hymns of the Medieval Church." She read and reread the various translations of *"Dies Irae."* But she was attracted most to the *"Hora Novissima,"* of Bernard of Cluni. Such a stanza as the 26th:

> "Thou hast no shore, fair ocean!
>   Thou hast no time, bright day!
> Dear fountain of refreshment
>   To pilgrims far away!
>
> "Upon the Rock of Ages
>   They raise thy holy Tower;
> Thine is the victor's laurel,
>   And thine the golden Dower."

And the 29th:

> "Jerusalem the golden,
>   With milk and honey blest,
> Beneath thy contemplation,
>   Sink heart and voice oppressed.
>
> "I know not, O, I know not,
>   What social joys are thine!
> What radiancy of glory,
>   What light beyond compare!"

But these and others were all eclipsed by the last, which seemed afterward to have been a prophecy of what was near at hand, and yet neither she nor we anticipated it:

> "*Exult, O dust and ashes!*
> *The Lord shall be thy part;*
> *His only, His forever,*
> *Thou shalt be, and thou art!*"

This was a fascination to her. We were blind at the time, and did not see afar off. Now it is manifest, that even then she was preparing to go to "Jerusalem the onely." *She was tenting in the Land of Beulah.*

For years past Mary had almost ceased to write letters. Neither her physical nor mental condition had permitted it. But a letter is found written on the 2d of February, 1869, which must have been the very last she ever wrote. Along with it she sent a copy of some of the stanzas from "*Hora Nov ssima*," which at this time were such an enjoyment to her. The letter is addressed to Isabella, in China. She writes: "Your last letter, written Oct. 5, '68, was received Jan. 5, 1869. All your letters are very precious to us, but this is peculiarly so. Perhaps I have written this before; but if I have, I am glad again to acknowledge the joy it gives me, that our Father gives you faith to look gratefully beyond the passing shadows of this life, into the abiding light of the life to come.

"Was the 19th of First Chronicles the last chapter we read in family worship before you left home? If so, the 13th verse must be the one you read: 'Be of good courage, and let us behave valiently for our people, and for the cities of our God; and let the Lord do that which is good in His sight.' Even so let it be. May you ever 'be strong in the Lord.'"

We had passed the nones of March. It was on Tuesday, the 10th, as I well remember the day of the minister's meeting, which was held at the house of the Presbyterian minister, Rev. Mr. Alexander. Mary had been planning to attend in the evening. But the day was chill and cold, as March days often are. She had been out in the yard seeing to the washed clothes, and had taken cold. In the evening she was not feeling so well, and decided to stay at home. For several days she thought—and we thought—it was only an ordinary cold, that some simple medicines and care in diet would remedy.

On Saturday, as she seemed to be growing no better, but rather worse, I called in Dr. Taggart, who pronounced it a case of pneumonia. The attack he said was a severe one, and her lungs were very seriously affected. Her hold on life had been so feeble for several years, that we could not expect she would throw off disease as easily as a person of more vigor. But at this time, her own impression was that she would recover. And the doctor said he saw nothing to make him think she would not

But soon after the physician's first visit, the record is, "She was occasionally flighty and under strange hallucinations, caused either by the disease or the medicines." On the following Thursday, she evidently began to be impressed with the thought that she possibly would not get well. She said she felt more *unconscious* and *stupid* than she had ever felt before in sickness. When, in answer to her inquiry as to what the doctor said of her case, I told her he was very hopeful, she said, "He does not know much more about it than we do." At one time she remarked, "I feel very delicious, the taking down of the tabernacle appears so beautiful;" and she desired me to get Bernard's Hymn, and read such passages as "Jerusalem the Golden," and "Exult, O dust and ashes."

"Friday, March 19, Noon.

"I watched with your mother last night. Her strength seems to keep up wonderfully well, but the disease has quite affected her power of speech. When it came light, I perceived a livid hue about her eyes, and became alarmed. We sent for Dr. Taggart. The propriety of continuing the whisky prescriptions seemed quite doubtful, especially as the mother was taking them under a conscientious protest. When the doctor came he appeared to be alarmed also, and changed his treatment from Dover's powders to quinine, but wished the whisky continued.

"During the morning she spoke several times about the probabilities of life. 'God knows the best time,' she said; 'but if I am to go now, I do not wish to linger long.' She had been able, she said, to do but little for years, and there was not much reason for her living—but she would be glad to stay longer for the children's sake. At one time she remarked in substance—'I have tried all along to do right, I don't know that I should be able to do better, if the life was to be lived over again.'"

"Saturday noon, March 20.

"It is a privilege that I never knew before, to watch and wait in a sick chamber, where one is in sympathy and contact with the spirit that is mounting upward. It does seem as if the pins of the tabernacle were indeed being taken out one by one, and the taking of it down is beautiful—how much more beautiful will be its rebuilding!

"Anna and I watched the first part of last night—or rather she watched, and I lay on the lounge and got up to help her. In the latter part, Alfred took Anna's place. So we watch and wait. Her mind-wandering continues at intervals, and she complains of her dullness—*so stupid*, she says. Christ, she says, has been near to her all winter, and is now. A little while ago, she remarked that she had been once, at Saint Anthony, as low as she is now, and God had restored her. So she wanted us to pray that God would restore her yet again. This forenoon she had a talk with Henry, Robbie and Cornelia separately. When Mr. Warner came in she asked to see him, and said she hoped to have seen him under different circumstances than the present—and then commended Anna to his gentle care."

"Saturday evening.

"One feels so powerless by the side of a sick loved one! How we would like to make well, if we could! But the fever continues to burn, and we can only look on. Then the mind wanders and fastens on all kinds of impossible and imaginary things. We would set that right, but we cannot. Dr. Taggart has just been here, and speaks encouragingly of your mother. He thinks if we can keep her along until the fever runs its course, then careful nursing will bring her up again. The neighbors are very kind in offering us help and sympathy."

"Sabbath morning.

"The mother is still here. But the hopes Dr. Taggart encouraged are not likely to be realized. Alfred and I watched with her until after midnight, and Mrs. Bushnell and Anna the rest of the night. As the *bourbon* continued to be so distasteful the doctor substituted *wine;* but that was no more desirable.

"When told it was the Sabbath morning, she looked up brightly and said, 'I think He will come for me to-day.' Over and over again, she said, 'He strengthens me.' Mrs. Carr and Mrs. Benson came in this morning and were very helpful. The doctor has been up again, and says he is *still* hopeful. So *we* hope and watch."

"Sabbath evening.

"The sick one continues much the same as earlier in the day. Mrs. Blaisdell and Mrs. Merrill came to offer their sympathy. Dr. Taggart came again and desired that she might renew the whisky. This she promised to do. Mr. Bushnell has been in and expressed his confidence in the *minne-wakan* for those who are ready to perish."

"Monday morn, 5:30 o'clock.

"The end seems to be coming on apace. Anna and Alfred watched the first part of the night, and Mrs. Wheeler and I have been watching since. The difficulty of breathing has increased within the last few hours, and added to it is a rattling in the throat. Your mother called my attention to it about three o'clock. It seems now, as if we can't do much but smooth the way, which we do tenderly—lovingly."

"Seven o'clock A. M.

"The battle is fought, the conflict is ended, the victory is won, and that *sooner* than we expected. Your mother's life's drama is closed—the curtain is drawn.

"About one hour ago she called for some tea. Mrs. Wheeler hasted and made some fresh. When she had taken that, we gave her also the medicine for the hour. She then appeared to lie easily. I sat down to write a note to Thomas, who was in the Freedman's work in Mississippi. But I had written only a few lines when Mrs. Wheeler called me. She had noticed a change come on very suddenly. When I reached the bed-side, your mother could not speak, and did not recognize me by any sign. She was passing through the deep waters, and had even then reached the farther shore.

"Mrs. Wheeler called up the children, and sent Robbie for Alfred. But before he could come, the mother had breathed her last breath. Quietly, peacefully, without a struggle, only the gasping out of life, she passed beyond our reach of vision.

"Yesterday she had said to me, 'I have neglected the flowers.' I asked, 'What flowers?' She replied, 'The Immortelles.' *Dear, good one, she has gone to the flower-garden of God.*"

CHAPTER XVI.

1869-1870.—Home Desolate.—At the General Assembly.—Summer Campaign.—A. L. Riggs.—His Story of Early Life.—Inside View of Missions.—Why Missionaries' Children Become Missionaries.—No Constraint Laid on Them.—A. L. Riggs Visits the Missouri Sioux.—Up the River.—The Brules.—Cheyenne and Grand River.—Starting for Fort Wadsworth.—Sun Eclipsed.—Sisseton Reserve.—Deciding to Build there.—In the Autumn Assembly.—My Mother's Home.—Winter Visit to Santee.—Julia La Framboise.

As Abraham, a stranger and sojourner in the land of the children of Heth, bought of them the cave of Machpelah wherein to bury Sarah, so it seemed to me that I had come to Beloit to make a last resting place for the remains of Mary. The house seemed desolate. Sooner or later it involved the breaking up of the family. Indeed it commenced very soon. Robert went up to Minnesota to spend a year at Martha's. In the meantime Anna had become mistress of the home, and had with her Mary Cooley, an invalid cousin.

That year of 1869, I was Commissioner from the Dakota Presbytery, to the General Assembly which met in New York City. It was an Assembly of more than ordinary interest, as at that meeting, and the one that followed in the autumn, the two branches of the Presbyterian Church North were again united. During this stay in New York City, I was the guest of Hon. Wm. E. Dodge.

That was quite a contrast to living among the Dakotas. But at the close of the Assembly, I hastened westward to join Dr. Williamson at St. Peter. He had procured a small double wagon and a pony team, with which we together should make our summer campaign. Having fitted ourselves out, as we always did, with tent and camping materials, our first objective point was Sioux City, where we had arranged to meet and take in Alfred L. Riggs.

Since a little previous to the outbreak in 1862, he had been preaching to white people; first at Lockport, Ill., where he was ordained and continued with the church five years, and then for a year at Center, Wis., and now at Woodstock, Ill. But all this time he seemed to be only waiting for the Dakota work to assume such a shape as to invite his assistance. For sometime he had been especially acquainting himself with the most approved methods of education, that he might fill a place, which, year by year, was becoming more manifestly important to be filled.

As in the progress of modern missions a large and increasing share of the new recruits are the children of missionaries, it will be interesting to know, from one of themselves, how they grow up *in* and *into* the Missionary Kingdom.

My first serious impression of life was, that I was living under a great weight of something; and as I began to discern more clearly, I found this weight to be the all-surrounding, overwhelming presence of heathenism, and all the instincts of my birth, and all the culture of a Christian home, set me at antagonism to it at every point. The filthy savages, indecently clad, lazily lounging about the stove of our sitting-room, or flattening their dirty noses on the window pane, caused such a disgust for everything Indian, that it took the better thought of many years to overcome the repugnance thus aroused. Without doubt our mothers felt it all as keenly as we, their children, but they had a sustaining ambition for souls which we had not yet gained.

This feeling of disgust was often accompanied with, and heightened by, fear. The very air seemed to breathe dangers. At times violence stalked abroad unchallenged, and dark, lowering faces skulked around. Even in times when we felt no personal danger, this incubus of savage life all around weighed on our hearts. Thus it was, day and night. Even those hours of twilight, which brood with sweet influences over so many lives, bore to us on the evening air only the weird cadences of the heathen dance, or the chill thrill of the war-whoop.

Yet our childhood was not destitute of joy. Babes prattle beside the dead. So, too, the children of the mission had their plays, like other children. But it was lonesome indeed when the missionary band was divided, to occupy other stations, and the playmates were separated. Once it was my privilege to go one hundred and twenty miles—to the nearest station—to have a play-spell of a week, and a happy week it was.

Notwithstanding our play spells, ours was a serious ife. The serious earnestness of our parents in the pursuit of their work could not fail to fall, in some degree, on the children. The main purpose of Christianizing that people was felt in everything. It was like garrison life in time of war. But this seriousness was not ascetical or morose. Far from it. Those Christian missionary homes were full of gladness. With all the disadvantages of such a childhood, was the rich privilege of understanding the meaning of cheerful earnestness in Christian life. Speaking of peculiar privileges, I must say that I do not believe any other homes can be as precious as ours. It is true everyone thinks his is the best mother in the world, and she is to him; but I mean more than this; I mean that our missionary homes are in reality better than others. And there is reason for it. By reason of the surrounding heathenism the light and power of Christianity is more centered and confined in the home. And then again its power is developed by its antagonism to the darkness and wickedness around it. For either its light must ever shine clearer, or grow more dim until it expires.

Next to our own home, we learned to love the homeland in "the States," whence our parents came. A longing desire to visit it possessed us. We thought that there we should find a heaven on earth. This may seem a strange idea, but as you think of us engulphed in heathenism and savage life, it will not seem so strange. It was like living at the bottom of a well, with only one spot of brightness overhead. Of course it would be natural to think that upper world all brightness and beauty. Thus all our glimpses of another life than that of heathenism came from "the States." There all our ideas of Christianized society were located. The correspondence of our parents with friends left behind, the pages of the magazines and papers of the monthly mail, and the yearly boxes of supplies, were the tangible tokens which in our innocent minds awakened visions of the wonderful world of civilization and culture in "the East."

These supplies were in reality, perhaps, very small affairs, but we thought them of fabulous value. Indeed they were everything to us. With the opening of the new year the lists of purchases began to be arranged.

Each item was carefully considered, and the wants of each of the family remembered. This was no small task when you had to look a year and a half ahead. What debates as to whether B could get on with one pair of shoes, or must have two; or whether C would need some more gingham aprons, or could make the old ones last through. And then it was so hard to remember musquito bars and straw hats in January; but if they were forgotten once, the next January found them first on the list. It was fun to make up the lists, but not so exhilarating when, on summing up the probable cost, it was found to be too much, and then the cruel pen ran through many of our new-born hopes. Then the letter went on its way to Boston, or maybe to Cincinnati, and we waited its substantial answer. Sometimes our boxes went around by lazy sloops from Boston to New Orleans; thence the laboring steamboat bore them almost the whole length of the Father of Waters; then the flatboatmen sweated and swore as they poled them up the Minnesota to where our teams met them to carry them for another week over the prairies. Now it was far on into rosy June. After such waiting, no wonder that everything seemed precious—the very hoops of the boxes and the redolent pine that made them; even the wrappers and strings of the packages were carefully laid away. And, thanks to the kind friends who have cared for this work at our several purchasing depots, our wants were generally capitally met; and yet sometimes the packer would arrange it so that the linseed oil would give a new taste to the dried apples, anything but appetizing, or turn the plain white of some long-desired book into a highly "tinted" edition.

When the number of our years got well past the single figures, then we went to "the States" to carry on the education begun at home. Then came the saddest disappointment of all our lives. We found we were yet a good ways from heaven. For me, the last remnant of this dream was effectually dispelled when I came to teach a Sabbath-school in a back country neighborhood, where the people were the driftwood of Kentucky and Egyptian Illinois. Thenceforth the land of the Dakotas seemed more the land of promise to me. From that time the claims of the work in which my parents were engaged grew upon my mind.

Of late years the children of missionaries have everywhere furnished a large portion of the new reinforcements. This is both natural and strange. It is natural that they should desire to stay the hands of their parents, and go to reap what they have sown. On the other hand, they go out in face of all the hardships of the work, made vividly real to them by the experience of their childhood. They are attracted by no romantic sentiment. The romance is for them all worn off long ago. For instance, those of us on this field know the noble red man of the poet to be a myth. We know the real savage, and know him almost too well. Thus those who follow in the work of their missionary fathers do not do it without a struggle—often fearful. On the one hand stands the work, calling them to lonesome separation, and on the other the pleasant companionship of civilized society. But if the word of the Lord has come to them to go to Nineveh, happy are they if they do not go thither by way of Joppa.

I have spoken of the drawbacks to entering the work, but the inducements must also be remembered. They are greater than the drawbacks. We know them also better than strangers can. If we have known more of the discouragements of the work, we also know more of its hopefulness. We know the real savage, but we now know, and fully believe in, his real humanity and salvability by the power of the cross. Now, too, when the work is entered, the very difficulties which barred the way grow less or disappear. We find the dreaded isolation to be more in appearance than reality. We here are in connection with the best thought and sympathy of the civilized world, whether it be in scholarship, statesmanship or Christian society. And not unfrequently do we have the visits of friends and the honored representatives of the churches. One may be much more alone in Chicago or New York.

The difficulties of the work in earlier years are also changing. We have a different standing before the people among whom we labor. We also have matured and tested our methods of operation, and can be generally confident of success. We have also an ever increasing force in the native agency, which adds strength and hopefulness to the campaign. The people we come to conquer are themselves furnishing recruits for this war, so that we, the sons of the mission, stand among them as captains of the host, and our fathers are as generals.

With such a growing up, it would seem that he was *attracted* to the life work of his father and mother. And yet our children will all bear witness, that no special influence was ever used to draw them into the missionary work. Some ministers' sons, I understand, have grown up under the burden of the thought that they were expected to be ministers. It was certainly my endeavor not to impose any such burden on my boys. But we certainly did desire—and our desire was not concealed—that all our children should develop into the most noble and useful lives, prepared to occupy any position to which they might be called. Accordingly, when a boy, while pursuing his education, has shown a disposition "to knock off," I have used what influence I had to induce him to persevere. But beyond this, it has been my desire that each one should, under the divine guidance, *choose*, as is their right to do, what shall be their line of work in life. At the same time, it is but just to myself, as well as to them, to say that it gives me great joy, now in my old age, to see so many of Mary's children making the life work of their father and mother their own.

This visit of Alfred to the Santee and Yankton Agencies, was made for the purpose of looking over the field, and forming an intelligent judgment as to whether the way was open and the time had come to commence some higher educational work among the Dakotas. The place for such an effort was evidently the Santee Agency. And John P. Williamson, who had so long and so well carried on the mission work among the Santees, had, for several years past, been more and more attracted to the Yanktons, where there was an open door; and to the Yankton Agency he had removed his family, in the early spring, before our visit. So the hand of God had shaped the work. It required only that we recognize His hand, and put ourselves in accord with the manifestations of His will. After a few weeks, Alfred returned to his people in Woodstock, and made his arrangements to close his labors there in the following winter, when he accepted an appointment from the American Board, to take charge of its work at the Santee Agency.

Our summer campaign now commenced. The Williamsons, father and son, with Titus, one of the Santee pastors, and myself, proceeded up the Missouri. We made a little stop, as we had done in former years, with the *Sechangoos,* or Brules, near Fort Thompson, preaching to them the gospel of Christ. Some interest was apparent. At least, a superstitious reverance for the *name* that is above every name was manifest. "What is the name?" one asked, "I have forgotten it." And we again told them of JESUS.

Our next point was the Cheyenne Agency, near Fort Sully, a hundred miles above Fort Thompson at Crow Creek. There we spent a week, and met the Indians in their Council House. Our efforts were in the line of sowing seed, much of which fell by the way side, or on the stony places. And then we passed on another hundred miles to the agency at the mouth of Grand River, where were gathered a large number of Yanktonais, as well as Teetons. This agency is now located farther up the river, and is called Standing Rock. Among these people we found some who desired instruction, but the more part did not want to hear. Our attempt to gather them to a Sabbath meeting seemed quite likely to fail. But there had been a thunder storm in the early morning, and out a few miles, on a hill-top, a prominent Dakota man was struck down by the lightning. He was brought in to the agency, and before his burial, at the close of the day, we had a large company of men and women to listen to the divine words of Jesus, who is the Resurrection and the Life. It was an impressive occasion, and it was said by white men, that many of those Indians listened that day, for the first time, to Christian song and Christian prayer. But that agency has since passed into the hands of the Catholics, and David, one of our native preachers, who visited there recently, was not permitted to remain.

15

At this point—Grand River—our company separated. John P. Williamson and Titus returned down the Missouri, and Dr. Williamson and I took a young man, Blue Bird by name, and crossed over to Fort Wadsworth. On Saturday we traveled up the Missouri about thirty miles, where we spent the Sabbath, and where we were joined by a Dakota man who was familiar with the country across to the James River, and who could find water for us in that "dry and thirsty land." As we journeyed that Saturday afternoon, the day grew dark, the sun ceased to shine, our horses wanted to stop in the road. It was a weird, unnatural darkness—an eclipse of the sun. We stopped and watched its progress. For about five minutes the eclipse was annular—only a little rim of light gleamed forth. The moon seemed to have a cut in one side, appearing much like a thick cheese from which a very thin slice had been cut out. We all noted this singular appearance. The Dakotas on the Missouri represent that year by the symbol of a *black sun with stars shining* above it.

When we reached the Sisseton Reservation, we held our usual camp-meeting again at Dry Wood Lake, regulating and confirming the churches, and receiving quite a number of additions, though not so many as in the year previous. The place for the Sisseton Agency had been selected, some log buildings erected, and the agent, Dr. Jared W. Daniels, with his family, was on the ground. The time seemed to have come, when, to secure the fruits of the harvest, some more permanent occupation should be made in the reservation. Mary was gone up higher. The boys, for whose sakes, mainly, we had made a home in Beloit, were no longer in college. Thomas had graduated, and spent a year in teaching Freedmen in Mississippi, and was now in the Chicago Theological Seminary; while Henry had commenced to seek his fortune in other employment. Without apparent detriment, I could break up housekeeping in Beloit, and build at Sisseton. The plan was formed during this visit, and talked over with Dr. Williamson and Agent Daniels. God willing, and the Prudential Committee at Boston approving, it was to be carried into effect the next spring.

And so I returned to my home in Beloit, and went on to attend the meeting of the two General Assemblies at Pittsburg, where their union became an accomplished fact. At the close of this meeting, I spent a couple of weeks in visiting friends in Fayette County, and the old stone church of Dunlap's Creek, which had been the church-home of my mother when as yet she was unmarried.

For several winters preceding this, I had been working on translations of the book of Psalms, and Ecclesiastes and Isaiah. They were printed in 1871. But this winter of 1869–'70 was mostly spent with the Santees. Mr. Williamson had left that place and gone to the Yankton Agency, where he has since continued with great prosperity in the missionary work. And so there came to me a pressing invitation from Mrs. Mary Frances Pond and Miss Julia La Framboise, to come out and help them that winter.

Julia La Framboise was the teacher of the mission school at Santee. She was born of a Dakota mother, and her father always claimed that he had Indian blood mixed with his French. Julia was a noble, Christian woman, who had been trained up in the mission families, completing her education at Miss Sill's Seminary, in Rockford, Illinois. I found them all actively engaged in carrying forward mission work. But we conceived more might be done, to bring children into the school, and men and women to the church. Accordingly, I called together the pastors and elders of the church, and engaged them to enter upon a system of thorough church visitation, which had the effect of greatly increasing the numbers in attendance on both the school and the church.

Even then, as it afterward appeared, Julia was entering upon the incipient stages of pulmonary consumption. She was not careful of herself. After teaching school until one o'clock, she was ever ready to go with the Agent's daughters to interpret for them in the case of some sick person, or to relieve the wants of the poor. Before I left in March, her cough had become alarming. And so it increased. The second summer after this, she was obliged to stop work, and simply wait for the coming of the messenger that called her to the Father's house above.

CHAPTER XVII.

1870-1871.—Beloit Home Broken up.—Building on the Sisseton Reserve.—Difficulties and Cost.—Correspondence with Washington.—Order to Suspend Work.—Disregarding the Taboo.—Anna Sick at Beloit.—Assurance.—Martha Goes in Anna's Place.—The Dakota Churches.—Lac-qui-parle, Ascension.—John B. Renville.—Daniel Renville.—Houses of Worship.—Eight Churches.—The "Word Carrier."—Annual Meeting on the Big Sioux.—Homestead Colony.—How it Came about.—Joseph Iron Old Man.—Perished in a Snow Storm.—The Dakota Mission Divides.—Reasons Therefor.

The spring of 1870 brought with it a breaking up of the Beloit home. Some months before Mary's death, she had invited to our house an invalid niece, the daughter of her older sister, Mrs. Lucretia Cooley. A dear good girl Mary Cooley was. She had, during the war, acted as nurse, in the service of the Christian Commission. But her health failed. It was hoped that a year in the West might build her up. After her aunt had gone from us, Mary Cooley remained with us. But the malady increased; and this spring her brother Allan came and took her back to Massachusetts. And now, only a little while ago, we heard of her release in California, whither the family had removed. The good Lord had compassion upon her, and took her to a land where no one says, "I am sick."

Then the house was rented. The household goods and household gods were scattered, the major part being taken up into the Indian country. Anna would spend the summer with friends in Beloit, and Cornelia, the youngest, I took up to Minnesota and left with Martha on the frontier.

My plan was to put up two buildings, a dwelling-house and a school-house, for the erection of which the Committee at Boston had appropriated twenty-eight hundred dollars. That may seem quite an amount; but the materials had to be transported from Minneapolis and the Red River of the North. What I purchased at Minneapolis was carried by rail and steamboat one hundred and fifty miles. There remained one hundred and thirty, over which the lumber was hauled in wagons in the month of June, when the roads were bad and the streams swimming. And so the cost was very great—dressed flooring coming up to $75 per 1,000 feet; dressed siding, $65; shingles about $15 per 1,000, and common lumber, $60 a thousand feet.

When the materials were on the ground, but little money was left for their erection. But with one carpenter and two or three young men to assist, I pushed forward the work, and by the middle of September, the houses were up and ready to be occupied, though in an unfinished state.

During this time there were some things transpired which deserve to be noticed.

Before commencing to build, I had received the written approval of the Agent. In regard to the locality, we differed. He wished me to build in the immediate vicinity of the agency, while I, for very good reasons, selected a place nearly two miles away. But that, I think, could have made no difference in his feeling toward the enterprise. However, soon after I commenced, I was visited by

Gabriel Renville, who was recognized as the head man on the reservation. He did not forbid my proceeding, but wanted to know whether I had authority to do so. I replied that I had the approval of Agent Daniels, which I regarded as sufficient. When I reported this to Mr. Daniels, he advised me to write to the Commissioner of Indian Affairs, and obtain a permit, which, he said, might save me trouble.

Accordingly, I wrote immediately to the Department of the Interior, stating the life-long connection we had had with these Indians, and the work we had done among them, and that now, I was authorized by the A. B. C. F. M. to erect mission buildings among them, and asking that our plan be approved.

After three or four weeks, when I was in the very middle of my work of building, there came an order from Washington that I should suspend operations, until they would settle the question to what religious denomination that part of the field should be assigned. That subject was then under advisement, they said.

Should I obey? If I did so, much additional expense would be incurred, and my summer's work, as planned, would be a failure. Really no question could be raised about it. The American Board had been doing missionary work among those Indians for a third of a century, and no other denomination or missionary board pretended to have any claim on the field. It was unreasonable, under the circumstances, that we should be asked to suspend, and thus suffer harm and loss. So I placed my letter safely away and went on with my work. No human being there knew that I had received such a command.

By the return mail, I wrote to Secretary Treat, rehearsing the whole case, and asking him, without delay, to write to the authorities at Washington. I told him I had concluded to disregard the *Taboo*, and would not, in consequence thereof, drive a nail the less. When the summer months were passed, and my houses were both up, I received a letter from the Commissioner commending my work, and telling me to go forward.

In the latter end of August, there came to me a letter written in a strange hand, saying that Anna was lying sick at Mr. Carr's of typhoid fever. The intention of the letter evidently was not to greatly alarm me, but it conveyed the idea that she was very sick, and the result was doubtful. Ten or twelve days had passed since it was written. My affairs were not then in a condition to be left without much damage, and so I determined to await the coming of another mail. When I heard again, a week later, there was no decided change for the better. So the letter read. But in the meantime, this word had come to me—"This sickness is not unto death, but for the glory of God." It came to me like a revelation. I seemed to know it. It quieted my alarm. All anxiety was not taken away, but my days passed in comparatively quiet trust. About the middle of September I started down with my own team, and, on reaching St. Peter and Mankato, I received letters from Anna written with her own hand. She had come up gradually, but a couple of months passed before she was strong.

Before I commenced building at Good Will, which was the name we gave to our new station, the understanding was that Anna would be married in the coming autumn, and she and her husband would take charge of the mission work there. Anna seemed to have grown up into the idea that her life-work was to be with the Dakotas. But it was otherwise ordered. In the October following, when we all again met in Beloit, she was married to H. E. Warner, who had lost an arm in the war of the rebellion, and they have since made their home in Iowa.

Martha Taylor Riggs had been married to Wyllys K. Morris, in December, 1866. For a time they made their home in Mankato, Minnesota, and then removed to a farm twenty miles from town. Life on the extreme frontier they found filled with privations and hardships, and so were quite willing to accept the new place; and before the winter set in, they were removed to Good Will. Robert, who had gone up after his mother's death, and spent a year with Martha at Sterling, returned to Beloit, and entered the preparatory department of the college. Cornelia went with us to Good Will, and remained two years.

The Home was again in Dakota land. We at once opened a school, which has since been taught almost entirely by W. K. Morris. The native churches needed a good deal of attention. At Lac-qui-parle a number of families had stopped and taken claims. There a church was organized of about forty members, which, for two or three years, was in the charge of Rev. John B. Renville. But about this time Mr. Renville removed to the Reservation, and from that time the Dakota settlement gradually diminished, until all had removed, and the Lac-qui-parle church was absorbed by those on the Reserve.

ASCENSION, or *Iyakaptape*, so named from its having been, from time immemorial, the place where the Coteau was ascended by the Dakotas on their way westward, was the district in which a number of the Renville families took claims. Daniel Renville, one of our licentiates, had been preaching to the church gathered there. But it was understood all along that John B. Renville was to be their pastor. And so it came about, as he now transferred his home to that settlement.

In the spring of 1863, Mr. Renville had purchased a little house in St. Anthony, where they made their home for several years, Mrs. Renville teaching a school of white children for a part of the time. Removing from there, they pre-empted a piece of land on Beaver Creek. During these years they had in their family from four to six half-breed or Dakota children, whom they taught English very successfully, and for the most part, maintained them out of their own scanty means. While living in St. Anthony, Mr. Renville had translated "Precept upon Precept," which was printed in Boston, and became thenceforth one of our Dakota school-books.

As Mr. Daniel Renville was now released from labor at Ascension, I proposed his name to the Good Will church, and advised them to elect him to be their religious teacher. But when the election took place, they all voted for me. I thanked them for the honor they did me, and told them that it could not be. Our plan of missionary work was changed. Henceforth the preaching and pastoral work were to be done almost exclusively by men from among themselves. It was better for them that it should be so, for only in that way would they learn to support their own gospel. We missionaries had never asked them to contribute anything toward our support. It was manifestly incongruous that we should do so. And yet, they were so far advanced in the knowledge of Christian duties, that they ought to assume the burden of contributing to the support of their own religious teachers. It would be a means of grace to them. Moreover, a man who spoke the language natively had great advantage over us, both in preaching and pastoral work.

When I had made this speech to them, they went again into an election, and chose Daniel Renville to be their pastor. He was soon afterward ordained and installed by the Dakota Presbytery, and continued with the Good Will church about six years. Previous to this time, the original Dakota Presbytery had been divided into the *Mankato* and *Dakota*, the latter of which was again confined to the Dakota field, as it had been when first formed in 1845.

At this time Solomon was the pastor of the Long Hollow church, and Louis was stated supply at Fort Wadsworth, or Kettle Lakes, and Thomas Good a licentiate preacher at Buffalo Lake. Sometime after this the Mayasan church was organized, and Louis called to take charge of it, David Gray Cloud coming into his place at Fort Wadsworth.

The General Assembly of the Presbyterian Church had set on foot their Million Thank Offering effort, which was available for poor churches in erecting houses of worship. By means of this outside help, the Ascension church and the Long Hollow church, as well as the Homestead Settlement church on the Big Sioux, were enabled to build houses—two of them of logs. The building at Long Hollow continues to be occupied by the church, while the other two houses have given place to larger and better frame buildings.

In the spring of 1871 our Dakota church organizations were eight, viz: The Pilgrim Church, at Santee, with 267 members; Rev. Artemas Ehnamane and Rev. Titus Ichadooze, pastors; The Flandreau or River Bend church, on the Big Sioux, with 107 members, Joseph Iron-oldman, pastor elect; the Lac-qui-parle church, with 41 members, now without a pastor; the Ascension church, on the Sisseton Reservation, with 69 members, Rev. John B. Renville, pastor; the Dry Wood Lake or Good Will church, with 42 members, Rev. Daniel Renville, pastor; the Long Hollow church, with 80 members, Rev. Solomon Toonkan-shaecheya, pastor; the Kettle Lakes or Fort Wadsworth church, with 38 members, Rev. Louis Mazawakinyanna, stated supply; and the recently organized church at Yankton Agency, with 19 members, in charge of Rev. John P. Williamson.

In the month of May of this year, the first number of the "Iapi Oaye" appeared. It was a very modest little sheet of four pages, eight by ten inches, and altogether in the Dakota language, with the motto, "Taku washta o-kiya, taku shecha kepajin," which, being interpreted, would read, "To help what is good, to oppose what is bad." Rev. John P. Williamson, who had the sole charge of it for the first twelve numbers, in his first Dakota editorial, thus accounts for its origin: "For three years I have prepared a little tract at New Year, which Mr. E. R Pond printed, and I distributed gratuitously to all who could read Dakota. And many persons liked it, and some said, 'If we had a newspaper, we would pay for it.' I have trusted to the truth of this saying, and so this winter have been preparing to print one. But I have found many obstacles in the way, and have not gotten out the first number until now." As it was to be the means of conveying the thoughts and speech of one person to another, it was proper, he said, to call it "Iapi Oaye," or "Word Carrier." The subscription price was placed at fifty cents a year. This was not increased after the paper was doubled in size, as it was the first of January, 1873, at the commencement of the second volume. When this change was made, I was taken in as associate editor, and henceforth, about one-third of the letter press was to be in the English language. By this means, we could communicate missionary intelligence to white people, and thus secure their aid in supporting the paper, as well as extend the interest in our work. And as an attraction to the Dakotas, a full-page picture has been generally added.

In starting the paper, the main object proposed was to stimulate education among the Dakotas, so that we were not disappointed to find that, in addition to all that came in from subscriptions, several hundred dollars were required from missionary funds to square up the year. But we lived in hope, and do so still, that the time will come when the enterprise will be self-supporting. It has proved itself to be an exceedingly important assistant in our missionary work, which we cannot afford to let die.

With the homesteaders on the Big Sioux, on the 23d of June, 1871, we held our first General Conference of the Dakota churches. From the Sisseton Agency there went down John B. Renville, Daniel Renville, and Solomon, of the pastors, with several elders and myself. Dr. Williamson came up from St. Peter; and John P. Williamson, A. L. Riggs, and Artemas Ehnamane and others came over from the Missouri River. Year by year, from that time on, we have continued to hold these meetings, and they have constantly increased in interest and importance. On this first occasion, four or five days were spent, and religious meetings held each day. The circumstances by which we were surrounded intensified the interest. As yet there was no church or school-house in which we could assemble, and our meetings were held out of doors, or under a booth in connection with Mr. *All Iron's* cabin.

This colony, of more than one hundred church members, had located near the eastern line of Dakota Territory, in the beautiful and fertile valley of the Big Sioux River. Their settlement lay along that stream for twenty-five or thirty miles, its center being about forty miles above the thriving town of Sioux Falls.

The most of these men were, in 1862, engaged in the Sioux outbreak in Minnesota. For three years they were held in military prisons. Meanwhile their families and the remnants of their tribe had been deported to the Missouri River; so that when they found themselves together again, it was at Niobrara, Nebraska, or soon afterward, at the newly established Santee Agency a few miles below.

What impulse stirred them up to break away from their own tribe, to which they had but just returned, and try the hard work of making a home among coldly disposed, if not hostile, whites? What made them leave all their old traditional ties and relationships and go forth as strangers and wanderers? It must be borne in mind that they left behind them the food, which the Government issued weekly on the Agency, to seek a very precarious living by farming, for which they had neither tools nor teams. They also gave up the advantage of the yearly issue of clothing, and the prospect of such considerable gifts of horses, oxen, cows, wagons, and plows, as were distributed occasionally on the Agency. More than this: Those who had already received such gifts from the United States Indian Civilization Fund had to leave all behind, though they went out for the very purpose of seeking a higher civilization. They went forth in the face, moreover, of great opposition and derision from the chiefs of their tribe. The United States Indian Agent was also against them. Whence then did they have the strength of purpose which enabled them to face all this opposition, brave all these dangers?

The germs of this movement are only to be found in the resolves for a new life made by these men when in prison! There all were nominally, and the larger part were really, converted to Christ. All of them, in some sense, experienced a conversion of thought and purpose. There they agreed to abolish all the old tribal arrangements and customs. Old things were to be done away, and all things were to become new. And as they had been electing their church officers, so they would elect the necessary civil officers.

But when they came to their people they found the old Indian system in full power, backed by the authority of the United States. Of the old chiefs who ruled them in Minnesota, Little Crow and Little Six, the leaders of the rebellion, were dead; but the others, who had been kept out of active participation, not by their loyalty to the United States, but by their jealousy of these leaders, had saved their necks and were again in power. A few had been appointed to vacancies by the United States Agent, and the ring was complete. And our friends were commanded at once to fall in under the old chiefs before they could receive any rations. They must be Indians or starve! Nothing was to be hoped for from within the tribe, nor from Washington. The Indian principle was regnant there also. Nothing was left to them but to seek some other land. One said, "I could not bear to have my children grow up nothing but Indians;" so they all felt.

They made their hegira in March, 1869. In this region this is the worst month in the year, but they had to take advantage of the absence of their agent and the chiefs at Washington. Twenty-five families went in this company. A few had ponies, but they mostly took their way on foot, packing their goods and children one hundred and thirty miles over the Dakota prairies. About midway a fearful snow-storm burst upon them. They lost their way, and one woman froze to death. The next autumn fifteen other families joined them, and twenty more followed the year after. Even one of the chiefs, finding the movement likely to succeed, left his chieftainship and its emoluments, to join them. He thought it more to be a man than to be a chief.

Existence was a hard struggle for several years; for these Indians had neither plows nor working teams. But they exchanged work with their white neighbors, and so had a little "breaking" done. And in the fall and early spring they went trapping, and by this means raised a little money to pay entry fees on their lands and buy their clothes. On one of these hunting expeditions, Iron Old-man, the acting pastor of their church and a leader in the colony, was overtaken, while chasing elk, by one of the Dakota "blizzards," and he and his companion in the hunt perished in the snow-drifts.

JOSEPH IRON OLD MAN was not an old man, notwithstanding his name, but a man in middle life. He had been a Hoonkayape or elder in the prison, re-elected on the consolidation of the Pilgrim Church in Nebraska, and thus elected to the same office a third time in the River Bend church on the Big Sioux. After this, when the church met to elect a religious teacher, he was chosen almost unanimously. It was expected that the Presbytery would have confirmed the action of the church, at this gathering in June. But this was not to be. On the

7th day of April, when it was bright and warm, he and another Dakota man, as they were out hunting, came upon a half a dozen elk. They chased them first on horseback, until their horses were jaded. Then, leaving the horses, they kept up the pursuit on foot, in the meantime divesting themselves of all superfluous clothing. In this condition, the storm came upon them suddenly, when they were out in the open prairie between the Big Sioux and the James River. Escape was impossible, and to live through the storm and cold in their condition was equally impossible, even for an Indian. Far and near their friends hunted, but did not find them until the first day of May.

So the hopes and plans of the colony and the church were disappointed. At our meeting, we expressed sorrow and sympathy, and endeavored to lead the people to a higher trust in God. The young men might fail and fall, but the command was still, "Hope thou in God." Before we left them, they elected another leader—Williamson O. Rogers—Mr. All Iron.

The Dakota mission had been, from its commencement, under the American Board of Commissioners for Foreign Missions. As Presbyterians, we had been connected with the New School branch. But now the two schools had been united. Many—nay most—of the New School Assembly, who had worked with the American Board, now thought it their duty to withdraw, and connect themselves and their contributions with the Assembly's Board of Foreign Missions. The plowshare must be run through the mission fields also. We in the Dakota mission were invited to transfer our relations. The Prudential Committee at Boston left us to act out our own sweet will. Dr. T. S. Williamson and Rev. John

P. Williamson elected to go over to the Presbyterian Board. For myself I did not care to do so. Although conscientiously a Presbyterian, I was not, and am not, so much of one as to draw me away from the associations which had been growing for a third of a century. Whether I reasoned rightly or wrongly, I conceived that I had a character with the American Board that I could not transfer; and I was too old to build up another reputation. Besides, Alfred L. Riggs had now joined the mission, and as a Congregational minister he could do no otherwise than retain his connection with the A. B. C. F. M.

The case was a plain one. We divided. Some questions then came up as to the field and the work. These were very soon amicably settled, on a basis which, so far as I know, has continued to be satisfactory from that day to this. The churches on the Sisseton Reservation and at the Santee were to continue in connection with the American Board; while the Big Sioux and Yankton Agency churches would be counted as under the Presbyterian Board. Henceforth, in regard to common expenses of Dakota publications, *they* were to bear *one-third*, and *we two-thirds*. And so it is still.

CHAPTER XVIII.

1870-1873.—A. L. Riggs Builds at Santee.—The Santee High School.—Visit to Fort Sully.—Change of Agents at Sisseton. —Second Marriage —Annual Meeting at Good Will.—Grand Gathering.—New Treaty Made at Sisseton.—Nina Foster Riggs.—Our Trip to Fort Sully.—An Incident by the Way.— Stop at Santee.—Pastor Ehnamane.—His Deer Hunt.—Annual Meeting in 1873.—Rev. S. J. Humphrey's Visit.—Mr. Humphrey's Sketch.—Where They Come From.—Morning Call.—Visiting the Teepees.—The Religious Gathering.—The Moderator.—Questions Discussed —The *Personnel.*—Putting Up a Tent.—Sabbath Service.—Mission Reunion.

From Flandreau the Dakota Homestead Settlement on the Big Sioux, I accompanied A. L. Riggs and J. P. Williamson to the Missouri. A year before this time, in the month of May, 1870, Alfred had removed his family from Woodstock, Illinois, to the Santee Agency. The mission buildings heretofore had been of the cheapest kind, only one small house had a shingle roof; the rest were "shacks." Before his arrival, some preparation had been made for building—logs of cottonwood had been cut and hauled to the government saw-mill. These were cut up into framing lumber. The pine boards and all finishing materials were taken up from Yankton, and Sioux City and Chicago, and so he proceeded to erect a family dwelling, and a school-house, which could be used for church purposes.

These were so far finished as to be occupied in the

autumn; and a school was opened with better accommodations and advantages than heretofore. In the December "Iapi Oaye," there appeared a notice of the Santee High School, *Rev. A. L. Riggs Principal*, with *Eli Abraham* and *Albert Frazier* assistants. The advertisement said, "If any one should give you a deer, you would probably say, 'you make me glad.' But how much more would you be glad, if one should teach you how to hunt and kill many deer. So likewise, if one should teach you a little wisdom he would make you glad, but you would be more glad if one taught you how to acquire knowledge." This the Santee High School proposed to do.

On reaching the Santee, I met by appointment Thomas L. Riggs, who had come on from Chicago at the end of his second Seminary year. Together we proceeded up to Fort Sully, where we spent a good part of the summer that remained. But this, with what came of our visit, will be related in a following chapter. In the autumn I returned to Good Will, and the winter was one of work, on the line which we had been following.

During the early part of this winter 1871–'72, a change was made of agents at Sisseton; Dr. J. W. Daniels resigned, and Rev. M. N. Adams came in his place. Dr. Daniels was Bishop Whipple's appointee, and as the Episcopalians were not engaged in the missionary work on this Reservation, it was evidently proper, under the existing circumstances, that the selection should be accorded to the American Board. As, many years before, Mr. Adams had been a missionary among a portion of these people, he came as United States Indian Agent, with an earnest wish to forward, in all proper ways, the cause of education and civilization, and the general uplifting of the whole people. He met with a good deal of opposition, but continued to be agent more than three years, and left many memorials of his interest and efficiency, in the school-houses he erected, as well as in the hearts of the Christian people.

The object that had been paramount in taking our family to Beloit in 1865, was but partly accomplished when Mary died in the spring of 1869. Since that time three years had passed. Robert had gone back to Beloit to school, and was now ready to enter the Freshman class of the college. Corneille was in her fourteenth year, and her education only fairly begun. It was needful that she should have the advantages of a good school. To accomplish my desire for their education, it seemed best to reoccupy our vacant house. That spring of 1872, I was commissioner from the Dakota Presbytery to the General Assembly, which met in Detroit. At the close of the Assembly, I went down to Granville, Ohio, and in accordance with an arrangement previously made, I married Mrs. Annie Baker Ackley, who had once been a teacher with us at Hazelwood, and more recently had spent several years in the employ of the American Missionary Association, in teaching the Freedmen. We at once proceeded to the Good Will mission station, where the summer was spent, and then in the autumn, opened our house in Beloit.

The meeting of the ministers and elders and representatives of the Dakota churches, which was held with the River Bend church on the Big Sioux, had been found very profitable to all. At that time a like conference had been arranged for, to meet on the 25th of June, 1872, with the church of Good Will, on the Sisseton Reservation. The announcement was made in the April "Iapi

Oaye." In the invitation nine churches are mentioned; viz., *The Santee, Yankton, River Bend, Lac-qui-parle, Ascension, Good Will, Buffalo Lake, Long Hollow*, and *Kettle Lakes*. It was said that subjects interesting and profitable to all would be discussed; and especially was the presence of the Holy Spirit desired and prayed for, since without God present with us, the assembly would be only a dead body.

In the green month of June, when the roses on the prairie began to bloom, then they began to assemble to our Dakota Conference. Dr. T. S. Williamson came up from his home at St. Peter—200 miles. John P. Williamson, from the Yankton Agency, and A. L. Riggs, from Santee, brought with them Rev. Joseph Ward, pastor of the Congregational church in Yankton. As they came by Sioux Falls and Flandreau, their whole way would not be much under 300 miles. Thomas L. Riggs, who had commenced his new station in the close of the winter, came across the country from Fort Sully on horseback, a distance of about 220 miles, having with him a Dakota guide and soldier guard. They rode it in less than five days. From all parts came the Dakota pastors and elders and messengers of the churches. The gathering was so large that a booth was made for the Sabbath service. It was an inspiration to us all. It was unanimously voted to hold the next year's meeting with the Yanktons at the Yankton Agency.

At the Sisseton Agency, in the month of September, a semi-treaty was made by Agents M. N. Adams and W. H. Forbes, and James Smith, Jr., of St. Paul, United States Commissioners, with the Dakota Indians of the Lake Traverse and Devil's Lake Reservations, by which they relinquish all their claim on the country of Northeastern

Dakota through which the Northern Pacific Railroad runs. By this arrangement, education would have been made compulsory, and the men would have been enabled to obtain patents for their land within some reasonable time; but the senate struck out everything except the ceding of the land and the compensation therefor. Our legislators do not greatly desire that Indians should become white men.

When Thanksgiving Day came this year, Mr. Adams dedicated a fine brick school-house, which he had that summer erected, in the vicinity of the agency. Of this occasion he wrote, "It was indeed a day of thanksgiving and praise with us, and to me an event of the deepest interest. And I hope that good and lasting impressions were made there upon the minds of some of this people."

In the work of Bible translation, I had been occupied with the book of Daniel in the summer, and, in the winter that followed, my first copy of the Minor Prophets was made. When the spring came, I hied away to the Dakota country. This time my course was to the Missouri River. Thomas had been married in Bangor, Maine, to Nina Foster, daughter of Hon. John B. Foster, and sister of Mrs. Charles H. Howard, of the "Advance." They came west, and as the winter was not yet past, Thomas went on from Chicago alone, and Nina remained with her sister until navigation should open. And so it came to pass that she and I were company for each other to Fort Sully.

As we left Yankton in the stage for Santee, where we were to stop a few days and wait for an up-river boat, an incident occurred which must have been novel to the girl from Bangor. The day was just breaking when the stage had made out its complement of passengers, except one. There were six men on the two seats before us, and Nina and I were behind. At a little tavern in the suburbs of the town, the ninth passenger was taken in. As he came out, we could see that he was the worse for drinking. I at once shoved over to the middle of the seat, and let him in by my side. He turned out to be a burly French half-breed, or a Frenchman who had a Dakota family. We had gone but a little distance, when he said he was going to smoke. I objected to his smoking inside the stage. He begged the lady's pardon a thousand times, but said he must smoke. By this time he had hunted in his pockets, but did not find his pipe. "O mon pipe!" The stage-driver must turn around and go back—it cost $75. He worked himself and the rest of us into quite an excitement. By and by he said to me: "Do you know who I am?" I said I did not. He said, "I am Red Cloud, and I have killed a great many white men." "Ah," said I, "you are Red Cloud? I do not believe you can talk Dakota"—and immediately I commenced talking Dakota. He turned around and stared at me. "Who are you?" he said. From that moment he was my friend, and ever so good.

It was now the month of May, but there were deep snow banks still in the ravines on the north side of the river. A terrible storm had swept over the country from the northeast about the middle of April. A hundred Indian ponies, and forty or fifty head of cattle, at the Santee Agency, had perished. This made spring work go heavily.

I was interested in examining the building erected last summer for the girls' boarding school. It should have been completed before the winter came on, according to the agreement. But now it is intended to have it ready for occupancy the first of September. When finished, it will accommodate twenty or twenty-four girls and also the lady teachers.

On the Sabbath we spent there, I preached in the morning, and Pastor Artemas Ehnamane preached in the afternoon. The " Word Carrier " tells a good story of this Santee pastor. In his younger days, Ehnamane was one of the best Dakota hunters. Tall and straight as an arrow, he was literally as swift as a deer. And he learned to use a gun with wonderful precision. Only a few years before this time, I was traveling with him, when, in the evening, he took his gun and went around a lake, and brought into camp twelve large ducks. He had shot three times.

Well, in the fall of 1872 his church gave him a vacation of six weeks, and " he turned his footsteps to the wilds of the Running Water, where his heart grew young, and his rifle cracked the death-knell of the deer and antelope."

" Being on the track of the hostile Sioux who go to fight the Pawnees, one evening he found himself near a camp of the wild Brules. *He* was weak, *they* were strong, and perhaps hostile. It was time for him to show his colors. His kettles were filled to the brim. The proud warriors were called, and as they filled their mouths with his savory meat, he filled their ears with the sound of the gospel trumpet, and gave them their first view of eternal life. Thus the *deer hunt* became a *soul hunt*. The wild Brules grunted their friendly " Yes," as they left Ehnamane's teepee, their mouths filled with venison, and their hearts with the good seed of truth, from which some one will reap the fruit after many days."

On the 13th of June, 1873, the second regular annual meeting of the Dakota Conference commenced its sessions at Rev. John P. Williamson's mission at the Yankton Agency. The "Word Carrier" for August says this was a very full meeting—"Every missionary and assistant missionary, except Mrs. S. R. Riggs and W. K. Morris, was present, also every native preacher and a full list of other delegates." I came down from Fort Sully with T. L. Riggs and his wife, who had only joined him a few weeks before. Martha Riggs Morris and her two children came over from Sisseton—three hundred miles—with the Dakota delegation. They had a hard journey. The roads were bad and the streams were flooded. There was no way of crossing the Big Sioux except by swimming, and those who could not swim were pulled over in a poor boat improvised from a wagon bed. It was not without a good deal of danger. Those from the Santee Agency had only the Missouri River to cross, and a day's journey to make. The interest of our meeting was greatly increased by the presence of Rev. S. J. Humphrey D.D., District Secretary of the American Board, Chicago; and Rev. E. H. Avery, pastor of the Presbyterian church in Sioux City.

Mr. Williamson's new chapel made a very pleasant place for the gatherings. *Pastoral Support, Pastoral Visitation,* and *Vernacular Teaching* were among the live topics discussed. Their eager consideration and prompt discussion of these questions were in strong contrast with the stolid indifference and mulish reticence of the former life of these native Dakotas, and showed the working of a superhuman agency. Our friend S. J. Humphrey wrote and published a very life-like description of what he saw and heard on this visit, and it does me great pleasure to let him bear testimony to the marvels wrought by the power of the Gospel of Christ.

"The annual meeting of the Dakota Mission was held at Yankton Agency, commencing June 13. We esteem it a rare privilege to have been present on that occasion and to have seen with our own eyes the marvelous transformations wrought by the gospel among this people. Thirty-six hours by rail took us to Yankton, the border town of civilization. Twelve hours more in stage and open wagon along the north bank of the Missouri—the Big Muddy, as the Indians rightly call it—carried us sixty miles into the edge of the vast open prairie, and into the heart of the Yankton Reservation. Here, scattered up and down the river bottom for thirty miles, live the Yanktons, one of the Dakota bands, about 2,000 in number. Thirty miles below, on the opposite bank, in Nebraska, are the Santees. Up the river for many hundreds of miles at different points other Reservations are set off, while several wilder bands still hunt the buffalo on the wide plains that stretch westward to the Black Hills. The Sissetons, another family of this tribe, are located near Lake Traverse, on the eastern boundary of Dakota Territory. This is the field of the Dakota Mission. The chief bands laid hold of thus far are the Sisseton, the Santee and the Yankton. A new point has recently been taken at Fort Sully among the Teetons.

"It was from these places, lying apart in their extremes at least 300 miles, that more than a hundred Indians gathered to this annual meeting. On Thursday afternoon the hospitable doors of Rev. J. P. Williamson's spacious log house opened just in time to give us shelter from a fierce storm of wind and rain. The next morning the Santees, fifty of them, from the Pilgrim Church, some on foot, some on pony-back, and a few in wagons, straggled in, and pitched their camp, in Indian fashion, on the open space near the mission house. About noon the Sissetons appeared, a dilapidated crowd of more than forty, weary and footsore with their 300 miles tramp through ten tedious days. Among them was one white person, a woman, with her two children, the youngest an infant, not a captive, but a missionary's wife, traveling thus among a people whom the gospel had made captives themselves, chiefly through the labors of an honored father and a mother of blessed memory. It intimates the courage and endurance needed for such a trip to know that there were almost no human habitations on the way, and that swollen rivers were repeatedly crossed in the wagon-box, stripped of its wheels and made sea-worthy by canvas swathed underneath.

"An hour afterward, from 200 miles in the opposite direction, the Fort Sully delegation appeared. For Father Riggs, and the younger son, famous as a hard rider, this journey was no great affair. But the tenderly-reared young wife—how she could endure the five days of wagon and tent life is among the mysteries.

"That this was no crowd of Indian revelers (come to a sun-dance, as it might have been of yore) was soon manifest. The first morning after their arrival a strange, chanting voice, like that of a herald, mingled with our daybreak dreams. Had we been among the Mussulmans we should have thought it the muezzin's cry. Of course, all was Indian to us, but we learned afterward that it was indeed a call to prayer, with this English rendering:

'Morning is coming! Morning is coming!
Wake up! wake up! Come to sing! come to pray!'

"In a few minutes, for it does not take an Indian long to dress, the low cadence of many voices joining in one of our own familiar tunes rose sweetly on the air telling us that the day of their glad solemnities had begun. This was entirely their own notion, and was repeated each of the four days we were together.

"On this same morning another sharp contrast of the old and the new appeared. By invitation of the elder Williamson, we took a walk among the *teepees* of the natives who live on the ground. Passing, with due regard for Dakota etiquette, those which contained only women, we came to one which we might properly enter. The inmates were evidently of the heathen party. A man, apparently fifty, sat upon a skin, entirely nude save the inevitable blanket, which he occasionally drew up about his waist. A lad of sixteen, in the same state, lounged in an obscure corner. The mother, who, we learned, occasionally attended meeting, wore a drabbled dress, doubtless her only garment. Two or three others were present in different stages of undress, and all, lazy, stolid, dirty. As we looked into these impassive faces we could understand the saying of one of the missionaries, that when you first speak to an audience of wild Indians you might as well preach to the back of their heads, so far as any responsive expression is concerned. And yet, now and then, the dull glow of a latent ferocity would light up the eye, like that of a beast of prey looking for his next meal. Alas! for the noble red man! In spite of what the poets say, we found him a filthy, stupid savage. All this we have time to see while Mr. Williamson talks to them in the unknown tongue. But now the little church bell calls us to the mission chapel. It is already filled—the men on one side, the women on the other. The audience numbers perhaps two hundred.

"All classes and ages are there. All are decently dressed. Were it not for the dark faces, you would not distinguish them from an ordinary country congregation. The hymn has already been given out, and each, with book in hand, has found the place. The melodeon sets the tune, and then, standing, they sing. It is no weak-lunged performance, we can assure you. Not altogether harmonious, perhaps, but vastly sweeter than a war-whoop, we fancy; certainly hearty and sincere, and, we have no doubt, an acceptable offering of praise. A low-voiced prayer, by a native pastor, uttered with reverent unction, follows. Another singing, and then the sermon. One of the Renvilles is the preacher. We do not know what it is all about. But the ready utterance, the mellifluent flow of words, the unaffected earnestness of the speaker, and the fixed attention of the audience, mark it as altogether a success. While he speaks to the people, we study their faces. They are certainly a great improvement upon those we saw in the teepee. But not one, or two generations of Christian life will work off the stupid, inexpressive look that ages of heathenism have graven into them. There is a steady gain, however. Just as in a dissolving view there comes slowly out on the canvas glimpses of a fair landscape, mingling strangely with the dim outlines of the disappearing old ruin, so there is struggling through these stony faces an expression of the new creation within, the converted soul striving to light up and inform the hard features, and displace the ruin of the old savage life. But the poor women! Their case is even worse. They start from a lower plane. Some of these are young, some are mothers with their infants, many are well-treated wives, not a few take part with propriety in the women's meetings, and yet you look in vain among them all for one happy face. They wear a beaten and abused look, as if blows and cruelty had been their daily lot, as if they lived even only by sufferance. This is the settled look of their faces when in repose. But speak to them; let the missionary tell them you are their friend; and their eyes light up with a gentle gladness, showing that a true, womanly soul only slumbers in them. This came out beautifully at a later point in the meeting. A motion was about to be put, when some one insisted that on that question the women should express their minds. This was cordially assented to, and they were requested to stand with the men in a rising vote. The girls, of course, giggled; but the women modestly rose in their places, and it was worth a trip all the way from Chicago to see the look of innocent pride into which their sad faces were for once surprised.

"But sermon is done. There is another loud-voiced hymn, and then the meeting of days is declared duly opened. It is to be a composite, a session of Presbytery, for they happen to have taken that form, and a Conference of churches. A leading candidate for moderator is Ehnamane, a Santee pastor. How far the fact that he is a great hunter and a famous paddleman, affects the vote, we cannot say. This may have had more weight: his father was a great conjurer and war prophet. Before he died he said to his son:

"'The white man is coming into the country, and your children may learn to read. But promise me that you will never leave the religion of your ancestors.'

"He promised. And he says now that had the Minnesota outbreak not come, in which his gods were worsted by the white man's God, he would have kept true to his pledge. As it is, he now preaches the faith which once he destroyed, and they make him moderator.

"We will not follow the meeting through the days.

There are resolutions, and motions to amend, and all that, just like white folks, and plenty of speech-making. Now a telling hit sends a ripple of laughter through the room; and now the moistened eyes and trembling lip tell that some deep vein of feeling has been touched. Grave questions are under discussion: Pastoral Support, opening out into general benevolence; Pastoral Visitation, its necessity, methods, difficulties, and also as a work pertaining to elders, deacons, and to the whole membership; Primary Education—shall it be in the vernacular or in English? a most spirited debate, resulting in this: '*Resolved*, That so long as the children speak the Dakota at home, education should be *begun* in the Dakota.' Then the 'Iapi Oaye—the Word Carrier,' for they have their newspaper, and it has its financial troubles, comes up. All rally to its support. But the hundred-dollar deficit for last year, *that*, we suspect, comes out of the missionaries' meager salaries. All along certain more strictly ecclesiastical matters are mingled in. James Red Wing is brought forward to be approbated as a preacher at Fort Sully. An application is considered for forming a new church on the Sisseton Reserve. The church at White Banks asks aid for a church building, and a Yankton elder is examined and received as a candidate for the ministry. The Indians, in large numbers, share freely in all these deliberations. Everything is decorous and dignified, sometimes evidently intensely interesting, we the while burning to know what they are saying, and getting the general drift only through a friendly whisper in the ear. While they are discussing, we will make a few notes: About one-third of these before us were imprisoned for the massacre of 1862, although, probably, none of them took active part in it. The larger portion of them were made freemen of the Lord in that great prison revival at Mankato, as a result of which 300 joined the church in one day. They were also of that number who, when being transferred by steamer to Davenport, 'passed St. Paul in chains, indeed, but singing the fifty-first Psalm, to the tune of Old Hundred.' Seven of these men are regularly ordained ministers, pastors of as many churches; two others are licentiate preachers. Quite a number are teachers, deacons, elders, or delegates of the nine churches belonging to the mission, and they report a goodly fellowship of 775 Dakota members, 79 of whom have come into the fold since the last meeting.

"Two or three of these men are of some historic note. John B. Renville, who sits at the scribe's desk, was the main one in inaugurating the counter revolution in the hostilities of 1862. Yonder is Peter Big Fire, who, by his address, turned the war party from the trail of the fleeing missionaries. And there is Grey Cloud, for five years in the United States army, a sergeant of scouts; and Chaskadan, the Elder Brewster of the prison church; and Lewis Mazawakinyanna, formerly chaplain among the Fort scouts, now pastor of Mayasan Church, and Hokshidanminiamani, once a conjurer, now no longer raising spirits in the teepee, but humbly seeking to be taught of the Divine spirit—and all these—ah, our eyes fill with tears as we think that but for the blessed gospel they would still be worshipers of devils.

"The meeting is adjourned, and the brethren are coming forward to greet us. We never grasped hands with a heartier good will. But somehow our sense of humor will not be altogether quiet as, one after another, we are introduced to Elder Big-Fire, Rev. Mr. All-good, Deacon Boy-that-walks-on-the-water, Pastor Little-Iron-Thunder,

Elder Grey-Cloud, and Rev. Mr. Stone-that-paints-itself-red. But they are grand men, and their names are quite as euphonious as some English ones we could pick out.

"While supper is preparing, we will look a moment at a phase of tent life. A sudden gust of wind has blown over two of the large teepees. And now they are to be set up again. One is occupied by the men, the other by the women. Under the old regime the women do all this kind of work. But now the men are willing to try their hand at it, at least upon their own tent. It is new work, however, and while they are making futile attempts at tying together the ends of the first three poles, the mothers and wives have theirs already up and nearly covered. At length a broad-chested woman steps over among them, strips off their ill-tied strings, repacks the ends of the poles, and with two or three deft turns binds them fast, and all with a kind of nervous contempt as if she were saying—she probably is: "O you stupid fellows!" The after work does not seem to be much more successful, and they stand around in a helpless sort of way, while the young women are evidently bantering them with good-natured jests, much as a bevy of white girls would do in seeing a man vainly trying to stitch on a missing button, each new bungling mistake drawing the fire of the fair enemy in a fresh explosion of laughter. How the thing comes out we do not stay to see, but we suspect that the practiced hands of the good women finally come to the rescue.

"Sunday is the chief day of interest, and yet there is less to report about that. In the morning at nine o'clock, Rev. A. L. Riggs conducts a model Bible class, with remarks on the art of questioning. At the usual hour of service the church is crowded, and Rev. Solomon Toonkanshaichiye preaches, we doubt not, a most excellent sermon. Immediately following is the sacrament of the Lord's Supper with the fathers of the mission, Revs. Dr. Riggs and Williamson officiating, a tender and solemn scene, impressive even to us who understand no single word of the service, for grave Indian deacons reverently pass the elements; and many receive them which but for a knowledge of this dear sacrifice might have reckoned it their chief glory that their hands were stained with human blood.

"Just as we close, in strange contrast with the spirit of the hour, two young Indian braves go by the windows. They are tricked out with all manner of savage frippery. Ribbons stream in the wind, strings of discordant sleigh-bells grace their horses' necks and herald their approach. Each carries a drawn sword which flashes in the sunlight, and a plentiful use of red ocher and eagles' feathers, completes the picture. As they ride by on their scrawny little ponies the effect is indescribably absurd. But they think it very fine, and, like their cousins, the white fops, have simply come to show themselves.

"In the afternoon, is an English service, and then one wholly conducted by the natives themselves. No evening meetings are held, as these people that rise with the birds are not far behind them in going to their rest. On Monday the business is finished, and the farewells are said. And on Tuesday morning the various delegations start for their distant homes.

"We have no space to speak of the meeting of the mission proper. It was held at Mr. Williamson's house during the evenings. Nearly all its members were present—a delightful re-union it was to them and us—and many questions of serious interest were amply discussed.

We dare not trust our pen to write about these noble men and women as we would. The results of their labors abundantly testify for them, and their record is on high. May they receive an hundred fold for their work of faith, and labor of love, and patience of hope in our Lord Jesus Christ."

CHAPTER XIX.

1873-1874.—The American Board at Minneapolis.—The *nidus* of the Dakota Mission.—Large Indian Delegation.—Ehnamane and Mazakootemane.—"Then and Now."—The Woman's Meeting.—Nina Foster Riggs and Lizzie Bishop.—Miss Bishop's Work and Early Death.—Manual Labor Boarding School at Sisseton.—Building Dedicated.—M. N. Adams, Agent.—School Opened.—Mrs. Armor and Mrs. Morris.— "My Darling in God's Garden."—Visit to Fort Berthold.-- Mandans, Rees and Hidatsa.—Dr. W. Matthews' Hidatsa Grammar.—Beliefs.—Missionary Interest in Berthold.—Down the Missouri.—Annual Meeting at Santee.—Normal School. —Dakotas Build a Church at Ascension.—Journey to the Ojibwas with E. P. Wheeler.—Leech Lake and Red Lake.— On the Gitche Gumme.—"The Stoneys."—Visit to Odanah. —Hope for Ojibwas.

The American Board of Commissioners for Foreign Missions was to hold its annual meeting, in the autumn of 1873, in the city of Minneapolis. That was almost the identical spot where our mission had been commenced, nearly forty years before. And it was comparatively near to the center of our present work. These were reasons why we should make a special effort to bring the Dakota mission, on this occasion, prominently before this great Christian gathering. Our churches on the Sisseton Reservation were only a little more than 200 miles away. Taking advantage of the Saint Paul and Pacific Railroad, it would only be a three days journey. Accordingly I applied to my friend Gen. Geo. L. Becker, of St. Paul, who was then President of the Road, to send me half-fares for a dozen Dakota men. He generously responded, and sent me up a *free pass* down for that number.

This made it possible for all the churches on the Sisseton Reservation to be represented by pastors and elders. A. L. Riggs brought over a good delegation from the Santee, so that we had there *seventeen* of our most prominent men. The present missionaries and assistant missionaries of the Board, except Mr. and Mrs. Morris, were all there. Our brother John P. Williamson was engaged in church building, and could not attend. But there were the Pond brothers and Dr. T. S. Williamson accepting with glad hearts the results of their labors commenced thirty-nine years before. And the presence of so large an Indian delegation added much to the popular interest of the occasion. So that the subject of Indian missions in general, and of the Dakota mission in particular, engaged the attention of this great meeting, for about one-third of their time. Artemas Ehnamane, the pastor of Pilgrim Church, at Santee, and Paul Mazakootemane, the hero of the outbreak of 1862, both made addresses before the Board, which were interpreted by A. L. Riggs.

In the Dakota "Word Carrier," we were at this time publishing a series of "Sketches of the Dakota Mission," which we gathered into a pamphlet and distributed to the thousands of Christian friends gathered there. Number twelve of these sketches is mainly a contrast between the commencement and the present state of our work among the Dakotas, from which I make the following extract:

"THEN AND NOW.

"In the first days of July, 1839, a severe battle was fought between the Dakotas and Ojibwas. The Ojibwas had visited Fort Snelling during the last days of June, expecting to receive some payment for land sold. In this they were disappointed. The evening before they started for their homes—a part going up the Mississippi, and a part by the St. Croix—two young men were observed to go to the soldiers' burying ground, near the Fort, and cry. Their father had been killed some years before by the Dakotas, and was buried there. The next morning they started for their homes; but these two young men, their people not knowing it, went out and hid themselves that night close by a path which wound around the shores of Lake Harriet. In the early morning following, a Dakota hunter walked along that path, followed by a boy. The man was shot down, and the boy escaped to tell the story.

"During their stay in the neighborhood of Fort Snelling, the Ojibwas had smoked and eaten with the Dakotas. That scalped man now lying by Lake Harriet was an evidence of violated faith. The Dakotas were eager to take advantage of the affront. The cry was for vengeance; and before the sun had set, two parties were on the war-path.

"The young man who had been killed was the son-in-law of *Cloud-man*, the chief of the Lake Calhoun village. *Scarlet Bird* was the brother-in-law of the chief. So Scarlet Bird was the leader of the war party which came to where the city of Minneapolis is now built, and about the setting of the sun, crossed over to the east side; and there, seating the warriors in a row on the sand, he distributed the beads and ribbons and other trinkets of the man who had been killed, and with them '*prayed*' the whole party into committing the deeds of the next morning. The morning's sun, as it arose, saw these same men smiting down the Ojibwas, just after they had left camp, in the region of Rum River. *Scarlet Bird* was among the slain on the Dakota side; and a son of his, whom he had goaded into the battle by calling him a woman, was left on the field. Many Ojibwa scalps were taken, and all through that autumn and into the following winter, the scalp dance was danced nightly at every Dakota village on the Mississippi and Minnesota rivers, as far up as Lac-qui-parle.

"That was the condition of things THEN. Between THEN and NOW there is a contrast. *Then* only a small government saw-mill stood where *now* stand mammoth mills, running hundreds of saws. *Then* only a little soldier's dwelling stood where *now* are the palaces of merchant princes. *Then* only the war-whoop of the savage was heard where *now*, in this year of grace, 1873, a little more than a third of a century after, is heard the voice of praise and prayer in numerous Christian sanctuaries and a thousand Christian households. *Then* it was the gathering place of the nude and painted war party; *now* it is the gathering place of the friends of the American Board of Commissioners for Foreign Missions. *Then* the dusky forms of the Dakotas flitted by in the gloaming, bent on deeds of blood; *now* the same race is here largely represented by pastors of native churches and teachers of the white man's civilization and the religion of Christ. *And the marvelous change that has passed over this country, converting it from the wild abode of savages into the beautiful land of Christian habitations, is only surpassed by the still more marvelous change that has been wrought upon those savages themselves.* The greater part of the descendants of the Indians who once lived here are now in Christian families, and have been gathered into Christian churches, having their native pastors. Some, too, have gone beyond to the still wild portions of their own people, and are commencing there such a work as we commenced, nearly forty years ago, among their fathers here.

"But the work is now commenced among the Teetons of the Missouri, under circumstances vastly different from those which surrounded us in its beginning here. *Then*, with an unwritten language, imperfectly understood and spoken stammeringly by foreigners, the gospel was proclaimed to unwilling listeners. *Now*, with the perfect knowledge of the language learned in the wigwam, a comparatively large company of native men and women are engaged in publishing it. Many ears are still unwilling to listen, and the hearts of the wild Indians are only a very little opened to the good news; but the contrast between the past and present is very great."

While this meeting of the American Board was in progress, the ladies of the Woman's Boards held a meeting, which was reported as full of interest. So many women publishers of the Word in all parts of the world were present, that the enthusiasm and Christ-spirit rose very high. Nina Foster Riggs, who had just arrived from Fort Sully, the center of Dakota heathendom, announced her wish for a female companion in labor there. Several young women present said, "I will go." From these, Miss Lizzie Bishop, of Northfield, Minn., was afterward selected. Her health was not vigorous, but she and her friends thought it might become more so in the Missouri River climate. She at once proceeded with T. L. Riggs and wife to Hope Station. There I met her, for the first time, in the first of June following. She impressed me as a singularly pure minded and devoted young woman. Two Teeton boys in the family belonged to her especial charge. She said she found the Lord's Prayer in Dakota too difficult of comprehension for their use, and desired me to make something more simple. I sat down and wrote a child's prayer, of which this is a translation:

> *My Father, God,*
>   *Have mercy on me;*
>   *Now I will sleep;*
>   *Watch over me:*
>   *If I die before the morning,*
>   *Take me to Thyself.*
> *For thy Son Jesus' sake, these I ask of Thee.*

Miss Bishop's missionary work for the Teeton Sioux was soon over. But I will let Nina Foster Riggs tell the story:

"After the meeting of the American Board in Minneapolis, in October, 1873, Miss Elizabeth Bishop, of Northfield, Minn., entered the Dakota work.

" Two years later, at the next western meeting of the Society, and during the session of the Woman's Board of Missions, her death was announced. Of the intervening twelve months twice told, it falls to my lot to speak, and I attempt the task with mingled feelings, for I know it is impossible to do justice to the beauty of Lizzie's character.

" Young, delicate, already suffering with a disease which made her to be over-fastidious in some things, sensitive to the discomforts of frontier life, and inexperienced in its ways of living, she came into the mission work.

" These hindrances were met and more than overbalanced by her singleness of purpose, her even temper, her devotion to her chosen labor, and her unwavering trust in Jesus.

"The first winter of her stay at Hope Station, on the bank of the Missouri River, opposite Fort Sully was a winter of trial and of danger. Indians had threatened to burn the mission house. Hostile ones crowded about the place, the camps were noisy with singing and dancing in preparation for war parties, and once a shot was fired into the house.

"None of these things disturbed Lizzie. 'I do not *choose* to be killed by the Indians,' she said, 'but if the Lord wills it so, it is all right.' And she went on as usual with her housework and her sewing-school, and the care of the two Indian boys who were taken into the family in the spring. While she taught the sewing-class, several little girls, some six or eight, made dresses of linsey-woolsey for themselves, and then, under Miss Bishop's supervision, combed their hair, bathed, and put on clean clothes. She also instructed several women in some branches of housework, and was always looking for the opportunity of doing good.

"Very early in the winter she had a slight hemorrhage from the lungs, which was followed by others more severe at intervals through the summer. But she still kept up.

"In the fall, after the removal to another mission station, her health gave way, and she was obliged to go to the Fort to rest and recuperate. After her return she was able to resume only a part of her former work; but she carried on, with great enthusiasm, the morning school for chilren, and aided somewhat in the sewing-school.

"Although, as the spring advanced, her health failed more and more, yet her courage would not give way, and she never but once expressed the opinion that she should not recover. Her plan had been to spend this second summer in her own home, though sometimes she was almost ready to stay on and work for 'my boys,' as she called them.

"Finally she concluded to go to Minnesota for the summer, but made every arrangement to return to the mission in the fall. After some hesitation because of her delicate health, she decided to make the journey with our mission party, overland, down the country. So she took the trip, enjoyed every day, and declared she felt better and slept better every night.

"The party camped out over the Sabbath, and on Monday evening, the seventh day after leaving Fort Sully, arrived at the Yankton Agency. Here at the mission home of our friend, J. P. Williamson, the welcome was so warm, and the companionship so pleasant, that Miss Bishop desired to spend a few days longer than she had intended. She wanted to visit the schools, and learn, both here and at Santee Agency, something to help her when she should go back to teach the Indian children on the Upper Missouri. So she stayed behind, full of hope and zeal. But her friends parted from her with foreboding in their hearts. In a few days she was again attacked with her old trouble; she rallied so as to get to her home and to be again with her mother and sister. But she sank rapidly, and after some weeks of severe suffering she entered into rest.

"Writing of her, her sister said: 'Her favorite motto was, "Simply to thy cross I cling." She trusted in Christ because he has promised to save all who come to him. She enjoyed hearing us sing, to the last, such hymns as, "Jesus, Lover of My Soul;" "Nearer, my God, to Thee;" "My Faith Looks Up to Thee;" "Father, Whate'er of Earthly Bliss;" "How Firm a Foundation," and others.'

"Resting on him who is able to save, she passed away.

"The work she loved and so conscientiously carried on, has fallen to other hands, but is not finished nor lost; and in the homes she helped to make happy she is missed, yet her memory is an abiding presence, cheering and encouraging.

"'And a book of remembrance was written before him for them that feared the Lord, and that thought upon His name. And they shall be mine, saith the Lord of Hosts, in that day when I make up my jewels.'"

The commencement of the Manual Labor Boarding School, on the Sisseton Reserve, was an event which indicated progress. Agent M. N. Adams had received authority from the Department to erect a suitable building. On the 4th of September, 1873, the foundation walls were so far completed that the *corner-stone* was laid with appropriate ceremonies. There was quite a gathering of the natives and white people on the Reservation. After prayer in Dakota by pastor Solomon, Mr. Adams made a speech which was interpreted, setting forth the advantages that would accrue to this people from such a school as this building contemplated. He then announced that he had in his hands copies of the Bible in Dakota and English, and a Dakota hymn-book, together with eight numbers of the "Iapi Oaye," a copy of the "St. Paul Press" and a Yankton paper, and also sundry documents, all of which he deposited in the place prepared for them. I added a few remarks, and then the corner-stone was laid and pronounced *level*. Speeches followed from Solomon, John B., and Daniel Renville, pastors; and from Robert Hopkins, Two Stars, and Gabriel Renville. They accepted this as the guarantee of progress in the new era on which they had entered.

That autumn the Boarding School was commenced. As only a part of the building could be made habitable for the winter, the girls alone were placed there, under the care and teaching of Mr. and Mrs. Armor. Mr. and Mrs. Morris took the boys and cared for them, in very close quarters, at the mission, only a little way off. In the summer of 1874 there appeared in the "Word Carrier" articles on "Our Girls," and "Our Boys," written by Mrs. Armor and Mrs. Morris, respectively. In each department they had about sixteen. Mrs. Armor classed her scholars as *large girls*, *little girls*, and *very little girls*. That first year was a good beginning of the school.

Mrs. Morris was willing to undertake the hard work these sixteen boys imposed upon her, because she had just met with a great sorrow. She had gone on east with *two* children, and came back with only *one*. "As I sit and mend," she writes, "the alarming holes which the boys make in their clothes, an unbidden tear sometimes falls when I think of *our* blue-eyed, sunny-haired boy, whose last resting place is in the valley of the Susquehanna. And I think how much rather I would have worked for him than for these boys. But I say to myself, '*My darling is safe and out of reach of harm;*' and these boys need the doing for that my darling one will never need more. For

>'Mine, in God's garden, runs to and fro,
> And that is best.'

And I know that somehow, the Lord knows what is best; and He does as He will with His own."

In the early spring of 1874, I was requested jointly by the American Board and the American Missionary Association, to visit and report upon various Indian agencies, where their appointees, or nominees rather, were agents. Accordingly I started in the month of May, by St. Paul, on the Northern Pacific Railroad, to Bismarck, and thence by steamboat up the Missouri to Fort Berthold. At this time Major L. B. Sperry, who had been a Professor in Ripon College, was the nominee of the American Missionary Association. It was not my good fortune to find Agent Sperry at home, but Mrs. Sperry, in a very lady-like way, gave me the best accommodations during the week I remained.

Here were gathered the remnant of the Mandans, only a few hundred persons, and the Rees, or Arricarees, a part of the Pawnee tribe, and the Gros Ventres, or Minnetaree, properly the Hidatsa. Altogether they numbered about two thousand souls. We had before this entertained the desire that we might be able to establish a mission among these people, and this thought or hope gave interest to my visit. The Mandan and the Hidatsa languages were both pretty closely connected with the Dakota; but what seemed to bring these nearer to us was the fact that many of all these people could understand and talk the Dakota, that forming a kind of common language for them.

Howard Mandan, or "The-man-with-a-*scared-face*," as his Indian name is interpreted, was the son of *Red Cow*, the principal chief of the Mandans, and had been taken down by Gen. C. H. Howard, a year before, and placed in A. L. Riggs' school at Santee. Howard had returned home before my visit, and also Henry Eaton, a Hidatsa young man, who had been East a good many years and talked English well.

George Catlin had, many years ago, interested us in the Mandans, by his effort to prove, from their *red hair* in some cases—perhaps only *redded* hair—and, in some instances, blue eyes, and the resemblances which he claims to have found in their languages—that they were the descendants of a Welsh colony that had dropped out of history a thousand years ago. And Dr. Washington Matthews, of the United States Army, had created in us a desire to do something for the spiritual enlightenment of the Hidatsa, by his admirable grammar and dictionary of their language. In his introduction to this book he gives us much valuable information about the people.

HIDATSA, he tells us, is the name by which they call themselves. They are better known to us by the names MINNETAREE and GROS VENTRE. This last is a name given them by the Canadian French, and without any special reason. It is a fact that Indians can eat large quantities of food, but it is very rarely indeed that you will find one whose appearance would justify the epithet *gros ventre*. The other term, Minnetaree, is the name given them by the Mandans, and means, *to cross the water*. The story is, that when the Hidatsa people came to the Missouri River from the northeast, the Mandan village was on the west side of the river. They called over, and the Mandans answered back in their own language " Who are you?" The Hidatsa not understanding it, supposed they had asked " What do you want?" And so replied *Minnetaree, to cross over the water.*"

Whence came the Hidatsa? Their legend says they originally lived *under* a great body of water which lies far to the northeast of where they now live. From this under-water residence some persons found their way out, and discovering a country much better than the one in which they lived, returned and gave to their people such glowing accounts of their discoveries that the whole nation determined to come out. But owing to the breaking of a tree on which they were climbing out of the lake, a great part of the tribe had to remain behind in the water, and they are there yet.

This is very much like the myth of another tribe, who lived under the ground by a lake. A large grape-vine sent its tap root through the crust of the earth, and by that they commenced to climb out. But a very fat woman taking hold of the vine, it broke, and the remainder were doomed to stay where they were. Do such legends contain any reference to the great Deluge?

After the Hidatsa came up they commenced a series of wanderings over the prairies. During their migrations they were often ready to die of hunger, but were always rescued by the interference of their deity. It was not manna rained down around their camp, but the stones of the prairie were miraculously changed into buffalo, which they killed and ate. After some time they sent couriers to the south, who came back with the news that they had found a great river and a fertile valley, wherein dwelt a people who lived in houses and tilled the ground. They brought back corn and other products of the country. To this beautiful and good land the tribe now directed their march, and, guided by their messengers, they reached the Mandan villages on the Missouri River. With them they camped and learned their peaceful arts.

Dr. Matthews says they have a tradition that, during these years of wandering, the Genius of the Sun took up one of the Hidatsa maidens, and their offspring came back, and, under the name of GRAND-CHILD, was the great prophet and teacher of his mother's people. Can that have any reference to the "Son of Man?"

These Indians, the Mandans, the Hidatsa and the Rees, live in one village at Berthold, in all numbering something over two thousand; and they have lived together, as we know, more than a hundred years, and yet the languages are kept perfectly distinct and separate. Many of them learn each other's language; and many of them talk Dakota also. "Many years ago they were considered ripe for the experiments of civilization; they stand to-day just as fit subjects as ever for the experiment, which never has been, and possibly never will be, tried." This is Dr. Matthew's statement. Let us hope that the latter part may not be prophetic.

"They worship a deity," says Dr. Matthews, "whom they call 'The First Made' or 'The First Existence.'" Sometimes they speak of him as "The Old Man Immortal." They believe in *shades* or *ghosts*, which belong not only to men, but to animals and trees and everything.

"In the 'next world' *human shades* hunt and live on the shades of the buffalo, and other animals who have lived here. Whether the shade of the buffalo then ceases to exist or not, I could find none prepared to tell me; but they seem to have a dim faith in shades of shades, and in shadowlands of shade-lands; belief in a shadowy immortality being the basis of their creed."

By all these means our interest in Fort Berthold and its people grew, and we became impatient of delay. But step by step we were led, by the hand of the Lord, until at the meeting of the American Board in Chicago, in the autumn of 1875, after an animated discussion on Indian Missions, and the debt of the Board was lifted by a special effort, Secretary S. B. Treat arose and said: "We are ready to send a man to Fort Berthold." The man and the woman, Charles L. Hall and Emma Calhoun, were ready, and the next spring they were commissioned to make their home among the Mandans, Arickarees and Hidatsa.

On leaving Berthold in May, 1874, I proceeded down the Missouri to Bismarck, where I was subjected to considerable delay; and then stopping a few days with Thomas at Hope Station, and making a short call at the Yankton Agency, I went to the Santee, to attend our Annual Meeting of the Dakota Conference, which commenced its sessions with the Pilgrim Church on the 18th of June.

A. L. Riggs had put up in large characters, the motto of the meeting—1834-1874. Thus we were reminded that FORTY years had passed since the brothers Pond had made their *log cabin* on the banks of Lake Calhoun. These gray-headed men were expected to have been present on this occasion but were not. T. L. Riggs and wife could not come down. Otherwise the attendance of whites and Indians was good. The presence of Rev. Joseph Ward, of Yankton, and of Mrs. Wood, the mother of Mrs. Ward, and also of Rev. De Witt Clark, of Massachusetts, greatly added to the interest. The question discussed by the native brethren with the most eagerness was, "Shall the eldership receive any money compensation?" This had come up to be a question solely because such native church helpers were receiving compensation among the Episcopalians. But our folks decided against it by an overwhelming vote.

So full an account has been given of the like meeting held a year previous, that this, which was in most respects equally interesting, may be passed over. Of the school here during the winter past, the "Word Carrier" had contained this notice: "The Normal School of the Dakota mission, at Santee Agency, has had a prosperous winter session, notwithstanding the dark days last fall, when its doors were closed, and many of its former pupils removed beyond the reach of earthly training by the small-pox." The whole number of scholars for the winter three months was *eighty-five.*

After this meeting closed, I spent six weeks with the churches in my own part of the field on the Sisseton Reservation. I found the people at Ascension church, J. B. Renville, pastor, in the midst of church building. Their log church had become too small, and they had for a year been preparing to build a larger and better house of worship. Mr. Adams took a great interest in this enterprise, and helped them much by obtaining contributions, and otherwise. The Dakota men and women also took hold of it as their own work, and the house went up, and was so far finished before the winter, that its dedication took place about the middle of December. The cost of the house was then given at $1,500. Two or three hundred more were afterward used in its internal completion. This was a great step forward. *Dakota Christians build,* with but little help, *their own house of worship !*

About the middle of August I left Sisseton to complete my work of visiting Indian agencies, which I had undertaken to do for the American Missionary Association. At Saint Paul I was joined by Rev. Edward Payson Wheeler, who was just from Andover Seminary. He was the son of the missionary Wheeler, who had spent his life with the Ojibwas, at Bad River. He had learned the language in his boyhood, and I was only too happy to have as my companion of the journey, one who was at home among the Ojibwas.

From St. Paul we went up the Lake Superior Road until we reached the Northern Pacific, on which we traveled westward to Brainerd, and then took stage seventy miles to Leech Lake. There we found white friends and Ojibwas, to whom we preached, Mr. Wheeler trying the language he had not used for years. We then proceeded by private conveyance, over a miserable road through the pine woods, to Red Lake. Rev. Mr. Spees and wife, who were there doing work under the American Missionary Association, and Agent Pratt received us kindly. My friend Wheeler talked with the Indians—the old men remembered his father, and seemed to warm very much toward the son. It appeared to me that there was a grand opening for an educational work and preaching the gospel. When we left Red Lake I fully believed that E. P. Wheeler would return there as a missionary before the snow fell. But I was disappointed. The American Missionary Association was heavily in debt, and had no disposition whatever to enlarge work among the Indians.

We then returned by the way we came, and went on to Du Luth, where we took a steamer on the Gitche Gumme (Lake Superior), for Bayfield. On the down lake steamer we formed the acquaintance of Rev. John McDougall, a Methodist minister, who, with his family, was going to the Canadian Conference, from the far off country of the Saskatchawan. For more than a quarter of a century, he had been a missionary among the *Crees*, and *Bloods*, and *Piegans*.

But what interested me most, was the account he gave of a small band of about seven hundred Indians called STONEYS. They talk the Dakota language, and, as their name indicates, they are evidently a branch of the Assinaboines.

The name *Assinaboine* means *Stone Sioux*, and is a compound of French and Ojibwa. The last part is *Bwan*, which is the name the Ojibwas give the Dakotas or Sioux.

These *Stoneys* are said to be *all Christians.* They have their school-house and church, and *Rev. John McDougall*, son of the old gentleman, is their missionary. They live on Bow River, which, I suppose, is a branch of the Saskatchawan, about two hundred miles northwest from Fort Benton, and one hundred north of the Canada line. To us who labor among the Dakotas, it is very cheering to know, that this small *outlier* of the *fifty thousand* Dakota-speaking people have all received the gospel. We clap our hands for joy.

Landing at Bayfield, we were kindly received by the Indian Agent, Dr. Isaac Mahan.

Nestled among the hills, and looking out into the bay, filled with the Apostle Islands, this town has rather a romantic position. And just out a little ways, on Magdalen Island, is LA POINTE, the old mission station. We passed around it in a sail-boat, on our way to *Odanah.*

Very soon after reaching Bayfield, we found a boat going over to *Odanah*, which I understand is the Ojibwa for *town* or *village*, and which is the name by which the mission station on Bad River has long been known. As I entered the boat, Mr. Wheeler introduced me to the Ojibwa men who were to take us over. When I shook hands with one of them, he said, " My father, Mr. Riggs." Was he calling me his father, or was it the Indian? I wondered which, but asked no questions. Two or three days after, I learned that *adoption* was one of the Ojibwa customs, and that when Mr. Wheeler was a little boy, this man lost his boy. He came to the mission and said to the missionary, " My boy is gone; you have a great many boys, let me call this one mine." And so they said he might so call him; and from that time Edward Payson Wheeler became the adopted child of an Ojibwa.

Now, after he had been gone ten years, going away a boy and coming back a man, they all seemed to regard him like a son and a brother. It was very interesting for me to see how they all *warmed* toward him. They came to see him and wanted him to go to their houses. They all wanted to talk with him; and when we came to leave, they all flocked to the mission to shake hands, and to have a last word and a prayer; and they gave him more *muckoks* of *manomin* (wild rice) than he could bring away with him.

For four days we were the guests of the Boarding School which is in charge of Rev. Isaac Baird. We became much interested in the school and the teachers—Mrs. Baird, Miss Harriet Newell Phillips, Miss Verbeek, Miss Dougherty and Miss Walker. Naturally I should be prejudiced in favor of the Dakotas, but I was obliged to confess, that I had not seen anywhere twenty-five boys and girls better looking, and more manly and womanly in their appearance than those Ojibwas. The whole community gave evidence of the good work done by the school in past years—many of the grown folks being able to talk English quite well.

But there was one impression that came to me without bidding—it was that *civilization* had been pressed farther and faster than *evangelization*. While houses and other improvements attested a great deal of labor expended, the native church is quite small, only now numbering about twenty-eight, and the *metawa*, their sacred heathen dance, was danced while we were there, within a stone's throw of the church. My spirit was stirred within me, and I said to the members of that native church, that they ought so to take up the work of evangelizing their own people in good earnest, that the dancing of the *metawa*, thus publicly, would become an impossibility.

My visit to various points in the Ojibwa country has interested me very greatly. From what I have seen and heard, the conviction grew upon me, that the whole Ojibwa field comprizing thirteen or fourteen thousand people, in the State of Wisconsin and Minnesota, is now open to the gospel, as it never has been before. The old laborers sowed the good seed, but they saw little fruit. No wonder they became discouraged. For years the field was almost entirely given up. But although the servants retired, the Master watched the work, and here and there the seed has taken root and sprung up. This appears in the new desire prevailing, that they may again have schools and missionaries. Shall we not take advantage of this favorable time to tell them of Jesus the Savior?

CHAPTER XX.

1875-1876.—Annual Meeting of 1875.—Homestead Settlement on the Big Sioux.—Interest of the Conference.—' Iapi Oaye."—Inception of Native Missionary Work.—Theological Class.—The Dakota Home.—Charles L. Hall ordained.—Dr. Magoun, of Iowa.—Mr. and Mrs. Hall sent to Berthold by the American Board.—The "Word Carrier's" good words to them.—The Conference of 1876.—In J. B. Renville's Church.—Coming to the Meeting from Sully.—Miss Whipple's Story.—"Dakota Missionary Society."—Miss Collins' Story.—Impressions of the Meeting.

More and more the important events of the year culminate in, and are brought out by, the meeting of our Annual Conference. Heretofore this gathering had been in June. In the year 1875, it was held in September, at the Homestead Settlement on the Big Sioux. Only four years had passed since we were here before, but in this time great changes had taken place. They had erected a log church, and outgrown it, and sold it to the government for a school-house, and had just completed, or nearly completed, a commodious frame building. In this our meetings were held. Their farms and dwelling houses had also greatly improved. In several of these years they had been visited by the grasshoppers, and by this visitation they had lost their crops. But they held on—somewhat discouraged it is true. When their prospects and hopes from Mother Earth failed, they went to hunting, and thus they had worked along. This year they had a fair crop, and by exerting themselves they were able to entertain more than a hundred Dakota guests. Besides what they could furnish from their own farms, they had raised about $70 in money, which they expended in fresh beef. Thus they made princely provision for the meeting, which was, as usual, rich and full of interest.

Our Conference meetings began on the afternoon of Thursday, Sept. 16, and by that time we were all on the ground and ready. We had journeyed, camping by-the way, some over from the Missouri and others down from the head of the Coteau. The native delegates and visitors were encamped by the river-side, convenient to wood and water and the place of meeting. The missionaries pitched their tents by the house and enjoyed the hospitality of P. A. Vannice and his good wife.

At the time appointed we gathered at the church and had a sermon by one of the native pastors—Louis. Then came the business organization followed by short speeches of greeting and welcome. On the following day the real work of the Conference began. Questions relating to the proper training and education of children, and the training and preparation needful for the ministry, were discussed with interest and profit. The next day, which was Saturday, was taken up in the discussion of two prominent subjects of interest—the homestead act in its relation to Indians, and our Dakota paper. On the first of these topics there was a full and healthy expression of opinion. It was said that the plan of depending on the government for support tended to bad. Said Ehnamane: "If when we are hungry we cry out to our great Father 'Give us food,' or when we are cold we say, 'Send us clothes,' we become as little children—we are not men. Here at this place we see that each man takes care of himself; he has a farm and a house, and some have a cow and a few chickens. We go into their houses and we see tables and chairs, and when they eat they spread a cloth over the table, as do white people, and there are curtains to the windows, and we see the women dressed like white women —here we find men. We who look to the government for food and clothing are not men but little children, and the longer we depend on the government the lower down we find ourselves." Others differed: they said one could grow into manhood anywhere supported by the government or caring for themselves. Besides, it would not do to be too confident. It was hard work to strike out alone; some had starved, some had been frozen to death, and others had turned back. It means *work* to become a self-supporting citizen.

Perhaps there was as much real feeling expressed when the IAPI OAYE was discussed, as at any other time during Conference. Last year it was hoped that by another year the paper would become self-sustaining. Owing to several reasons, however, the subscription receipts for the past year are very much smaller than for the year previous, necessitating the meeting of a considerable deficiency by the missionaries themselves. It was thought best for our native membership to know the facts in order to stimulate action lest we be obliged to discontinue the paper. However, they would listen to nothing of that kind.

The paper has so strong a hold on the people as to be almost a necessity, and thereby a means of great and growing good. Sabbath morning was devoted to communion services, and the 113 native delegates and visitors from other stations united with their brothers at Flandreau around the table of our Lord.

In the afternoon we had a grand missionary meeting

which was the closing of the Conference. Speeches were made by the Fathers in the mission and by the older native membership, contrasting the darkness of the past with the light of the present. It seemed as we listened to the words of joy and thanksgiving spoken by those who have come up from heathenism, that the cup of joy and gladness must be full to overflowing for the Fathers of our mission, who went through the great trials and dangers of early days, and who are permitted to look upon the wonderful success of their lives spent thus in the Master's service.

The last topic discussed had somewhat of a history. Sometime during the year before, it had been published that the American Board had *great grand-children*. The mission to the Sandwich Islands had commenced Christian work on the Marquesas, and they again had extended it to other islands. In an article which Dr. Williamson furnished to the "Iapi Oaye," under the heading of *Children and Grand-children*, he recited these facts. A month or two afterward, I wrote an article on the *Children of Grand-children*, in which I said I was thankful for children, but wanted grand-children.

These statements worked like leaven in some of the natives' minds. *David Grey-cloud*, who opened the subject of missionary work to be undertaken by the native churches, had been stimulated thereby. The whole assembly seemed to be ready to take the first steps in the organization of a native Foreign Mission Society. A commitee was appointed for that object, consisting of J. P. Williamson, A. L. Riggs, John B. Renville, Robert Hopkins and Iron Track. In the mean time the churches were exhorted to take up collections for the Foreign Mission Fund.

In the beginning of the year 1876, at the Santee Agency, in connection with the Mission Training School, a THEOLOGICAL CLASS was organized.

For a few years past, we have been realizing more and more the want of a higher education in our native pastors and preachers. To supply this defect, and prepare the young men who are coming up to the work to fill the places of the fathers, with a higher grade of scholarship, and especially with a more thorough knowledge and appreciation of Bible truth, this plan was undertaken. It is only a beginning.

The regular class consisted of *John Eastman*, *Eli Abraham*, *Albert Frazier*, *Henry Tawa*, *Peter Eyoodooze*, and *Solomon Chante*, with *Rev. Artemas Ehnamane*, the pastor of the Santee church. Some others have been in attendance on evening exercises.

The object has been to give them as much knowledge and training as could be imparted and received in the limited space of four weeks, in Bible geography and history, in the main doctrines of the Christian faith, in the best methods of teaching Bible truth, the founding and growth of the Christian Church, in its orders of laborers, in its ordinances, in its service, and in its benevolent and saving work.

For the first two weeks of the term A. L. Riggs was assisted by Rev. J. P. Williamson, from the Yankton Agency, which is the home of three of the young men attending the class.

I had received an urgent invitation to come on from Beloit, to aid in the instructions of the last two weeks, which I quite willingly accepted. While at the Santee on this visit, I became better acquainted with the working of the Normal school, and especially of that part of it called the "Dakota Home." The following is A. L. Riggs' description of it:

THE DAKOTA HOME is one of a group of buildings for educational purposes, belonging to the Dakota Mission at their principal educational center, Santee Agency, Nebraska. It was built by the funds of the Woman's Board of Missions at a cost of about $4,200. It was commenced in 1872, but not completely finished until 1874, although it has been in use now for two years.

"It is a large, well-proportioned frame building, two stories high, and 42x48 feet on the ground. On the first floor is the teachers' suit of rooms, the large dining-hall, which is also sewing and sitting-room for the girls, the Home kitchen and the necessary pantries and closets. Underneath is the commodious cellar and milk-room.

"In the second story are the dormitories. There are ten sleeping-rooms and a bath-room. Each room is intended to be occupied by only two girls, though three of them can accomodate four, if necessary. Every sleeping room is automatically and thoroughly ventilated without opening a door or window."

The object of the Dakota Home is to train up house-keepers for the future Dakota homes. Hence our effort is to train them into the knowledge and habit of all home work, and to instill in them the principles of right action, and cultivate self-discipline.

They learn to cook and wash, sew and cut garments, weave, knit, milk, make butter, make beds, sweep floors, and anything else pertaining to house-keeping, and they can make *good* bread.

At this time the Home was in the charge of Miss Marie L. Haines—since become Mrs. Joseph Steer—and Miss Anna Skea.

Before I left the Santee to return to my home in Beloit, the ordination of Mr. Charles L. Hall was announced to take place at Yankton on the 22d of February, and I was sorry I could not remain and take part. The marriage of Mr. Hall and Miss Calhoun was consummated at the Yankton Agency a week previous to this time.

For the ordination the Congregational churches of Yankton and Springfield had united in calling the Council. The call included the neighboring Congregational churches and three of our native churches. The Santee Agency church was represented by Pastor Artemas Ehnamane and Deacon Robert Swift Deer. The Council convened in Mr. Ward's church. The venerable Rev Charles Seccombe, of Nebraska, was moderator, and Rev. A. D. Adams, of Sioux Falls, was scribe.

The sermon was preached by Rev. Geo. F. Magoun, D. D., of Iowa College; and his theme was "The Christian Ambassadorship." It was said to be a sermon worthy of the occasion and the preacher. It was eminently fitting that Dr. Magoun should preach the sermon on the sending off of this new mission. For among those who bore such effective testimony in behalf of Indian missions, on the platform of the American Board in Chicago, was President Magoun. The ordaining prayer was made by Rev. John P. Williamson; the charge was given by Rev. Joseph Ward, and the right hand of fellowship by Rev. A. L. Riggs.

Thus Mr. and Mrs. Hall were set apart and sent off to plant the standard of the cross at Fort Berthold, among the Mandans and Rees and Hidatsa, at a point on the Missouri, 1,500 miles above its mouth. The "Word Carrier," for April, 1876, gave them the right hand of fellowship. It said: "They must be a part of us. They will, in fact, form a part of the Dakota Mission. We will work with them, by our prayers and sympathies, and Dakota books and native help, so far as they can use them." It said to them: "Go and plant the standard of the cross at Berthold, and 'Hold the Fort' for the Master. You have the old promise ' Lo! I AM WITH YOU ALL DAYS.' It is ever new and ever inspiring. And yet there may be dark days and lonesome nights perhaps. You will have to learn the way into dark, human hearts, which must be done 'by the Patience of Hope, and the Labor of Love.' You will tell them, in the heart's language, of that strange love of the Great Father, who sent His Son to seek and save the lost. You will entreat the Holy Spirit to beget in the Hidatsa and Ree and Mandan people, a soul-hunger that can only be satisfied with the Bread and the Water of Life. And may the good Lord keep you evermore and give you showers of blessing."

According to previous announcement in the "Word Carrier," the annual meeting of the Dakota Mission and Conference of the native churches, commenced its sessions on the afternoon of Sept. 7, 1876, in the new and beautiful church of Ascension, J. B. Renville, pastor. The house was crowded. The delegations and visitors from Yankton, Santee, Flandreau and Brown Earth amounted to 106.

The convention was opened with prayer and singing, Rev. A. L. Riggs and Rev. David Grey Cloud, English and Dakota secretaries, presiding. A new Dakota hymn of welcome was sung by the choir and church, when words of welcome were spoken by Pastor J. B. Renville, and by Agent J. G. Hamilton, of the Sisseton Agency, and by S. R. Riggs. These were responded to by J. P. Williamson, for the Yanktons; by Rev. Artemas Ehnamane, for the Santees, and by Rev. John Eastman, for the large delegation from the Big Sioux.

The Conference then proceeded to make out the roll and perfect its organization. All the native pastors were present, with elders, and deacons, and teachers, and messengers from the churches, numbering together fifty-nine, and missionaries, eleven. T. L. Riggs and David Grey Cloud were chosen secretaries for the next two years. The Conference then listened to an address on family worship from Dr. T. S. Williamson.

From the speeches of welcome and the responses it was manifest that, for months, the convention has been looked forward to with great interest; all parties have come up to the meeting with joyful expectations. Major J. G. Hamilton, the representative of the government on this Reserve, has made liberal arrangements to feed all the Dakota visitors, for which he has our thanks in advance.

Rev. A. D. Adams, pastor of the Congregational church, at Sioux Falls, we are glad to welcome to our hospitalities and discussions.

Although for the greater part of the time we were together, the clouds were over us, and sometimes enveloped us, all the services were very largely attended; and on Sabbath the crowd was so great that we were obliged to hold our morning service out of doors. The subjects brought before the Conference for discussion were of vital practical interest, and were entered into with enthusiasm by the native speakers, and the action taken upon them was usually very satisfactory.

While our meetings were in progress, there came a message to us from the white man's country, asking that our Dakota churches unite with white Christians all along the western border, in a *Prayer League* against the grasshoppers. While Sitting Bull and the hostile Dakotas are fighting with the white soldiers in one part of the country, and it may be, by the cruelties of one side or both, bringing upon us this scourge from the hand of God, it is eminently fitting that the praying Dakotas and the praying white people should together humble themselves before Him. So said the Dakotas.

It will give variety and interest to the circumstances and proceedings of this meeting to have them recounted by others.

MISS EMMARETTA J. WHIPPLE'S STORY.

" The morning of September 1st found the Missionaries of Bogue Station, near Fort Sully, on their way to the Annual Meeting of the Dakota Mission. The party consisted of five—Mr. and Mrs. Riggs, Misses Collins and Whipple and little Theodore. The carriage was heavily loaded with articles needed for the overland journey, consisting of tent, tent poles and pins, ax, gun, stove, cooking utensils, provision boxes, traveling bags, blankets and robes.

" A number of the Indians had promised to accompany them, but the coming Council of the Commissioners proved a greater attraction than the gathering together of their Christian brethren, and they remained at home.

" The day was cool but pleasant, and all enjoyed the ride, which gave them keen appetites for the dinner taken on the bank of the Huhboju. In the afternoon Mr. Riggs shot some ducks, while others gathered willows to carry along for the night's fire, as at that camping place there was no wood.

" The second day proved to be the most eventful of the

trip. A village of prairie dogs was passed, a rabbit chased, and an antelope seen. But the great event was the *tip over*—not an ordinary upset, but a complete revolution of the carriage. The large grasses grew so thickly across the track that a deep rut was concealed from view; and had it been thought necessary to drive from the track, the bluff on one side and a water hole on the other would have prevented.

"The upper part of the carriage was too heavy to keep its balance when the wheels went into the rut, and the whole outfit was precipitated six feet down the bank into the water hole, which, fortunately, was dry. Mrs. Riggs slipped from her seat and was held down by the provisions, boxes and blankets, which fell upon her when the carriage passed over. Mr. Riggs found himself upon the axletree. Miss Collins gave a faint '*Oh, oh!*' and said 'Don't hurt the baby.' The baby was the safest of all. He was nearly asleep on Miss Whipple's arm, and was there held while she went through a series of circus performing hitherto unknown. When all were safely out and it was known that no one was seriously injured, exclamations of joy and thankfulness were uttered.

"Mr Riggs started in pursuit of the team, which had become detached from the carriage by the breaking of a bolt, and, frightened by the confusion, had run away. They were easily caught, as one ran faster than the other and thus running went in a circle. Miss Collins commenced searching for the whiffletree and found it nearly a half mile away.

"The boxes, bags, blankets, &c., were taken out, the carriage drawn into the road and the bows of the top mended by means of a tent pin and a strap. The broken bolt was replaced by a lariat and picket-pin, and the dashboard found a place in the feed-box in the rear. Other things were arranged in their respective places, the team hitched to the conveyance, and in a little more than an hour from the time of stopping they were again journeying onward. Mr. and Mrs. Riggs and Miss Collins had a few bruises, the other two not a scratch of which to boast.

"At noon they lunched under the trees beside a dry lake bed. All the water they had they brought with them in a canteen.

"The head of Snake Creek was the next place where water could be found, and this place they hoped to reach by six o'clock. But the road was long and the horses weary. It was eight o'clock when the creek was reached, and then it was found to be dry. There was nothing to be done but to drive ten miles farther, where there were both wood and water.

"Little Theodore seemed to realize that all was not quite right, and knowing his bed-time was passed asked his mamma to sing. Then said, 'Mamma, keep still while I pray.' Folding his hands he lisped in sweet baby accents,—'Dear Father in Heaven, take care of little Theodore, Grandma and Grandpa, Papa and Mamma, Aunt May and Miss Whipple, for Jesus' sake, Amen.' Then he settled down in the seat to sleep. Happy, trusting child! He that careth for sparrows would not fail to hear the prayer of the little two-year-old who had expressed the thought of each heart. It was nearly midnight when supper was over and camp work done.

"All were thankful that the next day was the Day of Rest. The horses not less than the people.

"The Sabbath was bright and beautiful, and though nearly a hundred miles from any habitation they felt they were not alone, but that the God, who is worshiped in temples not made by hands, was with them, through all the pleasant hours of the holy day.

"Old Sol now concluded to veil his face awhile, and Monday morning was ushered in by a heavy rain. About nine o'clock the clouds broke away and preparations were made to start. Before these were completed the rain again commenced falling. They, however, did not tarry, but rode ten miles in the moist atmosphere, which took the starch out of the ladies' sunbonnets, wet the robes and bedding, but did not dampen the spirits of the party.

"Then they decided to wait until the storm abated. Pitched the tent in the rain and remained there until the next morning, when the journey was resumed, though the rain-drops were still falling.

"Wednesday forenoon they saw an Indian house and met four Indians,—the first house passed and the first persons seen since Bogue Station was left.

"That evening, just at dusk, the Jim River was forded, and that night spent on its bank in fighting mosquitoes.

"Thursday they ascended the Coteau Range and made a call at Fort Wadsworth. Two hundred miles had been traveled and they had now arrived at the first settlement. A few miles on their camp was made, and early the next morning they started, hoping to reach Good Will in time for dinner. Good Will was reached, but no person could be found. Bolted doors prevented an entrance, and now they must go eight miles to Ascension church, where the Conference was in session.

"After riding up and down the many hills over which the road runs, they stopped at an Indian house to inquire the way. Out rushed a multitude of men and women.

One old lady, a mother in Israel, came hurrying along on her staff, saying, 'That's Thomas, that's Thomas.' They all shook hands and expressed their joy, because of the safe arrival. The thought came, 'It is worth all the trouble of a journey across the wide prairie to see so many Christian Indians.'

"A little farther on the *old* church, now used for a school building, was reached and found to be occupied by most of the missionaries who were attending the meeting. They kindly welcomed the weary travelers who had come so far from the wild Teeton band, and took them in and warmed and fed them.

"But the subject which pre-eminently engaged the attention of the Conference, on this occasion, and drew from our native pastors and laymen enthusiastic words, was that of carrying the Gospel to the regions beyond."

T. L. Riggs has written the following account, of the formation of a native

DAKOTA MISSIONARY SOCIETY:

"A year since, steps were taken at our *Ptaya Owohdaka* gathering for the formation of a *Native Missionary Society*. The question was 'Are not the native Christians ready and able to support a special agency for the spread of the gospel among the still heathen Dakotas?' A committee was appointed to canvass the matter and report at the next Annual Conference. At this meeting, which has just adjourned, the missionary committee reported over $240 *cash in hand*, and recommended that (1) a Missionary Board of three members—one the Secretary, another Treasurer—be elected; and (2) a full discussion and expression of opinion on the part of the Conference. This discussion was earnest, and showed an understanding of the subject and a readiness to grapple with its difficulties that was very gratifying. The Missionary Board was carefully chosen and instructed to select a fit man and send him out at once. After some consideration, David Grey Cloud, pastor of the Ma-ya-san church, was chosen by the Board. His acceptance being received, the Sabbath afternoon service was mainly devoted to his special setting apart for the new work.

"This is the first effort of the kind. Heretofore our own Missionary Boards have fathered every such attempt. The support of native workers has come in part or entirely from white people. Now in this new attempt all this is changed. The native Christians send and support their own man. We thank God that they are ready to do this.

"The new missionary will have for his special field the Standing Rock Agency, though during the colder winter months, he will probably spend the most of his time in the neighborhood of Fort Sully and Cheyenne Agency. To those in official position, as well as all others, whom he may meet, we commend him for the work's sake and the Master's.'"

MISS MARY C. COLLINS' STORY

"We had just come from a region where they are still abiding in the shadow of death, and where they are just beginning to learn that they may have life and have it more abundantly, through our Lord Jesus Christ. No wonder that when I saw so many rejoicing in His love I felt like exclaiming, 'God has said, Let there be Light,' and all the powers of earth cannot withhold it, for God's time is at hand. Could all the Christians in our land have beheld with me such a multitude, partaking of the Lord's supper and obeying that loving command, 'This do in remembrance of me,' their hearts would, I think, have been filled with thanksgiving, and a long and earnest shout of 'Glory to God in the Highest, and on earth peace, good will toward men,' would have resounded through the land.

"They have the spirit of Christ and are not satisfied with being saved themselves only, but desire the salvation of their benighted brethren. They have organized a missionary association and raised in one year about two hundred and fifty dollars to support a missionary. He is sent forth from this meeting, and how it must have rejoiced the hearts of those good men who have grown grey in the service, to see this young man arising from the degradation of his forefathers, standing on the Christian platform, receiving the blessings of his people, and pledging himself faithfully to perform his work toward them, and to his God. They must have had feelings akin to those of Simeon when he beheld the Savior, 'For mine eyes have beheld thy salvation.' When I saw the work these women had done to help sustain their paper, again I was amazed. Twenty dollars worth of fancy work was sold, and the women had done it all themselves Well may we say, 'They have done what they could.' They only have one paper, the 'Word Carrier,' and it was about to fail for want of means to carry it on, and these women, with a truly Christian spirit, went to work to sustain this important disseminator of truth. That was far more for them to give than for our Christians at home to subscribe for the paper and make it self-supporting. On Sabbath there was not room in their large church to hold the people, and we were obliged to hold services in the open air, and seven or eight hundred Dakotas were present to hear God's message to them. And to me it seemed the most beautiful sight I ever beheld. There were several admitted into the church, and one girl who was about sixteen years old, who was baptized in infancy, now in youth, comes out on the Lord's side. A little boy about twelve years old was baptized, and I thought of many of the little boys at home even older than that, who had not accepted the Savior, and although they have so many blessings, yet 'he hath chosen the good part which shall not be taken away from him.'

"I think the angels in Heaven rejoiced when these people lifted up their hearts and voices in praise to Him. And as the old missionary hymn rang out on the air I thought it seemed even grander than ever before."

CHAPTER XXI.

1871–1877.—The Wilder Sioux.—Gradual Openings.—Thomas Lawrence.—Visit to the Land of the Teetons.—Fort Sully.—Hope Station.—Mrs. Gen. Stanley in the Evangelist.—Work by Native Teachers.—Thomas Married to Nina Foster.—Nina's First Visit to Sully. - Attending the Conference and American Board.—Miss Collins and Miss Whipple.—Bogue Station.—The Mission Surroundings.—Chapel Built.—Mission Work.—Church Organized.—Sioux War of 1876.—Community Excited.—Schools.—" Waiting for a Boat."—Miss Whipple Dies at Chicago.—Mrs. Nina Riggs' Tribute.—The Conference of 1877 at Sully.—Questions Discussed.—Grand Impressions.

We had been long thinking of, and looking toward, the wilder part of the Sioux nation, living on, and west of, the Missouri River. More than thirty years before this, in company with Mr. Alex. G. Huggins, I had made a trip over from Lac-qui-parle to Fort Pierre. The object of that visit was to inform ourselves in regard to the Teetons—their numbers and condition, and whether we ought then to commence mission work among them. And since the Santees were brought to the Missouri, we had made several preaching tours up the river, stopping awhile with the Brules at Crow Creek, and with the Minnekanjoos, the Oohenonpa, the Ogallala and the Itazipcho of the Cheyenne and Standing Rock Agencies. The bringing of our Christianized people into proximity with the wild part of the nation, seemed to indicate God's purpose of carrying the gospel to them also.

The field was evidently now open, and waiting for the sower of the precious seed of the Word. There was no *audible* cry of, " Come over and help us," nor was there in the case of Paul with the Macedonian. But there was the same unrest, the same agony, the same reaching out after a knowledge of God, now as then. We listened to it, and assuredly gathered that the Lord would have us work among the Teetons.

THOMAS LAWRENCE was Mary's second boy. He could hardly be reconciled with the idea that his mother should go away to the spirit land, while he was down in Mississippi teaching the freedmen. Now he had been two years in Chicago Theological Seminary, and was asking what he should do when the other year was finished. The Prudential Committee of the American Board were looking around for some one to send to the Upper Missouri. Thomas had been born and brought up, in good part, in the land of the Dakotas; but they deemed it only fair that he should now, with a man's eyes see the field, and with a man's heart better understand the work, before committing himself to it. And so, in his summer vacation of 1871, they said to him, " Go with your father to the land of the Teetons, and see whether you can find your life work with them."

We came to the land of the Teetons, and stopped for five or six weeks at Fort Sully, which was in the neighborhood of Cheyenne Agency. There we found Chaplain G. D. Crocker, who had been much interested in our work among the Dakotas when stationed at Fort Wadsworth. We found, also, good and true Christian friends in Captain Irvine and his wife, and in the noble Mrs. General Stanley, the wife of the commandant of the post. In the mornings of our stay in the garrison, we often gathered buffalo berries—Mashtinpoota, *rabbit noses*, as the Indians called them. During the day we talked with the Dakotas, and studied the Teeton dialect, and also the Assinaboine and the Ree. In our judgment the time had fully come for us to commence evangelistic work in this part of the nation. Our friends at Sully thought so, and the Prudential Committee did not hesitate a moment. Indeed, they could not wait for Thomas to finish his Seminary course, but sent him off in midwinter to Fort Sully. He was ordained by a council which met in Beloit.

The Indians of the Cheyenne Agency, a portion of them, were distributed along down in the Missouri Bottom, in little villages and clusters of houses. In a village of this kind a little below the Fort, and on the opposite side of the river, T. L. Riggs erected his first house. It was a hewed log cabin with two rooms below, one of which was a school-room. The garret was arranged for sleeping apartments. This was called *Hope Station*, so named by Capt. Irvine's little daughter, who, about this time, came into the Christian hope.

Of this new enterprise, *Mrs. Gen. D. S. Stanley* sent a very pleasant notice to the *New York Evangelist*. "Six years ago," she says, "my lot was cast among the Sioux, or Dakota Indians, who inhabit the region bordering on the Missouri River, 500 miles above Sioux City, Iowa, and in the vicinity of Fort Sully, Dakota Territory. All this time it has been a matter of surprise to me that no Christian missionary was laboring among these heathens, while so many were sent to foreign lands. In reply to a suggestion to this effect, made to the American Board, it was stated that it is almost impossible to induce a competent person to undertake so difficult and dangerous a task.

"Meanwhile God was preparing the way. A boy had

grown up among the Dakotas, speaking their language, understanding their customs, and identifying himself with their best interests. He was at this time in college preparing for the ministry, and last spring this young man, Rev. T. L. Riggs, son of the veteran missionary and Dakota scholar of that name, came to this place, and entered upon the work for which he seemed to be so peculiarly fitted. Almost unassisted, except by a brother, and some facilities for work afforded by the commandant of Fort Sully, he has erected two log buildings, and, already, schools are in operation on both sides of the river, attended by about sixty Indians of various ages. Two native teachers were employed during the summer, and two are engaged for the winter. Mr. Riggs has surmounted great difficulties, inseparable from such efforts, in remote and unsettled regions; but he is full of energy, and his heart is in the work."

From the beginning, it has been the aim, at this station, to do the work of education very much by means of native teachers. The first summer, a young man from the Yankton Agency, Toonwan-ojanjan by name, was employed, and also Louis Mazawakinyanna from Sisseton. The next autumn, James Red Wing and his wife Martha, and Blue Feather (Śuntoto) were brought up from the Santees. Red Wing's wife taught the women in letters and the family arts, while the men taught the young men and children generally, and greatly aided in the religious teachings of the Sabbath. Afterward, Dowanmane, another Santee man, was employed in like manner. This was the commencement of educational and Christian work in this Teeton field.

At another point, some few miles below Hope Station, on the same side of the river, was another Dakota village, where Thomas immediately commenced holding a preaching service, and has kept up a school. It is one of his out stations, and called *Chantier*, from the name of the creek and bottom. While the opportunities for education and the new teaching were looked upon favorably, and gladly received by many, there were not wanting those who were savagely opposed. At different times while Henry M. Riggs, who spent several years aiding in the erection of buildings and other general work, was present with Thomas at Hope Station, their house and tent were fired upon by Indians, and residence there seemed hardly safe.

When he had thus started the work, leaving it to be cared for and carried on by Henry M. Riggs and Edmund Cooley and the native teachers, Thomas went down to the States to consummate a marriage engagement with Cornelia Margaret Foster (known as Nina Foster), daughter of Hon. John B. Foster, of Bangor, Maine. It was winter, and not considered advisable for Mrs. Riggs to return with her husband to his home among the Teetons. She made a visit with her sister, Mrs. C. H. Howard, at Glencoe, in the vicinity of Chicago, and in the spring month of May, I accompanied her up the Missouri. We had a particularly long voyage of eleven days, on the *Katie Koontz*, between the Santee Agency and Fort Sully : so long, that we picked up Thomas on the way, coming to meet us in his little skiff.

Thomas and Nina returned to Sully after our mission meeting at the Yankton Agency, and then, in September, went to the meeting of the Board at Minneapolis.

Sully was a far-off station. There were many reasons why a white woman should not be there alone. Miss Lizzie Bishop's election to go back with them, together with her beautiful life and early death, have been detailed in a preceding chapter.

She had fallen out of the working ranks, but others were ready to step to the front. In the previous spring, Secretary Treat had told me that there were two young ladies in Iowa, who were anxious to engage in mission work. They preferred to go to the Indians, as they desired to labor together. It was a David and Jonathan love that existed between Miss Mary C. Collins and Miss J. Emmaretta Whipple. They were immediately sent out by the Woman's Board of the Interior to labor at Bogue Station.

This place, selected in 1873, had, for various reasons, become in 1874, the home station—thenceforward Hope was only an out-station. Bogue Station is on Peoria Bottom, about fifteen miles below Fort Sully, and on the same side of the Missouri, called by the Indians, "Teetanka-ohe," meaning, "The place of a large house," so-called from a house built years ago by an Indian. General Harney selected this bottom as the place for an Agency, or rather, perhaps, where a scheme of civilization should be tried, and built upon it several log houses, which became the dwellings of Yellow Hawk and his people. The bottom has several advantages—considerable cottonwood timber, plenty of grass for hay, and as good land for cultivation as there is in this often "dry and thirsty land."

The first winter Oyemaza, or James Redwing, and his wife, lived here with Henry M. Riggs, and taught a school. The second winter, Thomas and Nina, with Miss Bishop, made it their abode. So that it was not quite a new place to which Miss Collins and Miss Whipple came, and yet new enough. The mission dwelling is made of logs—

one series of logs joined to another, so as to make four rooms below, one of which has served as school-room through the week and a chapel for the Sabbath. Additions have been made in the rear. The school-room has, for a long time back, overflowed on the Sabbath, and the women and children have been packed into the room adjoining, which is the family room. Hence a great and growing want of this station has been a chapel and larger school room. The name of Bogue was given to the station for Mrs. Mary S. Bogue, a special friend of Thomas, while he was in the Seminary, who has gone to her rest. It was, at one time, expected that Mr. Bogue would furnish the means to erect a chapel; but the shrinkage in values and financial losses made him a broken reed. And so the desired building has been postponed from year to year. But a small contribution of fourteen cents, made by little Bertie Howard, was the nucleus around which larger contributions gathered, chiefly from Nina's native Bangor. About $400 of special contributions were thus received, and the Prudential Committee made a loan of $500 toward it.* The building is going up—August, 1877—a neat and substantial frame, the material of which was brought up from Yankton by boat. It is forty by twenty feet, and will have a bell tower in one corner.

Let me now go back and take up the threads of the narrative which were dropped two years ago. The two young ladies, who desired to work together in some Indian field, found themselves here in Yellow Hawk's village. They entered into the labors of those who had been here longer. They grew into the work. The day schools, in books and sewing, together with the night school, employed all hands, during the winter especially. A number

---

*This was afterward made a gift.

have learned to read and write in their own language. Besides the school carried on at the home station, the two out stations have been occupied by native helpers. Edwin Phelps, from the Sisseton Agency, with his mother, Elizabeth Winyan, have been valuable assistants for two winters past. Also for the winter of 1876-7, David Grey Cloud, one of the native pastors at the head of the Coteau, did valuable service, both in teaching and preaching. He was sent to Standing Rock by the native Missionary Society, but not being able to get a footing there, he came down here to preach to these Teetons salvation by Jesus Christ. In the spring, when he was leaving for Sisseton, they begged him to stay, or at least to promise to come back again.

The Word, during these years, has not been preached in vain. While in the main it has been seed sowing— only seed sowing—breaking up the wild prairie land of these wild Dakota hearts, and planting a seed here and there, which grows, producing some good fruit; but in most cases, not yet the best fruit of a pure and holy life. Still, in the summer of 1876, one young man, the first fruits among the Teetons, *David Lee* (Upijate) by name, came out as a disciple of Jesus. This was the signal for the organization of a church at this station, which was effected in August. Another native convert, the brother of the first, was added in the autumn following; and still more a year or so afterward.

For two winters past, several boys and young men, who have made a good commencement in education in these schools, have been sent down to enjoy the advantages of A. L. Riggs' High School, at Santee. The Sioux war of the summer of 1876 produced a great excitement at all the Agencies on the Upper Missouri. The Indians in these villages were more or less intimately connected with the hostiles. Many of those accustomed to receive rations here were during the summer, out on the plains. Some of them were in the Custer fight. They say that Sitting Bull's camp was not large—only about two hundred lodges. The victory they gained was not, as the whites claimed, owing to the overwhelming numbers of the Dakotas, but to the exhausted condition of Custer's men and horses, and to their adventuring themselves into a gorge, where they could easily be cut off.

When the autumn came, the victories of the Sioux had been turned into a general defeat. Many of them, as they claim, had been opposed to the war all along. The attacks, they say, were all made by the white soldiers. *They*—these Dakota men—were anxious to have peace, and used all their influence to abate the war spirit among the more excited young men. This made it possible for the military to carry out the order to *dismount* and *disarm* the Sioux. But in doing this all were treated alike as foes. Such men as *Long Mandan* complain bitterly of this injustice. From him and his connections the military took sixty-two horses. He cannot see the righteousness of it.

As a matter of course this excited state of the community was unfavorable, in some respects, to missionary work during the winter. The military control attempted to interfere with the sending away of Teeton young men to the Santee school. But on the whole no year of work has proved more profitable. In all the schools, Thomas reported about two hundred and forty scholars. They were necessarily irregular in attendance, as they were frequently ordered up to the Agency to be counted. Still the willing hearts and hands had work to do all the time. And so the spring of 1877 came, when the women folks of Bogue Station had all planned to have a little rest. Mrs. Nina Riggs was to go as far as Chicago to meet her father and mother, from Bangor. Miss Collins and Miss Whipple were going to visit their friends in Iowa and Wisconsin. And so they all prepared for the journey, and *waited for a boat.* By some mischance boats slid by them. They put their tent on the river bank and waited. So a whole month had passed, when, at last, their patient waiting was rewarded, and they passed down the Missouri River and on to Chicago.

The ladies of the Woman's Board of the Interior had arranged to have them present and take an active part in several public meetings in and around Chicago. This was unwise for the toilers among the Dakotas. The excitement of waiting and travel—the summer season—the strain on the nervous system, incident to speaking in public to those unaccustomed to it—all these were unfavorable to the rest they needed. We must not quarrel with the Lord's plan, but we may object to the human unwisdom. So it was; before Miss Whipple had visited her friends she was stricken down with fever. Loving hearts and willing hands could not stay its progress. It is said, and we do not doubt it, that all was done for her recovery that kind and anxious friends could do. Miss Collins, her special friend, did not leave her. Delirium came on, and she was "*Waiting for the Boat.*" It was not now a Missouri steamer, but the boat that angels bring across from the Land of Life. She saw it coming. "The boat has come, and I must step in," she said. And so she did, and passed over to the farther shore of the river.

The Teetons say, "Two young women went away, and

one of them is not coming back. They say she has gone to the land of spirits. It has been so before. Miss Bishop went away, and we did not see her again. And now we shall not see Miss Whipple any more." So they mourn with us. But while the workers fall, their work will not fail. It is the work for which Christ came from the bosom of the Father; and as He lives now, so "shall He see of the travail of His soul, and shall be satisfied."

Dear Miss Whipple's death came upon us like a thunder-clap. We are dumb, because the Lord has done it. Nevertheless, it has made our hearts very sad, and interfered with our plans of work. But we can say, "Not in *our* way, but in *Thy* way, shall the work be done." A fitting tribute from Mrs. Nina Riggs will be found very interesting.

"Miss J. E. Whipple died of gastric fever at Chicago, August 11th, aged 24. For nearly two years she had been connected with the Dakota Mission among the Teeton Indians. And she left her work there last spring, in order to take a short vacation and visit among her friends. On her way from her sister's home in Knoxville, Illinois, to the home of her father, at Badger, Wisconsin, she was attacked by the disease which proved fatal. Through all her sickness to the end she was tenderly and lovingly cared for by Miss Mary Collins, her intimate friend and companion in missionary labor. In the summer of 1875, Miss Whipple gave herself to the cause of missions, and entered upon her work in the autumn of that same year. She had little idea of what she should be called to do, but self-consecration was the beginning of all, and so whatever work was given her to do she took it up cheerfully and earnestly, yielding time and strength and zeal to it. Though it seemed small she did not scorn it, though repugnant she did not shirk it, though hard she bravely bore it. Her merry smile, her thoughtful mind, her quick response, the work of her strong, shapely hands, all blessed our mission home. She came a stranger to us, but when she left us in the spring, only for a summer's vacation as we thought, she was our true and well-beloved friend.

"They tell me she is dead! When the word reached us, already was the dear form laid away by loving hands to its last rest.

"Dead! The house is full of her presence, the work of her hands is about us, the echo of her voice is in our morning and vesper hymns, the women and children whom she taught to sew and knit, and the men whom she taught to read and write, gather about the doorway. Even now beneath the workman's hammer is rising the chapel, for which she hoped and prayed and labored.

"Dead? No! The power of her strong, young life is still making itself felt, though the bodily presence is removed from us, nor can that power cease so long as the work she loved is a living work.

"'The children all about are sad,' said an Indian woman. 'I too am sorrowful. I wanted to see her again.' The little Theodore whom she had loved and tended, folded his hands and prayed, 'Bless Miss Emmie up in heaven,—she was sick and died and went to heaven,—and bring her back some time.' Sweet, childish prayer that would fain reach out with benediction to her who is beyond the reach of our blessing, eternally blest.

"As she passed away from the fond, enfolding arms that would have detained her, she breathed a message for us all. Listen! Do you not hear her speaking? 'Work for the missions, work for the missions. Christ died for the missions.'

"On the wall of her room still hangs the Scripture roll as it was left. And this is the word of comfort it bears:

"'I shall be satisfied when I awake in thy likeness.'

"'His servants shall serve Him and they shall see his face.'"

THE DAKOTA CONFERENCE.

The annual meeting of the Conference of churches, connected with the Dakota Mission, took place at T. L. Riggs' Station on Peoria Bottom, near Fort Sully, commencing on Thursday, September 13, 1877, and closing on Sabbath, the 16th.

The very neat new chapel, which had been in building only a few weeks, was pushed forward so that it made a very convenient and comfortable place of meeting. The Sabbath immediately preceding, it was occupied for religious service. It was very gratifying to see the house filled by the Indians living here. In the general interest manifested in religious instructions, by the people of these villages, there is very much to encourage us. Old men and women, young men and maidens, flock to the new chapel, and express great gratification that it has been erected for their benefit.

On Wednesday, the 12th of the month, the delegates began to come in. The first to arrive were from the homestead settlement of Flandreau on the Big Sioux. They had come 260 miles and traveled ten days. Then came the delegation of more than twenty from the Sisseton Reservation, near Fort Wadsworth. And in the evening came the largest company from the Yankton and Santee Agencies. In all there were over sixty present, about forty-five of whom were members of the Conference, and all had traveled more than 200 miles The last to arrive were John P. Williamson and A. L. Riggs, who, being disappointed in getting a steamboat, had to come all the way in the stage.

Our meeting was opened with a sermon by the youngest of our Dakota pastors, Rev. John Eastman, of Flandreau. This was followed by greetings from T. L. Riggs and Mr. Yellow Hawk and Mr. Spotted Bear. Responses by S. R. Riggs, and pastors *Artemas, John Renville, Daniel Renville, Solomon, David, Louis,* and Joseph Blacksmith, followed by A. L. Riggs and John P. Williamson, who had just arrived. The meeting was very enjoyable and was followed by the organization. T. L. Riggs and David Grey Cloud were the English and Dakota secretaries, the only officers of the Conference. The roll contained fifty names, a number less than we have had present in years past, but quite large, considering the distance of the place from our churches, and the pressure of home work.

Friday, after a morning prayer meeting, at which the house appeared to be full, the Conference was opened with so large a gathering that it was found necessary to pack the house, when about two hundred were crowded in. As yet only a few of these Teetons have changed their dress, but they sit for three hours, and listen very attentively to discussions on the questions of "How to Study the Bible," and "Who shall be Received to Church Membership?" To the Teetons it was all new, but the native pastors endeavored to put their thoughts into such forms as to reach their understandings. Chaplain G. D. Crocker, of Sully, was present with his family, and added to the interest. On Saturday, Dr. Cravens, agent at Cheyenne, with his wife, made us a visit.

The Homestead question occupied us for a whole afternoon, and was one which attracted the most attention, as these Teetons, even, are greatly exercised to know how they shall secure a permanent habitation. Daniel Renville, Joseph Blacksmith, and Esau Iron Frenchman, all homesteaders, made eloquent appeals in favor of Indians becoming white men. But their stories of hard times showed that it had been no child's play with them.

The report of the executive committee of the native Missionary Society was read by A. L. Riggs, and David Grey Cloud gave an interesting account of his last winter's work on the Missouri. Speeches were made by John B. Renville, Joseph Blacksmith, S. R. Riggs, and John P. Williamson. By vote of the Conference the same committee was re-elected for another year—A. L. Riggs, Joseph Blacksmith, and John B. Renville. The money now in the treasury is about $160, besides certain articles contributed and not yet sold. The committee expect to engage the services of one of the pastors for the coming winter.

Another question discussed was "Household Duties;" when the Divine constitution of the family was made to bear against polygamy. This subject bore heavily upon the principal men of these villages, who were present and heard it all. It will doubtless cause some searchings of heart, which we hope will result in changed lives.

On Saturday afternoon a woman's meeting was held, which was peculiarly interesting in consequence of Miss Whipple's unexpected translation. She has worked herself very much into the hearts of these Teeton women.

Our whole meeting was closed by the services of the Sabbath. John P. Williamson preached an impressive sermon in Dakota; John Eastman led in the service of song at the organ; two of the native pastors administered the Supper of our Lord; Grey-haired Bear and Estelle Duprey were united in marriage; C. H. Howard, of "The Advance," made a good talk to the Dakotas on Christian work through the Holy Spirit's help, and led in an English Bible reading; and finally, John B. Renville gave us a wonderful series of pictures on the "Glory of Heaven"— what man's eye hath not seen—man's ear hath not heard —and man's heart hath not conceived. We shall long remember the meeting at Peoria Bottom, and we shall expect to see results in the progress of truth in the minds and hearts of these Teetons.

The Forty Years are completed. In the meantime many workers have fallen out of the ranks, but the work has gone on. It has been marvelous in our eyes. At the beginning, we were surrounded by the whole Sioux nation, in their ignorance and barbarism. At the close, we are surrounded by churches with native pastors. Quite a section of the Sioux nation has become, in the main, civilized and Christianized. The entire Bible has been translated into the language of the Dakotas. The work of education has been rapidly progressing. The Episcopalians, entering the field many years after we did, have nevertheless, with more men and more means at their command, gone beyond us in the occupation of the wilder portions. Their work has enlarged into the bishopric of Niobrara, which is admirably filled by Bishop Hare. Thus God has been showing us, by His providence and His grace, that the RED MEN, too, may come into the KINGDOM.

APPENDIX.

MONOGRAPHS.

Mrs. Nina Foster Riggs; Rev. Gideon H. Pond;
Solomon; Dr. T. S. Williamson;
The FAMILY Reunion;
and Others.

MRS. NINA FOSTER RIGGS.

A MONOGRAPH.

CORNELIA MARGARET, daughter of HON. JOHN B. FOSTER and CATHARINE McGAW FOSTER, was born in Bangor, Maine, March 19, 1848. Very soon after she left us, on August 5, 1878, there appeared appreciative testimonials of her life and character, in the ADVANCE, in the IAPI OAYE, and in LIFE AND LIGHT. In preparing this MONOGRAPH, the writer will make free use of all these materials.

REV. R. B HOWARD, while in the Theological Seminary at Bangor, knew her as Nina Foster, "a golden-haired, fair-cheeked, gracefully-formed little Sabbath-school scholar of ten, at the Central Church. Her quick, laughing eye, her sensitive face reflecting every changing thought, her constant companionship of an only sister a little taller, her ready answers to all Sabbath-school questions, her intelligent appreciation of the sermons, and her sunshiny presence at school and at home, were among the impressions which her childhood gave.

"She lacked no means of cultivating the rare powers of mind which she early developed. Many things she seemed to learn intuitively. Her scholarship was bright, quick, accurate. Literature was her delight. Her mother's father, Judge McGaw, whose white locks and venerable presence then honored Bangor, was an interested and judicious guide in the home reading.

"In social life few shone more brilliantly, or were more admired and sought after. In those days, the beauty of person of the young lady was of a rare and noticeable type. Her conversational powers were fascinating. She had by nature genuine histrionic talent, and in conversation, reading or reciting, seemed to be completely the person she sought to represent. On one occasion, by a slight change of dress, voice and manner, she appeared as an aged widow, pleading with a high officer of the Government at Washington, to help her find her son, lost in the troublous times of the war."

The "only sister a little taller," Mrs. KATIE FOSTER HOWARD, thus testifies of Nina's early life:

"When a little child, from eight to twelve years old, she and some of her companions formed 'a praying circle,' and had a little room in one of their homes, which they called THE HOUSE OF PRAYER. They met often in this room and delighted to decorate it after their childish fashion.

"Another favorite occupation was the teaching some poor children whom she and one or two friends brought out of their dreary homes to the church vestibule and there taught to sew and read.

"When eleven years old she was examined by the pastor and church officers for admission to the church; they asked her how long she had loved Jesus—and she answered, 'Oh, a great many years.'"

Mrs. Howard speaks of her sister as "the little girl in the Eastern home, whose *spirituelle* face, with its halo of golden hair, seemed so much more of heaven than of earth, as to cause the frequent, anxious comment, that this world could not long detain her. An active, happy child among her playmates, her thoughts were often upon heavenly things, and her desire was to turn theirs thitherward, yet without anything morbid or unchildlike in her ways.

"As she grew to womanhood, she was the delight of the home which so tenderly shielded her from every rude blast, and of a large circle of attached friends. She possessed those charms of person and manners and qualities of mind which won admiration, and peculiarly fitted her to enjoy and adorn society. So when the time came for her to change this for a secluded life, many regretted that the fine gold should be sent where baser metal, as they thought, would do as well; that the noble woman, so eminently fitted for usefulness in circles of refinement, should spend her life among the degraded and unappreciative savages. But the event has proved that only such a nature, abounding in resources, could be the animating spirit of a model home in the wilderness, which should be an object lesson of Christian culture, not only to the Indian, but to the Army people, who were her only white neighbors, and who, for her sake, could look with interest on a work too often an object of contempt. And thus the reflex influence upon those who missed her from their number, or met her as she journeyed to her field of labor, has been in proportion to the grace of her refinement, and the depth and breadth of her character. God, who spared not His own Son, still gives his choicest ones to the salvation of men."

While on a visit to Chicago in the family of her sister, she first became acquainted with Thomas L. Riggs, then a student in the Theological Seminary. Their mutual love soon compelled her to consider what it would be to share in his life-work. She recognized its hardships and deprivations, as could hardly have been expected in one so inexperienced in life's trials. She afterward often playfully said she was "not a missionary—only a missionary's wife." But it was a double consecration, joyous and entire, to the life of wife and missionary.

THOMAS and NINA were married at her home in Bangor, Dec. 26, 1872. It is said, "Christian people, and even Christian ministers were inclined to say, 'Why this waste?' Some did say it. Some spoke in bitter and almost angry condemnation of her course. That this beautiful and accomplished girl, eminently fitted to adorn any society, should devote herself to a missionary life, occasioned much comment in the social circle in which she had been prominent. What could she do for the coarse, degraded Indian women, that might not be better done by a less refined, sensitive and elevated nature? Why shut up her beauty and talents in the log cabin of an Indian missionary? It was a shock to some who had preached self-sacrifice, and a painful surprise to many who had been praying the Lord of the harvest to send laborers. But none of these things moved her. There has seldom been a sweeter and more lovely bride. The parents, too, made the consecration, while they wrestled in spirit. The father writes: "I gave her up when she left us on that winter's night. It was a hard struggle, but I think I gave her unconditionally to God, to whom she so cheerfully gave herself."

At this season of the year, it was not possible for Nina to accompany her husband to Fort Sully, and so he left her at Gen. C. H. Howard's, near Chicago, to come on in the early spring.

This was my first opportunity of becoming acquainted with "Mitakosh Washta," as I soon learned to call her. Gen. Howard accompanied her to Sioux City, and then I became her escort by railroad and stage to Santee Agency, and thence by steamboat to Sully. The boat was nearly two weeks on the way, and we took on two companies of United States troops at Ft. Randall. The officers soon manifested a marked admiration for the beauty and culture of the Bangor lady, so that afterward, in alluding to this little episode, I used playfully to say to Nina, that I was rejoiced when Thomas, coming down the Missouri in his skiff, met us, and took charge of his bride.

We had but a few weeks to spend at Fort Sully, until we should start down to the meeting of our Annual Conference, which was held in June that year, at the Yankton Agency. But those weeks were full of pleasure to Nina. Everything was new and strange. She was devoid of fear, when she sat in the iron skiff, and crossed the Big Muddy with her husband at the helm. The time came to go down. It was nearly noon on Monday when we were ready to start, but, by hard driving, we were able to reach Rev. John P. Williamson's—more than 200 miles—by the afternoon of Thursday. Secretary S. J. Humphrey, from Chicago, was there, and afterward wrote, that for T. L. Riggs and the father, who were accustomed to hard traveling and sleeping on the ground, it was nothing very strange; but for one reared as Nina had been, it was simply wonderful.

This was the first meeting of Martha Riggs Morris with her new sister. When the latter had gone beyond our ken, Martha wrote an appreciative article for the "Word Carrier": "Let me give something," she wrote, "of the little glimpses I have had of her brave, cheery life. I may first go back to the time when we first heard of Nina Foster—who thought enough of T. L. Riggs and the Indian work, to help him in it. That was in the spring time. A few months later, Thomas had a hard ride across from Fort Sully to Sisseton, on horseback, accompanied by a soldier for guard, and an Indian for guide. He came to attend the Annual Conference of the Dakota churches, and he showed us a picture of the young lady herself. A beautiful face we all thought it was. And from what we heard of Nina Foster, we were all prepared to take her into our hearts, as we did when we saw her afterward.

"It was in June of the year following that I had my first glimpse of her. I had myself taken a tedious journey of some three hundred miles, and the years as well as the journey had worn upon me. So I felt some trepidation about meeting the blooming bride. But on seeing her, that soon vanished, and I had nothing left but admiration for the beautiful sister. She told so merrily how they had strapped her in, to keep her from falling out of the wagon, and other incidents of her unaccustomed journey. There was an evident determination to make the best of every experience."

A little while after this Mrs. Morris was called to lay away her blue-eyed boy out of sight. Then Nina's letter was very comforting. "I have wept," she says, "with you for the dear little baby form laid away from your arms to its last sleep; and I think of your words, 'Nothing to do any more.' Ah! my dear sister, He will not so leave you comfortless. He, who forgot not in the last hours of his earthly life, to give to the aching mother-heart a new care and love, will not forget, I think, to bestow on your emptied hands some new duty which shall grow to be a joy."

At the meeting of the American Board at Minneapolis in the autumn of 1873, Mrs. Nina Riggs was present, and addressed the ladies of the Woman's Board, asking for a young lady companion in her far-off field. To this call Miss Lizzie Bishop, of Northfield, responded, and gave the remainder of her bright, true life, to help on the work at Fort Sully. Nina visited her sister in Chicago, and charmed them all by reciting her strange experiences of the summer. "Her buoyant spirits and faculty for seeing the droll side of everything, helped to make the sketch a bright one. Her sense of humor and keen wit has lightened many a load for herself and others; the more forlorn and hopeless the situation, the more elastic her spirits. How often have those of her own household, wearied with severe labor and weighed down with care, been compelled to laugh, almost against their will, by her irresistible drollery, and thus the current of thought was turned, and the burden half thrown aside."

In the summer of 1874, baby Theodore was born, and none from Fort Sully came to our annual meeting. On my way from a visit to Fort Berthold, down the Missouri River, I stopped off for a few days. They were then occupying Hope Station, across the river from the Fort. Both Miss Bishop and Mrs. Nina Riggs I found very enthusiastic over their work for the Teeton women.

When another year had been completed, Lizzie Bishop had gone home to die, and Nina Riggs made a visit to her friends in the East. The Board met in Chicago that autumn, and Mrs. Riggs again addressed the ladies. "Two years ago," she said, "at a meeting in Minneapolis, I made a request which was promptly answered. I asked for a young lady to go back with me to the mission work. I find her name is not on the rolls. But if ever a brave life should be recorded, and the name of an earnest woman be loved and remembered by all, it is that of Miss Lizzie Bishop, of Northfield, Minnesota. We had hoped that she might return, but the Lord has not seen fit to allow that. He calls her to himself soon. For the past two years I have been at different stations. I was at Hope Station, on the west side of the Missouri. Now I am at Bogue Station, fifteen miles below Fort Sully, on the east side. Since I have been there I have met a great many women. At first they all seemed to me very degraded; but I have come not only to feel interested in many of them, but to love some of them with a very deep love." So spake Nina; and when she sat down a telegram was read, that the good and brave Lizzie Bishop had already entered in through the gates of pearl, into "Jerusalem the golden."

Two others, Miss Mary C. Collins and Miss Emmarette Whipple, were ready to start back with Mrs. Riggs. So the vacant place was more than filled, and they all girded themselves for a hard winter's work.

A little before this time Nina sent to the "Word Carrier" a short bit of poetry, which seems to embody her own wrestling with doubt in others. The last stanza reads:

> "With daring heart, I too have tried
> To know the height and depth of God above;
> And can I wonder that I, too, walked blind,
> And felt stern Justice in the place of love?
> Above the child, the sun shines on;
> Above me, too, one reigns I cannot see;
> Yet all around I feel both warmth and power;
> *If God is not*, whence can *their* coming be?"

In September, 1876, the great gathering of the Dakota mission was held in the new Ascension church, on the Sisseton Reservation. Mrs. Morris writes: "We looked out eagerly for the travelers from Fort Sully way. We hoped they would come a few days beforehand, so that we might have more of their companionship. But they did not come. And as we had to be on hand in the Ascension neighborhood, ten miles away, to entertain the missionaries that might come, we shut up our house, and went on without the Fort Sully friends. It was Friday noon when they arrived, and received a glad welcome from all."

Thomas and Nina and their little lad Theodore, now two years old, who amused every one with his quaint sayings, together with Miss Collins and Miss Whipple, with all their personal and camping baggage, had been packed for eight days, into a small two-horse buggy. The journey of 250 miles, the way they traveled, over a country uninhabited, was not without its romance. "Not the least of the enjoyment of this 'feast of days,' were the bits of talk sandwiched in here and there, between meetings and caring for the children and providing for the guests. As we baked the bread and watched over the two cousins, Theodore and Mary Theodora, so nearly of an age, we had many a pleasant chat, —Nina and I. She gave me an insight into their happy home life, and I longed to know more. She told, too, of her special work in visiting the homes of the Teetons and prescribing for the sick. At the special meeting held for the women, Nina made a few remarks, winning all hearts by her grace of manners, as well as by her lovely face. Now that she is gone the Dakota women speak of her as 'the beautiful woman who spoke so well.'"

"To all who come, I wish my home to seem a pleasant home," is a remark which Miss Collins accredits to Nina. So indeed we found it in the months of August and September, of 1877. The dear Miss Whipple had just stepped into the boat at Chicago, which carried her to the farther shore. Miss Collins was mourning over her departed comrade while making out the visit to her friends. By appointment, I met, on the way, Gen. Charles H. Howard, of the ADVANCE, who, with his family, was bound for Fort Sully. We were prospered in our journey up the Missouri, and gladly welcomed into the mission home on Peoria Bottom. The two sisters met and passed some happy weeks in the home of the younger one. Mrs. Howard thus describes that home in those August days: "Its treeless waste lay under a scorching sun. Beneath a bluff which overlooks the river lowlands, nestled a solitary green enclosure around a long, low dwelling, whose aspect was of comfort and of home. The sunshine which withered the surrounding country, was not the gentle power under which had sprung up this oasis in the desert. The light within the house, whose sweet radiance beautified the humble dwelling, and shone forth upon the wilderness around, was the fair soul, whose heaven-reflected glory touched all who came within its ray."

To the same effect is Miss Collins' testimony: "I think no one ever entered her home without feeling that the very house was purified by her presence. I remember well just how she studied our different tastes. She knew every member of the family thoroughly; and our happiness was consulted in all things." So we all thought. Nina presided in her own home, albeit that home was in Dakota land, with a queenly grace.

About the middle of that September, our Annual Conference met in their new and not yet finished chapel, on Peoria Bottom. Miss Collins did not get back until the close of the meeting. Besides her guests, Mrs. Nina Riggs had a good deal of company from Fort Sully and the Agency. But it was all entertained with the same quiet dignity. Of this visit to her sister, Mrs. Howard wrote afterward: "I do not know how to be grateful enough that we spent last summer (1877) together; it is a season of blessed memory."

To this I add: I, too, have one last picture of Nina in my memory. I was to return to Sisseton with the Indians who had come over to our annual Conference. They went up on Monday to Cheyenne Agency to get rations for the journey. On Tuesday afternoon Thomas arranged to take me out fifteen miles to meet them. Thinking they would go out and return home that evening, a party was made up. The two sisters, Mrs. Howard and Nina, and little Theodore and Thomas and myself in a buggy, and Gen. C. H. Howard and "Mack" on ponies, we had a pleasant ride out. But it was too late for them to return. The Dakota friends gave us of their fresh meat, and with the provisions Nina had bountifully supplied for my journey, we all made a good supper and breakfast, and had an abundance left. The next morning we separated. That was my last sight of NINA.

In midsummer of 1878, the time for her departure came. She seemed to have a premonition of its coming. Miss Collins writes: "The last summer of her precious life seemed a very fitting one for the last. She labored earnestly for the conversion of her boy, and said: 'If I should die and leave my boy, I should feel so much better satisfied to go, if he had that strong-hold.'"

In the "Word Carrier" for September appeared this notice: "OUR BELOVED NINA FOSTER RIGGS, wife of REV. T. L. RIGGS, of Bogue Station, near Fort Sully, has heard the Master's call, and gone up higher. She was taken away in child-birth, on the 5th of August. Hers was a beautiful life, blossoming out into what we supposed would be a grand fruitage of blessing to the Dakotas. It is cut off suddenly! 'Even so, Father, for so it seemeth good in thy sight.' WE ARE DUMB, BECAUSE THOU DIDST IT!"

Two days after her death, Thomas wrote: "Dear Father—NITAKOSH-WASHTA has been taken from us. My good NINA has gone. She was taken sick Saturday night. Before the light of the Sabbath, violent convulsions had set in. We got the Post Surgeon and Mrs. Crocker here as soon as possible; but, though every effort was made, the spasms could not be prevented, and our dear one sank gradually out of reach. Early Monday morning, after child-birth, the mother seemed to brighten a bit; but soon our gladness was turned to sadness, for she did not rally. God took her. She was His. We buried the body—the beautiful house of the more beautiful spirit—in the yard near her window, yesterday. May God help us."

Only a few days before, a kind Providence had guided ARTHUR H. DAY, a cousin of Nina's, from his work in the office of the ADVANCE, in Chicago, and ROBERT B. RIGGS from his teaching in Beloit College, up to Peoria Bottom, for a little rest. And so they were there to help and give sympathy. Of this event, Mr. Day wrote: "Rarely is it the lot of one so blessed with loving relatives and friends, to pass away surrounded by so few to sympathize, and to be buried with so few to weep. Three relatives and nine other white friends stood alone by her grave, and the many hundreds in the far East knew not of the scene. I say *white* friends, because I would not ignore the presence of those many dusky faces which looked on in sorrow, because *their friend* was dead.

"About noon on Tuesday, August 6th, the funeral service was conducted by Chaplain Crocker. The same hymn was sung that, by Nina's own choice, had been sung at her wedding:

"'Guide me, O thou great Jehovah.'

One room of the house was filled with Indians, and the service was partly in the native language. Her grave was made near the window of her room, where she so often had beheld the sunset; and as kindly hands laid her body there, surrounded by beautiful flowers, the chaplain said: 'Never was more precious dust laid in Dakota soil—never more hopeful seed planted for a spiritual harvest among the Dakota people.'"

This beautiful summing up of her character appeared as an editorial in the *Advance*, by Rev. Simeon Gilbert.

Here was a young woman of extraordinary beauty of person, of still more noticeable symmetry and completeness of mental endowment, sweetness and nobility of disposition, brightness and elasticity of temperament; quickly, keenly sympathetic with others' joys and sorrows—but who had never known a grief of her own; converted in infancy, reared in one of the happiest of earnest Christian homes, and favored with as fine social and educational advantages as the country affords; with too much sense to be affected by mere "romance," yet deeply alive to all the poetry alike in literature and in real life; and withal, from early childhood, with a spiritual imagination exquisitely alive to the realness and the nearness of unseen things, and the all-controlling sweep of the motives springing therefrom;—rarely does one meet a young person better fitted at once to enjoy and to adorn what is best in American Christian homes. At the age of twenty-four she marries a young man just out of the Seminary, and goes forth with him beyond the frontiers of civilization, into the very heart of savage Indian tribes. What a sacrifice; what a venture; what certain-coming solicitudes, perils, cares, deprivations, hardships, loneliness, and mountainous discouragements. And there, for the short period of less than five years she lives, when suddenly the young missionary is left alone, longing for the "touch of a vanished hand and the sound of a voice that is still."

Now a case like this must set one to studying over again what, after all, is the true philosophy of life, and what, on the whole, is the wisest economy of personal forces in the church's work of Christianizing the world. As helping to a right answer, let us note a few facts:

1. It costs to save a lost world; and nothing is wasted that serves well that end. God himself has given for this purpose the choicest, the highest and the best, which it was possible for even Him to give.

2. Heathen people, even savages, as we call them, are not insensible to the unique fascination, and power to subdue and inspire, which belong to what is really most beautiful in aspect, manner, mind and character. Often it is to them as if they had seen a vision, or dreamed a startling dream of possibilities of which they had known nothing, and could have known nothing, until they *saw* it, and the sight awakened into being and action the diviner elements of their own hidden nature. The word of God is one form of revelation, but the work of God in a peculiarly complete and lovely character is another revelation, and one that unmistakably interprets itself. There is as much need of the one as there is of the other. The light of the knowledge of the glory of God in the face of Christ, must, in most cases, at least, first be seen reflected "in the face" of some of his disciples. The more dense the darkness, the more intense must be the shining of the love and the beauty of the truth which are to enlighten, captivate, lead forth, and refine. Among all the teepees and huts of that Indian Reservation, as also throughout the barracks and quarters of the military post at Fort Sully, Mrs. Riggs was known, and the potent charm of her personal influence and home-life was deeply felt. It is largely due to such persons, that the cause of missions, even among the most degraded, commands the respect, if not the veneration of those who otherwise might have looked on derisively.

3. Nor again are the lives of such persons wasted as regards their influence upon those who knew them, or shall come to know of them, at home. "How far that little candle throws its beams; so shines a good example;" and in instances like these, it shines more effectively than, perhaps, in any other circumstances would have been possible. If one were to mention a score of American women who have exerted most influence in determining the best characteristics of American women, half of them, we suspect, would be names of the women who, leaving home and country, went far forth seeking to multiply similar homes in other countries.

4. Nor, again, is the strangely beautiful life wasted because cut short so early in its course. The ointment most precious was never more so than when its box was broken and the odor of it filled all the house. This that this young missionary has done, animated by the love of the Master and a sacred passion for lifting up the lowly, will be spoken of as a memorial of her in all the churches; and in not a few homes, of the rich as of the poor, will be felt the sweet constraint of her beautiful, joyous, consecrated life. She was not alone; there are many more like her; and best of all, there are to be vastly more yet, who will not be

deaf to " the high calling." The Master has need of them. The way, on the whole, is infinitely attractive. Thanks for the life of this woman who did so much, from first to last, to make it appear so!

And thanks, too, for such a death, which, coming in the sweetest and completest blooming of life's beauty, when not a fault had stayed to mar it, and no wasting had ever touched it—an ending which transfigures all that came before it, and which now, in the mingling of retrospect and prospect, helps those who knew her to a deeply surprised sense of the fact that,

<blockquote>
To Death it is given,
To see how this world is embosomed in heaven."
</blockquote>

To us, who are blind and cannot see afar off, it is impossible to perceive, and difficult to believe, that the taking away, in the vigor of womanhood, of one who was showing such a capacity and adaptability for the work of elevating the Teetons, can be made to subserve the furtherance of the cause of Christ. But we must believe that God, who sees the end from the beginning, and who makes no mistakes, will bring out of this sore bereavement a harvest of joy; and that that grave under the window of the mission house in Peoria Bottom, will be a testimony to the love of Jesus, and the power of his Gospel, that will thrill and uplift many hearts from Bangor to Fort Sully. It was a beautiful life of faith and service; and it has only gone to be perfected in the shadow of the Tree of Life.   S. R. R.

REV. GIDEON H. POND.

A SUCCESSFUL LIFE.

Born and brought up in Litchfield county, in a town adjoining Washington, Connecticut, REV. GEORGE BUSHNELL visited that Hill country in his youth, and was deeply impressed with the manifest and pervading religious element in the community. Taken there by a special providence, more than a quarter of a century ago, and enjoying the privilege of a visit in some of the families, it seemed to me that it had been a good place to raise men. This was on the line of the impression made upon me years before that. When I first met, in the Land of the Dakotas, the brothers, SAMUEL W. and GIDEON H POND, they were both over six feet high, and "seemed the children of a king."

In this hill town of Washington, on the 30th of June, 1810, GIDEON HOLLISTER, the younger of the two brothers, was born. His parents were ELNATHAN JUDSON, and SARAH HOLLISTER, POND. Gideon was the fifth child, and so was called by the Dakotas *Hakay*. Of his childhood and youth almost nothing is known to the writer. He had the advantage of a New England common-school education; perhaps nothing more. As he grew very rapidly, and came to the size and strength of man early, he made a full hand in the harvest field at the age of sixteen. To this ambition to be counted a man and do a man's work, when as yet he should have been a boy, he, in after life, ascribed some of his infirmities. This ambition continued with him through life, and occasional over-work at least, undermined a constitution that might, with care and God's blessing, have continued to the end of the century.

He came to the Land of the Dakotas, now Minnesota, in the spring of 1834. The older brother, Samuel, had come out as far as Galena, Illinois, in the summer previous. The pioneer minister of that country of lead was REV. ARATUS KENT, who desired to retain Mr. Pond as an adjutant in his great and constantly enlarging work; but Mr. Pond had heard of the Sioux or Dakotas, for whose souls no one cared, and, having decided to go to them, he sent for his brother Gideon to accompany him.

When they reached Fort Snelling, and had made known their errand to the commanding officer of the post, Maj. Bliss, and to the resident Indian Agent, Maj. Taliaferro, they received the hearty approval and co-operation of both, and the Agent at once recommended them to commence work with the Dakotas of the Lake Calhoun village, where some steps had already been taken in the line of civilization. There, on the margin of the lake, they built their log cabin. Last summer Mr. King's grand Pavilion, so called, was completed on the same spot, which gave occasion for Mr. Gideon H. Pond to tell the story of this first effort in that line:

"Just forty-three years previous to the occurrence above alluded to, on the same beautiful site, was completed a humble edifice, built by the hands of two inexperienced New England boys, just setting out in life-work. The foundation stones of that hut were removed to make place for the present Pavilion, perchance compose a part of it. The old structure was of oak logs, carefully peeled. The peeling was a mistake. Twelve feet by sixteen, and eight feet high, were the dimensions of the edifice. Straight poles from the tamarack grove west of the lake, formed the timbers of the roof, and the roof itself was of the bark of trees which grew on the bank of what is now called 'Bassett's Creek,' fastened with strings of the inner bark of the bass-wood. A partition of small logs divided the house into two rooms, and split logs furnished material for a floor. The ceiling was of slabs from the old government saw-mill, through the kindness of Major Bliss, who was in command of Fort Snelling. The door was made of boards split from a log with an ax, having wooden hinges and fastenings, and was locked by pulling in the latchstring. The single window was the gift of the kind-hearted Maj. Lawrence Taliaferro, United States Indian Agent. The cash cost of the building was one shilling, New York currency, for nails used in and about the door. 'The formal opening' exercises consisted in reading a section from the old book by the name of BIBLE, and prayer to Him who was its acknowledged author. The 'banquet' consisted of mussels from the lake, flour and water. The ground was selected by the Indian chief of the Lake Calhoun band of Dakotas, Man-of-the-sky, by which he showed good taste. The reason he gave for the selection was, that 'from that point the loons would be visible on the lake.'

"The old chief and his pagan people had their homes on the surface of that ground, in the bosom of which now sleep the bodies of deceased Christians from the city of Minneapolis, the Lake Wood cemetery, over which these old eyes have witnessed, dangling in the night breeze, many a Chippewa scalp, in the midst of horrid chants, yells and wails, widely contrasting with the present stillness of that quiet home of those

'Who sleep the years away.'

That hut was the home of the first citizen settlers of Hennepin county, perhaps of Minnesota, the first school-room, the first house for divine worship, and the first mission station among the Dakota Indians."

The departure of Mr. Pond called forth from GEN. HENRY H. SIBLEY so just and beautiful a tribute, that I cannot forbear inserting a portion, from the "Pioneer-Press," of St. Paul:

"When the writer came to this country in 1834, he did not expect to meet a single white man, except those composing the garrison at Fort Snelling, a few government officials attached to the department of Indian affairs, and the traders and voyageurs employed by the great fur company in its business. There was but one house, or rather, log cabin, along the entire distance of nearly 300 miles between Prairie du Chien and St. Peters, now Mendota, and that was at a point below Lake Pepin, near the present town of Wabashaw. What was his surprise, then, to find that his advent had been preceded in the spring of the same year by two young Americans, Samuel W. Pond and Gideon H. Pond, brothers, scarcely out of their teens, who had built for themselves a small hut at the Indian village of Lake Calhoun, and had determined to consecrate their lives to the work of civilizing and Christianizing the wild Sioux. For many long years these devoted men labored in the cause, through manifold difficulties and discouragements, sustained by a faith that the seed sown would make itself manifest in God's good time. The efforts then made to reclaim the savages from their mode of life, the influence of their blameless and religious walk and conversation upon those with whom they were brought in daily contact, and the self-denial and personal sacrifices required at their hands, are, doubtless, treasured up in a higher than human record."

Gen. Sibley mentions an incident belonging to this period of their residence at Lake Calhoun, which never before came to my knowledge:

"Gifted with an uncommonly fine constitution, the subject of this sketch met with an accident in his early days from the effects of which it is questionable if he ever entirely recovered. He broke through the ice at Lake Harriet in the early part of the winter, and as there was no one at hand to afford aid, he only saved his life after a desperate struggle, by continuing to fracture the frozen surface until he reached shallow water, when he succeeded in extricating himself. His long immersion and exhaustive efforts brought on a severe attack of pneumonia, which, for many days, threatened a fatal termination."

My own personal acquaintance with Mr. Pond commenced in the summer of 1837. He was then, and had been for a year previous, at Lac-qui-parle. In September my wife and I joined that station, and the first event occurring after that, which has impressed itself upon my memory, was the marriage of Mr. Pond and Miss Sarah Poage, sister of Mrs. Dr. Williamson. This was the first marriage ceremony I had been called upon to perform; and Mr. Pond signalized it by making a feast, and calling, according to the Savior's injunction, "the poor, the maimed, the halt, and the blind." And there was a plenty of such to be called in that Dakota village. They could not recompense him, but " he shall be recompensed at the resurrection of the just."

Mr. Pond had long been yearning to see what was inside of an Indian. He sometimes said he wanted to be an Indian, if only for a little while, that he might know how an Indian felt, and by what motives he could be moved. When the early spring of 1838 came, and the ducks began to come northward, a half dozen Dakota families started from Lac-qui-parle to hunt and trap on the upper part of the Chippewa River, in the neighborhood of where the town of Benson now is. Mr. Pond went with them and was gone two weeks. It was in the month of April, and the streams were flooded and the water was cold. There should have been enough of game easily obtained to feed the party. But it did not prove so. A cold spell came on, the ducks disappeared, and Mr. Pond and his Indian hunters were reduced to scanty fare, and sometimes they had nothing for a whole day. But Mr. Pond was seeing inside of Indians, and was quite willing to starve a good deal. However, his stay with them, and their hunt for that time as well, was suddenly terminated, by the appearance of the Ojibwa chief, Hole-in-the-Day, and ten men with him. They came to smoke the peace-pipe, they said. They were royally feasted by three of the families, who killed their dogs to feed the strangers, who, in turn, arose in the night and killed the Dakotas. As God would have it, Mr. Pond was not then with those three tents, and so he escaped.

No one had started with more of a determination to master the Dakota language than Gideon H. Pond. And no one of the older missionaries suceeded so well in learning to talk just like a Dakota. Indeed, he must have had a peculiar aptitude for acquiring language; for in these first years of missionary life, he learned to read French and Latin and Greek, so that the second Mrs. Pond writes: "When I came, and for a number of years, he read from the Greek Testament at our family worship in the morning. Afterward he used his Latin Bible, and still later, his French Testament."

In this line of literary work Gen. Sibley's testimony is appreciative. He says:

"Indeed, to them, and to their veteran co-laborers, Rev. T. S. Williamson and Rev. S. R. Riggs, the credit is to be ascribed of having produced this rude and rich Dakota tongue to the learned world in a written and systematic shape, the lexicon prepared by their joint labors forming one of the publications of the Smithsonian Institute at Washington City, which has justly elicited the commendation of experts in philological lore, as a most valuable contribution to that branch of literature."

While Mr. Pond was naturally ambitious, he was also peculiarly sensitive and retiring. When the writer was left with him at Lac-qui-parle, Dr. Williamson having gone to Ohio for the winter, although so much better master of the Dakota than I was at that time, he was unwilling to take more than a secondary part in the Sabbath services. "Dr. Williamson and you are ministers," he would say. And even years afterward, when he and his family had removed to the neighborhood of Fort Snelling, and he and his brother had built at Oak Grove, with the people of their first love, Gideon H. could hardly be persuaded that it was his duty to become a preacher of the gospel. I remember more than one long conversation I had with him on this subject. He seemed to shrink from it as a little child, although he was then thirty-seven years old.

In the spring of 1847, he and Mr. Robert Hopkins were licensed by the Dakota Presbytery, and ordained in the autumn of 1848. We were not disappointed in our men. Mr. Hopkins gave evidence of large adaptation to the missionary work; but in less than three years he heard the call of the Master, and went up through a flood of waters. Mr. Pond, notwithstanding his hesitation in accepting the office, became a most acceptable, and efficient and successful preacher and pastor.

After the treaties of 1851, these lower Sioux were removed to the upper Minnesota. White people came in immediately and took possession of their lands. Mr. Pond elected to remain and labor among the white people. He very soon organized a church which, in a short time, became a working, benevolent church — for some years the *banner* Presbyterian church of Minnesota, in the way of benevolence. When, in 1873, Mr. Pond resigned his pastorate, he wrote in his diary, "I have preached to the people of Bloomington *twenty years.*" He received home mission aid only a few years.

We are very glad to have placed at our disposal so much of the private journal of the late REV. G. H. POND as relates to the wonderful work of God among the Dakotas, in prison at Mankato, Minn., in the winter of 1862-'3. The facts, in the main, have been published before; but the story, as told so simply and graphically by Mr. Pond, may well bear repeating. Mr. Pond arrived at Mankato Saturday, Jan. 31, 1863, and remained until the afternoon of Tuesday, Feb. 3:

"There are over three hundred Indians in prison, the most of whom are in chains. There is a degree of religious interest manifested by them which is incredible. They huddle themselves together every morning and evening in the prison, and read the Scriptures, sing hymns, confess one to another, exhort one another, and pray together. They say that their whole lives have been wicked—that they have adhered to the superstitions of their ancestors until they have reduced themselves to their present state of wretchedness and ruin. They declare that they have left it all, and will leave all forever; that they do and will embrace the religion of Jesus Christ, and adhere to it as long as they live; and that this is their only hope, both in this world and in the next. They say that before they came to this state of mind—this determination—their hearts failed them with fear, but now they have much mental ease and comfort.

"About fifty men of the Lake Calhoun band expressed a wish to be baptized by me, rather than by any one else, on the ground that my brother and myself had been their first and chief instructors in religion. After consultation with Rev. Marcus Hicks, of Mankato, Dr. Williamson and I decided to grant their request, and administer to them the Christian ordinance of baptism. We made the conditions as plain as we could, and we proclaimed there in the prison that we would baptize such as felt ready heartily to comply with the conditions—commanding that none should come forward to receive the rite who did not do it heartily to the God of heaven, whose eye penetrated each of their hearts. All, by a hearty—apparently hearty—response, signified their desire to receive the rite on the conditions offered.

"As soon as preparations could be completed, and we had provided ourselves with a basin of water, they came forward, one by one, as their names were called, and were baptized into the name of the Father, the Son, and the Holy Ghost, while each subject stood with his right hand raised and head bowed, and many of them with the eyes closed, with an appearance of profound reverence. As each one passed from the place where he stood to be baptized, one or the other of us stopped him and addressed to him in a low voice, a few words, such as our knowledge of his previous character and the solemnities of the occasion suggested. The effect of this, in most cases, seemed to very much deepen the solemnity of the ceremony. I varied my words, in this part of the exercises, to suit the case of the person; and when grey-haired medicine men stood, literally trembling before me, as I laid one hand on their heads, the effect on my mind was such that at times my tongue faltered. The words which I used in this part of the service were the following or something nearly like them in substance: 'My brother, this is the mark of God which is placed upon you. You will carry it while you live. It introduces you into the great family of God, who looked down from heaven, not upon your head, but into your heart. This ends your superstition, and from this time you are to call God your father. Remember to honor Him. Be resolved to do His will.' It made me glad to hear them respond heartily, 'Yes, I will.'

"When we were through, and all were again seated, we sung a hymn appropriate to the occasion, in which many of them joined, and then prayed. I then said to them, 'Hitherto I have addressed you as friends, now I call you brothers. For years we have contended together on this subject of religion, now our contentions cease. We have one Father—we are one family. I must now leave you, and probably shall see you no more in this world. While you remain in this prison, you have time to attend to religion. You can do nothing else. Your adherence to the Medicine Sack and the Wotawe has brought you to ruin. Our Lord Jesus Christ can save you. Seek him with all your heart. He looks not on your heads, nor on your lips, but into your bosoms. Brothers, I will make use of a term of brotherly salutation, to which you have been accustomed in your medicine dance, and say to you, "Brothers, I spread my hands over you and bless you."' The hearty answer of three hundred voices made me feel glad.

"The outbreak and events which followed it have, under God, broken into shivers the power of the priests of devils which has hitherto ruled these wretched tribes. They were before bound in the chains and confined in the prison of Paganism, as the prisoners in the prison at Philippi were bound with chains. The outbreak and its attendent consequences have been like the earthquake to shake the foundation of their prison, and every one's bonds have been loosed. Like the jailer, in anxious fear they have cried, 'Sirs, what must we do to be saved?' They have been told to believe on the Lord Jesus Christ, who will still save unto the uttermost all that come unto God by him. They say they repent and forsake their sins—that they believe on him, that they trust in him, and will obey him. Therefore they have been baptized into the name of the Father, and of the Son, and of the Holy Ghost, THREE HUNDRED IN A DAY."

In the spring of 1853, Mrs. Sarah Poage Pond departed, after a lingering illness of eighteen months, and left a "blessed memory." There were *seven* children by this marriage, all of which are living and have families of their own, but *George*, who died while in the Lane Theological Seminary. In the summer of 1854, Mr. Pond was married to his second wife, Mrs. Agnes C. J. Hopkins, widow of Rev. Robert Hopkins. The second Mrs. Pond brought her *three* children, making the united family of children at that time *ten*. *Six* have been added since. And there are *twenty-two grandchildren*, *six* of whom are members of the Church of Christ, together with all the children and their companions. Is not that a successful life? Counting the widowed mother and those who have come into the family by marriage, there are, I understand, just *fifty* who mourn the departure of the Patriarch father. A little more than two score years ago, he was *one*; and now behold a MULTITUDE!

Mary Frances Hopkins, who came into the family when a girl, and afterward married Edward R. Pond, the son, writes thus: "To me he was as near an own father as it is possible for one to be, who is so by adoption, and I shall always be glad I was allowed to call him *father*."

The members of the Synod of Minnesota will remember, with great pleasure, Mr. Pond's presence with them, at their last meeting at St. Paul, in the middle of October. For some years past, he has frequently been unable to be present. This time he seemed to be more vigorous than usual, and greatly entertained the Synod and people of St. Paul with his terse and graphic presentation of some of the Lord's workings in behalf of the Dakotas.

During the meeting I was quartered with Mrs. Gov. Ramsey. On Saturday I was charged with a message to Mr. Pond, inviting him to come and spend the night at the Governor's. We passed a profitable evening together, and he and I talked long of the way in which the Lord had led us—of the great prosperity he had given us in our families and in our work. Neither of us thought, probably, that that would be our last talk this side the golden city. The next day, Sabbath, he preached in the morning, for Rev. D. R. Breed, in the House of Hope, which, probably, was *his last sermon*. In the evening he was with us in the Opera House, at a meeting in the interest of Home and Foreign Missions.

"His health gradually failed," Mrs. Pond writes, "from the time of his return from Synod, though he did not call himself sick until the 11th of January, and he died on Sabbath, the 20th, about noon." She adds: "His interest in the Indians, for whom he labored so long, was very deep; and he always spoke of them with loving tenderness, and often with tears. One of the last things he did was to look over his old Dakota hymns, revised by J. P. W. and A. L. R., and sent to him for his consent to the proposed alterations."

"His *simple faith* in the Lord Jesus caused him all the time to live a life of self-denial, that he might do more to spread the knowledge of Jesus' love to those who knew it not." The love of Christ constrained him, and was his ruling passion.

Of his last days the daughter says:

"He really *died of consumption*. The nine days he was confined to bed he suffered much; but his mind was mostly clear, and he was very glad to go. I think the summons was no more sudden to him than to Elijah. He was to the last loving and trustful, brave and patient. To his brother Samuel, as he came to his sick bed, he said: 'So we go to see each other die.' Sometime before, he had visited Samuel when he did not expect to recover. 'My struggles are over. The Lord has taken care of me, and he will take care of the rest of you. My hope is in the Lord,' he said.

"Toward the last it was hard for him to converse, and he bade us no formal farewell. But the words, as we noted them down, were words of cheer and comfort: 'You have nothing to fear, for the present or the future.' And so was given to him the victory over death, through faith in Jesus."

Is that dying? He sleeps with his fathers. He has gone to see the King in His beauty, in a land not very far off.

As loving hands ministered to him in his sickness, loving hearts mourned at his death. On the Wednesday following, he was buried. A half a dozen brothers in the ministry were present at his funeral, and, fittingly, Mr. Breed, of the House of Hope, preached the sermon.

This is success. S. R. R.

SOLOMON.

In the summer of 1874, Rev. John P. Williamson made a tour up the Missouri River as far as Fort Peck. His judgment was, that there was no opening at that place for the establishment of a new mission, but that something might possibly be done by native Dakotas. In the mean time we had heard from the regions farther north than Fort Peck, where some of our church members had gone after the outbreak of 1862. Somewhere up in Manitoba, near Fort Ellice, was HENOK APPEARING CLOUD, with his relatives. His mother, Mazaskawin—*Silver-woman*—was a member of the Hazelwood church, and his father, Wamde-okeya—*Eagle Help*,—had been my old helper in Dakota translations. These were all near relatives of SOLOMON TOONKANSHAECHEYE, one of our native pastors.

Dr. Williamson, by correspondence with the Presbyterian Board, obtained an appropriation of several hundred dollars to send a native missionary to these Dakotas in Canada. Solomon gladly accepted the undertaking, and in the month of June, 1875, started for Manitoba, with SAMUEL HOPKINS for a companion.

They were received with a great deal of joy by their friends, who entreated them to stay, or come back again if they left. But provisions were very scarce, and hard to be obtained; and hence they determined to return to the Sisseton Agency before winter. While in Manitoba they had taught and preached the gospel, and baptized and received several persons to the fellowship of the church. Solomon wrote before he returned: "Indeed, there is no food; they have laid up nothing at all; so that when winter comes, where they will obtain food, and how they will live, no one knows. But I have already found something of what I have been seeking, and very reluctantly I turn away from the work."

Solomon and Samuel returned to Sisseton, but their visit had created a larger desire for education and the privileges of the gospel. In the March following, Henok Appearing Cloud wrote that he had taught school during the winter, and conducted religious meetings, as he "wanted the Word of God to grow." In much simplicity, he adds: "Although I am poor and often starving, I keep my heart just as though I were rich. When I read again in the Sacred Book, what Jesus the Lord has promised us, my heart is glad. I am thinking if a minister will only come this summer and stay with us a little while, our hearts will rejoice. If he comes to stay with us a long time, we will rejoice more. But as we are so often in a starving condition, I know it will be hard for any one to come."

Rev. John Black, of Keldonan Manse, near Winnipeg, heard o this visit of Solomon to Manitoba, and of the desire of those Dakotas to have a missionary. He at once became deeply interested in the movement, and wrote to Dr. Williamson at Saint Peter, proposing that the Presbyterian Missionary Society of Canada should take upon themselves the charge of supporting Solomon, as a missionary among the Dakotas of the Dominion. But when the matter was brought before the Missionary Committee, they decided that the condition of their finances would not allow them to add to their burdens at that time. It was not, however, given up, and a year later the arrangement was consummated. In the "Word Carrier" for December, 1877, appeared this editorial:

"The most important event occurring in our missionary work during the month of October, is the departure of REV. SOLOMON TOONKANSHAECHEYE, with his family, for Fort Ellice, in the Dominion of Canada. This has been under advisement by the Presbyterian Foreign Missionary Society of Canada for two years past. REV. JOHN BLACK, of Keldonan Manse, Manitoba, has been working for it. A year ago the funds of the society would not admit of enlargement in their operations. This year their way has b en made clear, and the invitation has come to Solomon to be their missionary among the Dakotas on the Assinaboine River. They pay his expenses of removal, and promise him $600 salary.

"He has gone. Agent HOOPER, of Sisseton Agency, furnished him with the necessary pass, and essentially aided him in his outfit, and so we sent him off on the 10th day of October, invoking God's blessing upon him and his by the way, a d abundant success for him in his prospective work. From the commencement of negotiations in regard to this matter, it has been of special interest to Dr. T. S. Williamson, of St Peter. He has conducted the correspondence with Mr. Black. And now, while the good doctor was lying nigh unto death, as he supposed, the arrangement has gone into effect. If this prove to be his last work on earth (may the good Lord cause otherwise), it will be a matter of joy on his part that thus the gospel is carried to regions beyond, by so good and trustworthy a man as we have found Solomon to be, all through these years."

Thus was the work commenced. Dr. Williamson did not pass from us then, but lived nearly two years longer, and was cheered by the news of progress in this far-off land. This being among our first efforts to do evangelistic work by sending away our native ministers, our hearts were much bound up in it. The church of Long Hollow was reluctant to give up their pastor, and to me it was giving up one whom I had learned to trust, and in some measure, to depend upon, among my native pastors. But it was evidently God's call, and He has already justified himself, even in our eyes. Solomon found a people prepared of the Lord, and in the summer of 1878, he reports a church organized, with *thirteen members*, which they named *Paha-cho-kam-ya*—MIDDLE HILL—of which Henok was elected elder.

In the next winter Solomon and Henok made a missionary tour of some weeks, of which we have the following report. The letter is dated "Feb. 22, 1879, at *Middle Hill*, near Fort Ellice, Northwest Territory:"

"This winter it seemed proper that I should visit the Dakotas living in the extreme settlements, to proclaim to them the Word of God. I first asked counsel of God, and prayed that he would even now have mercy on the people of these end villages, and send his Holy Spirit to cause them to listen to his Word. Then I sent word to the people that I was coming.

"Then I started with *Mr. Enoch*, my elder. The first night we came to three teepees of our own people at Large Lake, and held a meeting with them. The next morning we started, and slept four nights. On the fifth day we came to a large encampment on Elm River. There were a great number of tents which we visited and prayed with them, being well received. But as I came to where there were two men, and prayed with them, I told them about him whose name was Jesus—that he was the Helper Man, because he was the Son of God. That he came to earth, made a sacrifice of himself and died, that he might reconcile all men to God. That he made himself alive again, that although men have destroyed themselves before God, whosoever knows the meaning of the name of Jesus, and fears for his own soul, and prays, he shall find mercy, and be brought near to God. That is the Name. And he is the Savior of men, and so will be your Savior also, I said.

"Then one of them in a frightened way answered me: 'I supposed you were a Dakota, of those who live in cabins. It is not proper that you should say these things. As for me, I do not want them. Those who wish, may follow in that way; but I will not. You who hold such things should stay at home. What do you come here for?'

"WALKING-NEST then said: 'You are Cloudman's son, I suppose, and so you are my cousin. Cousin, when we first came to this country there was a white minister who talked to us and said: "Your hands are full of blood, therefore when your hands become white, we will teach you." So he said, and when you brought a book from the South, while they were looking at it, blood dropped from above upon it; and behold, as the white minister said, I conclude we are not yet good. Therefore, my cousin, I am not pleased with your coming,' he said.

"But there were only two men who talked in this way. We eft them and visited every house in the camp. Many may have elt as those men did, but did not say it openly. The men said they were glad, and welcomed us into their tents.

"The next day I came into a sick man's tent whose name was *Hepan*, lying near to death. I talked with him, and prayed to God for him. Then he told me how he longed to hear from his friends down South, and mentioned over a half a dozen names of his relatives. A woman also, who was present, said, 'I want to know if my friends are yet living.'

"Then we continued our visiting from house to house. Sometimes we found only children in the tent; sometimes there were men and women, and I prayed with them and told them a word of Jesus. So we came to the teepees in the Valley. Then I met Iron Buffalo. There we spent the Sabbath and held meeting, having twenty-three persons present. A chief man, whose name is War-club-maker, called them together.

"Our meetings there being finished, we departed and came to the Wahpaton village. They were making four sacred feasts. We did not go into them. But visiting other houses, we passed on about five miles, when night came upon us. Still we went on to the end of the settlement, where we held a meeting. The teepee was small, but there I found a sick man who listened to the word. This was *Chaskay*, the son of *Taoyatedoota*. He said he was going to die, and from what source he should hear any word of prayer, or any comforting word of God, was not manifest. But now he had heard these things, and was very glad, he said. This way was the best upon earth, and he believed in it now. So while we remained there, he wanted us to pray with and for him, he said.

"We spent one day there, and the second day we started home, and came to Hunka's tent, and so proceeded homeward. When we had reached the other end of the settlement, we learned that the white ministers were to hold a meeting of Presbytery. They sent word to us to come, and so in the night, with my Hoonkayape, Mr. Enoch, I went back. They asked us to give an account of our missionary journey among the Dakotas. And so we told them where we had been and what we had done. Also, we gave an account of things at Middle Hill, where we live. When we had finished, they all clapped their hands. Then they said they wanted to hear us sing a hymn of praise to God in Dakota. We sang 'Wakantanka Towaste,' and at the close they clapped their hands again.

"Then two men arose, one after the other. The first said: 'I have not expected to see such things so soon among the Dakotas. But now I see great things which I like very much.' The other man spoke in the same way.

"Men and women had come together in their Prayer House, and so there was a large assembly.

"Then the minister of that church arose and said: 'White people, who have grown up hearing of this way of salvation, are expected to believe in it, and I have been accustomed to rejoice in the multiplication of the Christian Church; but I rejoice more over this work among the Dakotas.'"

Both of these men came home to watch and wait by the sick bed of dear children. NANCY MAZA-CHANKOO-WIN—*Iron Road Woman*—the daughter of Henok, died April 28, 1879. She was thirteen years old, read the Dakota Bible well, and was quite a singer in the prayer assemblies. They say: "We all thought a great deal of her; but now she, too, has gone up to sing in the House of Jesus, because she was called."

From Middle Hill, near Fort Ellice in Manitoba, comes a letter written on May 20th, by our friend Solomon. He reports *seven* members added by profession of faith to his church in April, and ten children baptized. There, as here, the season has been a s‘ckly one, and many deaths have occurred. For three months he has had sickness in his own family. His story is pathetic· "Now," he says, "my son Abraham is dead. Seven years ago, at Long Hollow, in the country of the Coteau des Prairies, he was born on January 12, 1872. And on the 23d of June following, at a communion season at Good Will church, he was baptized. When Mr. Riggs poured the water on him, he was called ABRAHAM. And then in the country of the north, from Middle Hill,

May 9, 1879, on that day, his soul was carried home to the House of Jesus.

"Five months after he was born, I wanted to have him baptized. I always remember the thought I had about it. Soon after a child is born it is proper to have it baptized. I believed that baptism alone was not to be trusted in, and when one is baptized now it is finished, is not thinkable. But in Luke 18:16, our Lord Jesus says: 'Suffer the little children to come unto me;' and so taking them to Jesus is good, since his heart is set on permitting them to come. Therefore I wanted this my son to go to Jesus.

"And so from the time he could hear me speak, I have endeavored to train him up in all gentleness and obedience, in truth and in peace. Now for two years in this country he has been my little helper. When some could not say their letters, he taught them. He also taught them to pray. And when any were told to repeat the commandments, and were ashamed to do so, he repeated them first, for he remembered them all. Hence, I was very much attached to him. But this last winter he was taken sick, and from the first it seemed that he would not get well. But while he lived it was possible to help him, and so we did to the extent of our ability. He failed gradually. He was a long time sick. But he was not afraid to die. He often prayed. When he was dying, but quite conscious of everything that took place, then he prayed, and we listened. He repeated the prayer of the Lord Jesus audibly to the end. That was the last voice we heard from him. Perhaps when our time comes, and they come for us to climb up to the Hill of the Mountain of Jehovah, then we think we shall hear his new voice. Therefore, although we are sad, we do not cry immoderately."

That was a beautiful child life, and a beautiful child death. Who shall say there are not now Dakota children in heaven? To have been the means, under God, of opening in this desert such a well of faith and salvation, is quite a sufficient reward for a lifetime of work.

S. R. R.

DR. T. S. WILLIAMSON.

THE FATHER of the Dakota Mission has gone. THOMAS SMITH WILLIAMSON died at his residence in St. Peter, Minnesota, on Tuesday, the 24th of June, 1879, in the *eightieth* year of his life. My own acquaintance with this life-long friend and companion in work commenced when I was yet a boy, just fifty years ago in July. We were new-comers in the town of Ripley, Ohio, where Dr. Williamson was then a practicing physician of some five years' standing. My mother was taken sick and died. In her sick chamber our acquaintance commenced, which has continued unbroken for half a century.

THE SILVER WEDDING of the Dakota Mission was celebrated at Hazelwood, in the summer of 1860. Dr. Williamson himself furnished a sketch of his life and ancestry for that occasion, which has never been published. From this document, as well as from articles written by his son, PROF. ANDREW WOODS WILLIAMSON, and published in the "St. Peter Tribune" and the "Herald and Presbyter," much of this life-sketch will be taken.

THOMAS SMITH WILLIAMSON, M. D., was the son of REV. WILLIAM WILLIAMSON and MARY SMITH, and was born in Union District, South Carolina, in March, 1800.

WILLIAM WILLIAMSON commenced classical studies when quite young; but the school he attended was broken up by the appointment of the teacher as an officer in the revolutionary army When about sixteen years of age, while on a visit to an uncle's on the head waters of the Kanawha, in Virginia, several families in the neighborhood were taken captive by the Indians, and he joined a company of volunteers which was raised to go in pursuit. After more than a week's chase they were entirely successful, and lost only one of their own number.

When not yet eighteen years old, he was drafted into the North Carolina militia, and accompanied Gates in his unfortunate expedition through the Carolinas. After the war was over and the family had removed to South Carolina, William resumed his studies and was graduated at Hampton Sidney College—studied theology and was ordained pastor of Fair Forest church in April, 1793.

The grandfather of Thomas Smith Williamson, was THOMAS WILLIAMSON, and his grandmother's maiden name was ANN NEWTON, a distant relative of Sir Isaac, and Rev. John Newton. They were both raised in Pennsylvania, but removed first to Virginia and then to the Carolinas, where they became the owners of slaves, the most of whom were purchased at their own request to keep them from falling into the hands of hard masters.

Thus Rev. William Williamson was born into the condition of slaveholder. By both his first, and second marriage also, he became the owner of others, which by the laws of South Carolina would have been the property of his children. For the purpose of giving them their liberty he removed in 1805 from South Carolina to Adams county, Ohio. Before her marriage, Mary Smith had taught a number of the young negroes to read. And of their descendants quite a number are now in Ohio. It should be remembered that the Smiths and Williamsons of the eighteenth century thought it right, under the circumstances in which they were, *to buy and hold slaves, but not right to sell them.* THEY NEVER SOLD ANY.

THOMAS SMITH WILLIAMSON inherited from his father a love for the study of God's Word, and a practical sympathy for the down-trodden and oppressed, which were ever the distinguishing characteristics of his life. He was also blessed with a godly mother, and with five earnest-working Christian sisters, four of whom were older than himself. He was converted during his stay at Jefferson College, Cannonsburg, Pa., where he graduated in 1820. Soon after, he began reading medicine with his brother-in-law, Dr. William Wilson, of West Union, Ohio, and, after a very full course of reading, considerable practical experience, and one course of lectures at Cincinnati, Ohio, completed his medical education at Yale, where he graduated in medicine in 1824. He settled at Ripley, Ohio, where he soon acquired an extensive practice, and, April 10, 1827, was united in marriage with Margaret Poage, daughter of Col. James Poage, proprietor of the town. Perhaps no man was ever more blessed with a helpmeet more adapted to his wants than this lovely, quiet, systematic, cheerful, Christian wife, who for forty-five years of perfect harmony encouraged him in his labors.

They thought themselves happily settled for life in their pleasant home, but God had better things in store for them. His Spirit began whispering in their ears the Macedonian cry. At first they excused themselves on account of their little ones. They felt they could not take them among the Indians; that they owed a duty to them. They hesitated. God removed this obstacle in his own way—by taking the little ones home to himself. As this was a great trial, so was it a great blessing to these parents. This was one of God's means of so strengthening their faith that, having once decided to go, neither of them ever after for one moment regretted the decision, doubted that they were called of God to this work, or feared that their life-work would prove a failure.

In the spring of 1833, Dr. Williamson placed himself under the care of the Chillicothe Presbytery, and commenced the study of theology. In August of that year he removed with his family to Walnut Hills, and connected himself with Lane Seminary. In April, 1834, in the First Presbyterian Church of R d Oak, he was licensed to preach by the Chillicothe Presbytery.

Previous to his licensure, he had received from the American Board an appointment to proceed on an exploring tour among the Indians of the Upper Mississippi, with special reference to the Sacs and Foxes, but to collect what information he could in regard to the Sioux, Winnebagoes, and other Indians. Starting on this tour about the last of April, he went as far as Fort Snelling, and returned to Ohio in August. At Rock Island he met with some of the Sacs and Foxes, and at Prairie du Chien he first saw Dakotas, among others, Mr. Joseph Renv'lle, of Lac-qu'-parle. On the 18th of September he was ordained as a missionary by the Chillicothe Presbytery, in Union Church, Ross county, Ohio.

A few months afterward he received his appointment as a missionary of the A. B. C. F. M., to the Dakotas; and on the first day of April, 1835, Dr. Williamson, with his wife and one child, accompanied by Miss Sarah Poage, Mrs. Williamson's sister, who afterward became Mrs. Gideon H. Pond, and Alexander G. Huggins and family, left Ripley, Ohio, and on the 16 h of May they arrived at Fort Snelling. At this time the only white people in Minnesota, then a part of the Northwest Territory, were those connected with the military post at Fort Snelling, the only postoffice within the present limits of the State; those connected with the fur trade, except Hon. H. H. Sibley, were chiefly Canadian French, ignorant of the Engli h language; and Messrs. Gideon H. and Samuel W. Pond, who came on their own account as lay teachers of Christ to the Indians in 1834.

While stopping there for a few weeks, Dr. Williamson presided at the organization, on the 12th of June, of the First Presbyterian Church—the first Christian church organized within the present limits of Minnesota. This was within the garrison at Fort Snelling, and consisted of twenty-two members, chiefly the result of the labors of Maj. Loomis among the soldiers.

Having concluded to accompany Mr. Joseph Renville, Dr. Williamson's party embarked on the Fur Company's Mackinaw boat on the 22d of June; reached Traverse des Sioux on the 30th, where they took wagons and arrived at Lac-qui-parle on the 9th of July. There on the north side of the Minnesota River, and in sight of the "Lake that speaks," they established themselves as teachers of the religion of Jesus.

Of the "Life and Labors" pressed into the next forty-four years, only the most meager outline can be given in this article. It is now almost two round centuries since Hennepin and DuLuth met in the camps and villages of the Sioux on the upper Mississippi. Then, as since, they were recognized as the largest and most warlike tribe of Indians on the continent. Until Dr. Williamson and his associates went among them, there does not appear to have been any effort made to civilize and Christianize them. With the exception of a few hundred words gathered by army officers and others, the Dakota language was unwritten. This was to be learned—*mastered*, which was found to be no small undertaking, especially to one who had attained the age of thirty-five years. While men of less energy and pluck would have knocked off, or been content to work as best they could through an interpreter, Dr. Williamson persevered, and in less than two years was preaching Christ to them in the language in which they were born. He never spoke it easily, nor just like an Indian, but he was readily understood by those who were accustomed to hear him.

It was by a divine guidance that the station at Lac-qui-parle was commenced. The Indians there were very poor in this world's goods, not more than a half-dozen horses being owned in a village of 400 people. They were far in the interior, and received no annuities from the government. Thus they were in a condition to be helped in many ways by the mission. Under its influence and by its help, their corn-patches were enlarged and their agriculture improved. Dr. Williamson also found abundant opportunities to practice medicine among them. Not that they gave up their pow-wows and conjuring; but many families were found quite willing that the white Pay-zhe-hoo-ta-we-chash-ta (Grass-root man) should try his skill with the rest. For more than a quarter of a century his medical aid went hand in hand with the preaching of the gospel. By the helpfulness of the mission in various ways, a certain amount of confidence was secured. And through the influence of Mr. Renville, a few men, but especially the women, gathered to hear the good news of salvation.

Here they were rejoiced to see the word taking effect early. In less than a year after their arrival, Dr. Williamson organized a native church, which, in the autumn of 1837, when I joined the mission force at Lac-qui-parle, counted seven Dakotas. Five years after the number received from the beginning had been forty-nine. This was a very successful commencement.

But in the meantime the war-prophets and the so-called medicine men were becoming suspicious of the new religion. They began to understand that the religion of Christ antagonized their own ancestral faith, and so they organized opposition. The children were forbidden to attend the mission school; Dakota soldiers were stationed along the paths, and the women's blankets were cut up when they attempted to go to church. Year after year the mission cattle were killed and eaten. At one time, Dr. Williamson was under the necessity of hitching up milch cows to haul his wood—the only animals left him.

These were dark, discouraging years—very trying to the native church members, as well as to the missionaries. As I look back upon them I can but admire the indomitable courage and perseverance of Dr. Williamson. My own heart would, I think, have sometimes failed me, if it had not been for the "hold on and hold-out unto the end" of my earthly friend.

As Mr. Renville could only interpret between the Dakotas and French, Dr. Williamson applied himself to learning the latter language. Through this a beginning was made in the translation of the Scriptures into the Dakota. Late in the fall of 1839 the Gospel of Mark and some other small portions were ready to be printed, and Dr. Williamson went with his family to Ohio, where he spent the winter. The next printing of portions of the Bible was done in 1842–'3, when Dr. Williamson had completed a translation of the book of Genesis. We had now commenced to translate from the Hebrew and Greek. This was continued through all the years of his missionary life. So far as I can remember there was no arrangement of work between the Doctor and myself, but while I commenced the New Testament, and, having completed that, turned to the Psalms, and, having finished to the end of Malachi, made some steps backward through Job, Esther, Nehemiah and Ezra, he, commencing with Genesis, closed his work, in the last months of his life, with Second Chronicles, having taken in also the book of Proverbs.

Before leaving the subject of Bible translation, let me bear testimony to the uniform kindness and courtesy which Dr. Williamson extended to me, through all this work of more than forty years. It could hardly be said of either of us that we were very yielding. The Doctor was a man of positive opinions, and there were abundant opportunities in prosecuting our joint work for differences of judgment. But while we freely criticised, each the other's work, we freely yielded to each other the right of ultimate decision.

In the autumn of 1846, Dr. Williamson received an invitation, through the agent at Ft. Snelling, to establish a mission at Little Crow's Village, a few miles below where St. Paul has grown up, and he at once accepted it, gathering from it that the Lord had a work for him to do there. And indeed he had. During the five or six years he remained there, a small Dakota church was gathered, and an opportunity was afforded him to exert a positive Christian influence on the white people then gathering into the capital of Minnesota. Dr. Williamson preached the first sermon there.

When, after the treaties of 1851, the Indians of the Mississippi were removed, he removed with them—or rather, went before them—and commenced his last station at Pay-zhe-hoo-ta-zee, Yellow Medicine. There he and his family had further opportunities "to glory in tribulations." The first winter was one of unusual severity, and they came near starving. But here the Lord blessed them, and permitted them to see a native church grow up, as well as at Hazelwood, the other mission station near by. It was during the next ten years that the seeds of civilization and Christianity took root, and grew into a fruitage, which, in some good manner, bore up under the storm of the outbreak in 1862, and resulted in a great harvest afterward.

Twenty-seven years of labor among the Dakotas were past The results had been encouraging—gratifying. Dr. Williamson's oldest son, Rev. John P. Williamson, born into the missionary kingdom, had recently come from Lane Seminary, and joined our missionary forces. But suddenly our work seemed to be dashed in pieces. The whirlwind of the outbreak swept over our mission. Our houses and churches were burned with fire. The members of our native churches—where were they? Would there ever be a gathering again? But nothing could discourage Dr. Williamson, for he trusted not in an arm of flesh, but in the all-powerful arm of God. He found that he at least had the consolation of knowing that all the Christian Indians had continued, at the risk of their own lives, steadfast friends of the whites, that they had succeeded in saving more than their own number of white people, and that those of them who were unjustly imprisoned spent much of the time in laboring for the conversion of the heathen imprisoned with them.

It required just such a political and moral revolution as this to break the bonds of heathenism, in which these Dakotas were held. It seems also to have required the manifest endurance of privations, and the unselfish devotion of Dr. Williamson and others, to them in this time of trouble, to fully satisfy their suspicious hearts, that we did not seek *theirs*, but *them*. The winter of 1862-'3, Dr. Williamson, having located his family at St. Peter, usually walked up every Saturday to Mankato, to preach the gospel to the 400 men in prison. "That" said a young man, "satisfied us that you were really our friends." Sometimes it seems strange that it required so much to convince them! History scarcely furnishes a more remarkable instance of divine power on human hearts than was witnessed in that prison. For a particular account of this the reader is referred to the Monograph on Rev. G. H. Pond.

Ever since the outbreak, Dr. Williamson has made a home for his family in the town of St. Peter and its vicinity. For two years of the three in which the condemned Dakotas were imprisoned at Davenport, Iowa, he gave his time and strength chiefly to ministering to their spiritual needs. Education never progressed so rapidly among them as during these years. They almost all learned to read and write their own language; and spent much of their time in singing hymns of praise, in prayer and in reading the Bible. They were enrolled in classes, and each class placed under the special teaching of an elder. This gave them something like a Methodist organization, but it was found essential to a proper watch and care. This experience in the prison and elsewhere, made it more and more manifest that to carry forward the work of evangelization among this people, we must make large use of our native talent.

The original Dakota Presbytery was organized at Lac-qui-parle in the first days of October, 1844. Dr. Williamson and myself brought our letters from the Presbytery of Ripley, Ohio, and Samuel W. Pond brought his from an Association in Connecticut. The bounds of this Presbytery were not accurately defined, and so for years it absorbed all the ministers of the gospel of the Presbyterian and Congregational orders who came into the Minnesota country. By and by the Presbyteries of Saint Paul and Minnesota were organized; but the Dakota Presbytery still covered the country of the Minnesota River.

At a meeting of this Presbytery at Mankato in the spring of 1865, when our first Dakota preacher, Rev. John B. Renville, was licensed, an incident took place which illustrates the meekness and magnanimity of Dr. Williamson's character. On its own adjournment the Presbytery had convened and was opened with a sermon by Dr. Williamson, in the evening, in the Presbyterian church. He took occasion to present the subject of our duties to the down-trodden races, the African and the Indian. Doubtless some who heard the discourse did not approve of it. But no exceptions would have been taken if the Jewett family, out a few miles from the town, had not been killed that night by a Sioux war-party. Men were so unreasonable as to claim that the preaching and the preacher had some kind of casual relation with the killing. The next day, Mankato was in a ferment. An indignation meeting was held, and a committee of citizens was sent to the Presbyterian church, to require Dr. Williamson to leave their town. Some of the members of the Presbytery were indignant at this demand; but the good doctor chose to retire to his home at St. Peter, assuring the excited and unreasonable men of Mankato, that he could have had no knowledge of the presence of the war-party, and certainly had no sympathy with their wicked work.

In years after this, I traveled hundreds of miles, often alone with Dr. Williamson, and while we conversed freely of all our experiences, and of the way God had led us, I do not remember that I ever heard him refer to this ill treatment of the people of Mankato. Like his Master, he had learned obedience by the things he suffered.

Never brilliant, he was yet, by his capacity for long-continued, severe exertion, and by systematic, persevering industry, enabled to accomplish an almost incredible amount of labor. His life was a grand one, made so by his indomitable perseverance in the line of lifting up the poor and those who had no helper.

From the beginning he had an unshaken faith in his work. He fully believed in the ability of the Indians to become civilized and Christianized. He had an equally strong and abiding faith in the power of the gospel to elevate and save even them. Then add to these his personal conviction that God had, by special providences, called him to this work, and we have a three-fold cord of faith that was not easily broken.

No one who knew him ever doubted that Dr. Williamson was a true friend of the Red Man. And he succeeded wonderfully in making this impression upon the Indians themselves. They recognized, and, of late years, often spoke of his life-long service for them. With a class of white men, this was the head and front of his offending, that, in their judgment, he could see only one side —that he was always the apologist of the Indians—that in the massacres of the border in 1862, when others believed and asserted that a thousand or fifteen hundred whites were killed, Dr. Williamson could only count three or four hundred. He was honest in his beliefs and honest in his apologies. He felt that necessity was laid upon him to "open his mouth for the dumb." They could not defend themselves, and they have had very few defenders among white people..

In the summer of 1866, after the release of the Dakota prisoners at Davenport, Dr. Williamson and I took with us Rev. John B. Renville, and journeyed up through Minnesota, and across Dakota, to the Missouri River, and into the eastern corner of Nebraska. On our way we spent some time at the Head of the Coteau, preaching and administering the ordinances of the gospel to our old church members, and gathering in a multitude of new converts, ordaining elders over them, and licensing two of the best qualified to preach the gospel. When we reached the Niobrara, we found the Christians of the prison at Davenport and the Christians of the camp at Crow Creek now united; and they desired to be consolidated into one church, of more than 400 members. We helped them to select their religious teachers, which they did from the men who had been in prison. So mightily had the Word of God prevailed among them, that almost the entire adult community professed to be Christians. Rev. John P. Williamson was there in charge of the work.

For four successive summers, it was our privilege to travel together in this work of visiting and reconstructing these Dakota Christian communities. We also extended our visits to the villages of the wild Teeton Sioux along the Missouri River. Dr. Williamson claimed that Indians must be more honest than white people; for he always took with him an old trunk without lock or key, and in all these journeys he did not lose from a thread to a shoe-string.

For thirty-six years the Doctor was a missionary of the American Board. But after the union of the Assemblies, and the transfer of the funds contributed by the New School supporters of that Board to the Presbyterian Board of Foreign Missions, the question of a change of our relations was thoughtfully considered and fully discussed. He was too strong a Presbyterian not to have decided convictions on that subject. But there were, as we considered it, substantial reasons why we could not go over as an entire mission. And so we agreed to divide, Dr. Williamson and his son, Rev. John P. Williamson, transferring themselves to the Presbyterian Board, while my boys and myself remained as we were. The division made no disturbance in our mutual confidence, and no change in the methods of our common work. Rather have the bonds of our union been drawn more closely together, during the past eight years, by an annual Conference of all our Dakota pastors and elders and Sabbath-school workers. This has gathered and again distributed the enthusiasm of the churches; and has become the director of the native missionary forces. With one exception, Dr. Williamson was able to attend all these annual convocations, and added very much to their interest.

While the Synod of Minnesota was holding its sessions in St. Paul, in October, 1877, the good Doctor was lying at the point of death, as was supposed, with pneumonia. Farewell words passed between him and the Synod. But his work was not then done, and the Lord raised him up to complete it. At the next meeting of the Synod, he presented a discourse on Rev. G. H. Pond; and during the winter following, he finished his part of the Dakota Bible. Then his work appeared to be done, and he declined almost from that day onward.

On my way up to the land of the Dakotas, in the middle of May, 1879, I stopped over a day with my old friend. He was very feeble, but still able to walk out, and to sit up a good part of the day. We talked of many things. He then expressed the hope, that as the warm weather came on he might rally, as he had done in former years. But the undertone was, that as the great work of giving the Bible to the Dakotas in their own language was completed, there was not much left for him to do here. He remarked that, during the last forty-four years, he had built several houses, all of which had either gone to pieces, or were looking old, and would not remain long after he was gone. But the building up of human souls that he had been permitted to work for, and which, by the grace of God, he had seen coming up into a new life, through the influence of the Word and the power of the Holy Ghost, he confidently believed would *remain*.

When I spoke of the near prospect of his dissolution to his

Dakota friends, there arose in all the churches a *great prayer cry* for his recovery. This was reported to him, and he sent back this message, by the hand of his son Andrew; "Tell the Indians that Father thanks them very much for their prayers, and hopes they will be blessed both to his good and theirs. But he does not wish them to pray that his life here may be prolonged, for he longs to depart and be with Christ." And the testimony of Rev. G. F. McAfee, pastor of the Presbyterian church in St. Peter, who often visited and prayed with him in his last days, is to the same effect: "He absolutely forbade me to pray that he might recover, but that he might depart in peace."

And so his longing was answered. He died on Tuesday, June 24, 1879, in the morning watch.

He had no ecstacies, but he looked into the future world with a firm and abiding faith in Him, whom not having seen he loved. Of his last days, John P. Williamson writes thus:

"He seemed to be tired out in body and mind, with as much disinclination to talk as to move, and apparently as much from the labor of collecting his mind, as the difficulty of articulation. I think he talked very little from the time I was here going home from General Assembly (June 1st) till his death, and for some time was perhaps unconscious.

"You may know that father had a special distaste for what are called death-bed experiences. Still we thought that perhaps, at the last, when the bodily pains ceased, there might be a little lingering sunshine from the inner man, but such was not the case; and perhaps it was most fitting that he should die as he had lived, with no exalted feelings or bright imagery of the future, but a stern faith which gives hope and peace in the deepest waters."

He lived to see among the Dakotas ten native ordained Presbyterian ministers, and about 800 church members, beside a large number of Episcopalians, a success probably much beyond his early anticipations.

On the farther shore he has joined the multitude that have gone before. Of his own family there are the three who went up in infancy. Next, Smith Burgess, a manly Christian boy, was taken away very suddenly. Then Lizzie Hunter went in the prime of womanhood. The mother followed, a woman of quiet and beautiful life. And then the sainted Nannie went up to put on white robes. Besides these of his family, a multitude of Da-

"Grandmother Huggins was a sister of Rev. James Gilliland, of Red Oak, Ohio. She was a very earnest Christian, and often prayed that her descendants, to the latest generation, might be honest, humble followers of Jesus."

"Eliza was converted, and united with the church in Felicity, Ohio, under the pastorate of Rev. Smith Poage. She was, I think, about twelve years of age.

She was a most loving daughter, sister, and friend, because she had given herself unreservedly to him who yearns to be more than friend, mother or brother to us all. When heavy bereavements came upon the family, Jesus kept their hearts from breaking. The dear father went the way of all the earth. Then a brother-in-law, who was a brother indeed; then the elder brother, tried and true, in an instant of time, speeds home to heaven; and again a younger brother, in his bright youth; these three were the family's offering upon the altar of freedom. A costly offering! A heavy price paid! "Though he slay me, yet will I trust in him."

For seven years Miss Huggins taught school as continuously as her health permitted. Her methods as a teacher were followed by peculiar success. She loved children and had a most earnest desire to help them up to all that is best and wisest in life. Children know by instinct whose is the firm, yet loving, hand stretched out to lead them in the paths of pleasantness and peace. Some of this time she taught in the Mission school. Her sister says:

"I cannot write of her long sickness, her intense suffering, her patient waiting to see what the Lord had in store for her; all this is too painful for me. St. Anthony, where she first came with such bright hopes of finding health, was the place from which she went to her long rest. It was the place where she found cure.

"The Dakota text-book, which she and Nannie prepared, was a labor of much thought and prayer. It was not published until after she had gone home."

Mignonette and sweet violets may well be emblem-flowers for this lovely sister. Would that I might strew them on her grave, in the early summer-time, as a farewell till we meet again.

NANCY JANE WILLIAMSON.

BY M. R. M.

When an army marches on under fire, and one after another falls by the way, the ranks close up, that there may ever be an unbroken front before the foe. So in life's battle, as one by one drops out of the ranks, we who are left must needs *march on*. Yet if we stop a little to think and talk of the ones gone, it may help us as we press forward. Then to-day let us bring to mind something of the life of a sister departed.

NANNIE J. WILLIAMSON was born at Lac-qui-parle, Minnesota, on the 28th of July, 1840. From her birth she was afflicted with disease of the spine, so that she was almost two years old before she walked at all, and then her ankles bent and had to be bound in splints. "Aunt Jane" mentions that Nannie was in her fourth year when she first saw her, and at that time, when the children went out to play, her brother John either carried her or drew her in a little wagon, to save her the fatigue of walking. So she must have truly borne the yoke in her youth. That the burden was not lifted as the years went by, we may judge from the facts that when away at school, both in Galesburg, Ill., and Oxford, O., she was under the care of a physician; and she almost always studied her lessons lying on her back.

Though her days were stretched out to her 38th year, her body never fully ripened into womanhood, and her heart never lost the sweetness and simplicity of the child. It was not so with her mind. Overleaping the body with a firm and strong grasp, it took up every object of thought, and filled its storehouse of knowledge.

"The date of her conversion is not known. She loved Jesus from a child."

In the fall of 1854, our family moved to within two miles of Dr. Williamson's new station of Pajutazee, or Yellow Medicine. From that time we were intimately associated, and many delightful memories are connected with those days. In September, 1857, Nannie went to the W. F. Seminary at Oxford, O. She made many friends among her schoolmates, and all respected her for her consistent character, her faithfulness in her studies, and

A MEMORIAL.

ELIZA HUGGINS; NANNIE WILLIAMSON; JULIA LA FRAMBOISE.

ELIZA W. HUGGINS.

The Lord came to His garden, and gathered three fair flowers, which now bloom in the city of our God. We, who knew their beauty, come to lay our loving remembrances upon their graves.

ELIZA WILSON HUGGINS was the third child of Alexander G. and Lydia Huggins. She was born March 7, 1837, and died June 22, 1873.

She early gave herself to Jesus, and her lovely life was like a strain of sacred music, albeit its years of suffering brought out chords of minor harmony.

This young girl, in the dawn of womanhood, with gentle step and loving voice, was a revelation to us who were younger than she. Huguenot blood ran swiftly in her veins, and grief and joy were keen realities to her sensitive soul. But she quieted herself as a child before the Lord, and he gave her the ornament which is without price. Though she wist not, her face shone, and we, remembering, know that she had been with Jesus.

Her sister, Mrs. Holtsclaw, writes: "We are of Huguenot descent on our father's side. Our great great grandfather was born at sea in the flight from France to England. Two brothers (in that generation or the one following,) came to America, one settling in North Carolina, the other in New England. Our grandfather left North Carolina when father was a small boy, because he thought slavery wrong, and did not wish his children exposed to its influences.

kotas are there, who will call him father. I think they have gathered around him and sung, under the trees by the river, one of his first Dakota hymns:

   Jehowa Mayooha, nimayakiye,
    Nitowashta iwadowan.
   Jehovah, My Master, Thou hast saved me,
    I sing of Thy Goodness.

My friend—my long-life friend—my companion in tribulation and in the patience of work, I almost envy thee of thy *first* translation!   S. R. R.

her earnestness in seeking to bring others to Christ. One with more thankful humility never lived. She was always so very grateful for the least favor or kindness done her, and seemed ever to bear them in mind. She was exceedingly thoughtful for other people, never seemed to think evil of any one, and never failed to find kindly excuses for one's conduct if excuses were possible. After the burning of the Seminary building, the senior class, of which Nannie was one, finished their studies in a house secured for that purpose. Then followed the sorrowful days of '62, that broke up so many homes, ours among others. Some time after, Nannie wrote this: "It is a little more than a year since we left our dear old homes. I wonder if our paths will ever lie so near together again, as they have in times past. Who can tell? But though we may *seem* to be far apart, we trust we are journeying to the same place, and we shall meet *there.*"

During the months that Nannie's mother waited to be released from earthly suffering, the daughter spared none of her strength to do what she could for the faithful, patient mother. After there was nothing more to do on earth for that mother, then indeed Nannie felt the effects of the long strain on body and mind. Even then her nights were painful and unresting. But after recruiting a little, she entered upon the work to which her thoughts had often turned, that of uplifting the Dakota women and children. In 1873 "she joined her brother, Rev. J. P. Williamson, in missionary labor, at Yankton Agency, Dakota Ter., under the Presbyterian Board of Foreign Missions, and continued in it until her death, Nov. 18, 1877."

"Her knowledge of the Scriptures was such that the minister scarcely needed any other concordance when she was by, and during her last illness, every conversation was accompanied with Scripture quotations.

"Notwithstanding her physical weakness, she taught school and did much other work; and as all was consecrated to the Lord, we are sure she has much fruit in glory. Many in the Sabbath-schools of Traverse and St. Peter, received lessons from her, whose impression will last to eternity."

In the spring of 1876, she went to Ohio, on the occasion of a reunion of the first five graduating classes of the W. F. Seminary, Oxford, O. She desired with great desire to meet her classmates, and the beloved principal, Miss Helen Peabody; and also to visit relatives, among them two aged aunts, one of whom crossed over to the other side a little before her. She took great delight in her visit, and yet her nights were wearisome, and she was probably not entirely comfortable at any time. But she did not complain.

On her last visit home her face bore the impress of great suffering. It was with difficulty she could raise either hand to her head, and could only sleep with her arms supported on pillows. They would fain have kept her at home, but she longed to do what she could as long as she could. So she went back, taught in the school, visited the sick, read from the Bible in the tents, and prayed. In her last illness some of these women came and prayed with her, and so comforted her greatly. She did not forget her brother's children, in her anxiety for the heathen around them, and they will long remember Aunt Nannie's prayerful instructions.

With so little strength as she had, it was not strange that when fever prostrated her, she could not rally again. So she lay for nearly eight weeks, suffering much, but trusting much also. At times she hoped to be able to work again for the women, if the Lord willed. But when she knew that her earthly life was nearly ended, she sent this message to her aunt: "Do not grieve, dear aunt. Though I had desired to do much for these women and girls, the prospect of heaven is very sweet." For a while she had said now and then: "I wonder how long I shall have to lie here and wait," but one day she remarked, "I do not feel at all troubled now about how long I may have to wait: Jesus has taken that all away." When any one came in to see her, she said a few words, and as the school children were gathered around her one day she talked to them a little while for the last time. Two days before her death, she dictated a letter to her father, who had himself been very near death's door, but was recovering: "I do rejoice that God has restored you to health again. I trust that years of usefulness and happiness may still be yours. I am gaining both in appetite and strength. I feel a good deal better." But the night that followed was a sleepless one, and the next day she suffered greatly. About dark her brother said to her, "You have suffered a great deal to-day." She answered, "Yes, but the worst is over now." He said, "Jesus will send for you," and she replied, "Yes, I think he will, for he says, 'I will that they also, whom thou hast given me, be with me where I am.'"

She spoke now and then to different ones, a word or two, asked them to read some Scripture texts from the "Silent Comforter" that hung where she could always see it, wanted it to be turned over, and, with her face to the wall, she seemed to go to sleep. She so continued through the night, her breath growing fainter and fainter. And at daybreak on the morning of the Sabbath, the other life began. "*That is the substance, this the shadow; that the reality, this the dream.*"

JULIA LA FRAMBOISE.

JULIA A. LA FRAMBOISE was the daughter of a French trader, and of a Dakota mother. When nine years of age, her father placed her in Mr. Huggins' family. In that Christian home she learned to love her Savior, and, one year later, covenanted forever to be His. Her father was a Catholic, and would have preferred that his daughter remain in that church, but allowed her to choose for herself. His affection for her, and hers for him, was very strong.

After her father's death, Julia determined to use her property in obtaining an education. She spent two years in the Mission school at Hazelwood, then going to the W. F. Seminary, Oxford, Ohio, and for a short time to Painsville, Ohio, and afterward to Rockford, Ills. Having taken a full course of study there, she returned to Minnesota as a teacher.

Our mother had a warm affection for Julia, as indeed for each of the others of whom we write. Julia called our house one of her homes, and, whenever with us, she took a daughter's share in the love and labor of the household.

A story of my mother's childhood illustrates the spirit of benevolence, by which she influenced Miss La Framboise among others. Her surviving sister, Mrs. Lucretia S. Cooley, writes:

"When the first missionaries from the vicinity of my early home, Mr. and Mrs. Richards, of Plainfield, went to the Sandwich Islands, sister Mary was a little girl. She was deeply impressed by the story of the wants of the children, as portrayed by Mr. Richards, and expressed a strong desire to accompany him. She had just learned to sew quite nicely. Looking up to mother she said, 'I could teach the little girls to sew.' Here was the missionary spirit. Those who go to the Indians, to the Islands of the sea, to Africa, must needs be ready to teach all things, doing it as to the Lord.

When the call to teach among her own people came, Miss La Framboise gladly embraced the opportunity, laboring for them in season and out of season for two short years. Her health failing, she was taken to her old home in Minnesota, where she died, Sept. 20th, 1871, but twenty-eight years of age.

Mrs. Holtsclaw, one of her girlhood friends, went to her in that last sickness. She wrote: " I was with her when she died. It was beautiful to see the steady care and gentle devotion of her step-mother, of the rest of the family, and of the neighbors."

Miss La Framboise was thoroughly educated, thoroughly the lady; always loyal to her people even when they were most hated and despised; always generous in her deeds and words; always to be depended upon.

Oh, could we but have kept her to work many years for the ennobling and Christianizing of the Dakotas!

Bring lilies of the prairie for this grand-daughter of a chieftain, ay, more, this daughter of the King!   I. R. W.

THE FAMILY REUNION.
1879.
A MONOGRAPH.

EIGHTEEN YEARS had gone by since the family were all together. That was in the summer of 1861. In the summer of 1858, Alfred had graduated at Knox College, Illinois; and Isabella returned with him from the Western Female Seminary, Ohio. They gladly arrived at home, in borrowed clothes, having trod together "the burning deck" of a Mississippi River steamboat. All were together then. That fall, Martha went to the Western Female Seminary, and was there when the school building was burned in 1860. After that she came home, and Isabella went back to graduate. In the meantime, Alfred had become a member of the Theological Seminary, of Chicago. And so it happened, that all were not at home again together, until the summer of 1861. Then came the Sioux outbreak, and the breaking up of the mission home. Though a new home was made at St. Anthony, and then at Beloit, it never came to pass that all were together at any one time.

Then new home centers grew up. Alfred was married in June, 1863. Isabella was married in February, 1866, and very soon sailed for China. Martha was married in December of the same year, and went to live in Minnesota. The dear mother went to the Upper Home in March, 1869. Alfred moved to the mission field at Santee Agency, Nebraska, in June, 1870. Anna was married in October of the same year and moved to Iowa. While Martha, the same autumn, removed to open the Missionary Home at the Sisseton Agency. In May, 1872, a new mother came in, to keep the hearthstone bright at the Beloit home. In February of 1872, Thomas went to Fort Sully to commence a new station, and was married in December of the same year. Meanwhile

Henry, Robert and Cornelia were growing up to manhood and womanhood, and getting their education by books and hard knocks. Henry was married in September, 1878, and Robert was tutor in Beloit College, and Cornelia a teacher in the Beloit city schools.

At these new home centers children had been growing up At Kalgan, China, there were *six;* at Santee, Neb., *five;* at Sisseton, D. T., *four;* at Vinton, Iowa, *three,* and at Fort Sully, D. T., *one.* Another sister had also come at the Beloit home.

And now the Chinese cousins were coming home to the America they had never seen. So it was determined that, on their arrival, there should be a family meeting. But where should it be? Every home was open, and urged its advantages. But Santee Agency, Nebraska, united more of the requisite conditions of central position and roomy accommodations. And besides, it was eminently fitting that the meeting should be held on missionary ground. And so, from early in July on to September, the clan was gathering.

First came Rev. Mark Williams and Isabella, with their six children, fresh from China, finding the Santee Indian Reservation the best place to become acclimated to America gradually. Father Riggs and Martha Riggs Morris, with three of her children, from Sisseton Agency, arrived the 18th of August. On the 27th came Anna Riggs Warner, with her three children, from Vinton, Iowa. Mother Riggs with little Edna arrived on the 29th, from Beloit, Wis. Mr. Wyllys K. Morris and Harry, their eldest son, came across the country by wagon, and drove in Saturday evening, the 30th of August. Thomas L. Riggs and little Theodore, with Robert B. Riggs, and Mary Cornelia Octavia Riggs, and their caravan, did not arrive from Fort Sully until Tuesday afternoon of the 2d of September. Alfred L. and Mary B. Riggs, and Henry M. and Lucy D. Riggs were of course already there, as they were at home, and the entertainers of the gathering.

Now the family were gathered, and this is the ROLL:

STEPHEN RETURN RIGGS, born in Steubenville, Ohio, March 23, 1812; married February 16, 1837, to MARY ANN LONGLEY, who was born Nov. 10, 1813, in Hawley, Mass., and died March 22, 1869, in Beloit, Wisconsin.

I. *Alfred Longley Riggs*, born at Lac-qui-parle, Minn., December 6, 1837; married June 9, 1863, to *Mary Buel Hatch*, who was born May 20, 1840, at Leroy, N. Y.

Children: *Frederick Bartlett*, born at Lockport, Ill, July 14, 1865; *Cora Isabella*, born at Center, Wis., August 19, 1868; *Mabel*, born at Santee Agency, Neb., September 11, 1874; *Olive Ward*, born at Santee Agency, Neb., June 13, 1876; *Stephen Williamson*, born at Santee Agency, Neb., April 28, 1878.

II. *Isabella Burgess Riggs*, born at Lac-qui-parle, Minn., February 21, 1840; married February 21, 1866, to *Rev. W. Mark Williams*, who was born October 28, 1834, in New London, Ohio.

Children: *Henrietta Blodget*, born at Kalgan, China, September 25, 1867; *Stephen Riggs*, born at Kalgan, China, August 22, 1870; *Emily Diament*, born at Kalgan, China, May 23, 1873; *Mary Eliza*, born at Kalgan, China, August 3, 1875; *Margaret* and *Anna*, born at Kalgan, China, May 30, 1878.

III. *Martha Taylor Riggs*, born at Lac-qui-parle, Minn., January 27, 1842; married December 18, 1866, to *Wyllys King Morris*, who was born in Hartford, Conn., September 11, 1842.

Children: *Henry Stephen*, born at Sterling, Minn., June 21, 1868; *Philip Alfred*, born at Good Will, D. T., August 4, 1872, and died at Binghamton, N. Y., August 18, 1873; *Mary Theodora*, born at Good Will, D. T., July 31, 1874; *Charles Riggs*, born at Good Will, D. T., June 21, 1877; *Nina Margaret Foster*, born at Good Will, D. T., May 30, 1879.

IV. *Anna Jane Riggs*, born at Traverse des Sioux, Minn., April 13, 1845; married October 14, 1870, to *Horace Everett Warner*, who was born January 10, 1839, near Painesville, Ohio.

Children: *Marjorie*, born at Belle Plaine, Iowa, September 29, 1872; *Arthur Hallam*, born in Vinton, Iowa, October 28, 1875; *Everett Longley*, born in Vinton, Iowa, July 15, 1877.

V. *Thomas Lawrence Riggs*, born at Lac-qui-parle, Minn., June 3, 1847; married December 26, 1872, to *Cornelia Margaret Foster*, who was born in Bangor, Maine, March 19, 1848, and died August 5, 1878, at Fort Sully, D. T.

Child: *Theodore Foster*, born near Fort Sully, D. T., July 7, 1874.

VI. *Henry Martyn Riggs*, born at Lac-qui-parle, Minn., September 25, 1849; married September 24, 1878, to *Lucy M. Dodge*, who was born at Grafton, Mass., February 29, 1852.*

VII. *Robert Baird Riggs*, born at Hazelwood, Minn., May 22 1855.

VIII. *Mary Cornelia Octavia Riggs*, born at Hazelwood, Minn., February 17, 1859.

STEPHEN R. RIGGS married, May 28, 1872, MRS. ANNIE BAKER ACKLEY, who was born March 14, 1835, in Granville, Ohio.

IX. *Edna Baker Riggs*, born at Beloit, Wis., December 2, 1874.

The sons and daughters brought into the original family by marriage contributed much to the success of the reunion. The cousins will not soon forget the inimitable stories of Uncle Mark. Horace E. Warner wrote a charming letter, proving conclusively that he was really present; while Uncle Wyllys must have gained the perpetual remembrance of the boys, by taking them swimming. Mary Hatch Riggs was the unflagging main spring of the whole meeting. Lucy Dodge Riggs presided hospitably at the "Young men's hall," where many of the guests were entertained; and the new mother, Annie Baker Riggs, won the love of all.

It would not have been a perfect meeting without seeing the face of John P. Williamson, the elder brother of the mission. Then, too, there was our friend Rev. Joseph Ward, whose home at Yankton has so often been the "House Beautiful" to our missionary pilgrims. We were also favored with the presence of many of our missionary women: Mrs. Hall, of Fort Berthold, Misses Collins and Irvine, from Fort Sully, and Misses Shepard, Paddock, Webb and Skea, of Santee. The children will long remember the party given them by Miss Shepard in the Dakota Home, and the picnic on the hill.

It is impossible to give any adequate report of such a Reunion. The renewal of acquaintance, taking the bearings of one another's whereabouts in mental and spiritual advance, is more through chit-chat and incidental revelations, than in any of the things that can be told.

And so we gather in as memorials and reminders some of the

---

* NOTE.—After the family gathering, a child was born—*Lewis Ward*, October 19, 1879.

papers read at the evening sociables, and some paragraphs from reports of the Reunion published in the *Word Carrier* and *Advance*. First, we will have Isabella's paper, the story of that long journey home— By Land and by Sea:

Ding lang, ding lang, ding lang! Hear the bells. The litters are packed, the good-byes spoken. Thirteen years of work in sorrow and in joy are over. "Good bye. We will pray for you all; do not forget us."

Down the narrow street, past the closely crowded houses of more crowded inmates, beyond the pale green of the gardens, on the stony plain, and our long journey is begun.

Eight hours and the first inn is reached, we having made a twenty-five-mile stage. Over rocks and river, fertile lake bed, desert plain and through mountain gorge we creep our way, till, on the fifth day, the massive walls of Peking loom up before us.

Here there are cordial greetings from warm hearts, and willing hands stretched out to help. Best of all is the inspiration of mission meeting with its glad, good news from Shantung Province.

By cart and by canal boat again away. At Tientsin we ride by starlight in jinrickshas, to the steamer. How huge the monster! How broad seems the river, covered here and yonder, and again yonder, with fleets of boats!

We ensconse ourselves in the assigned state rooms, and little Anna's foster mother keeps a vigil by the child so soon to be her's no more. "Farewell, farewell."

Grey morning comes, and the ponderous engine begins his work. We move past boats, ships, steamers, past the fort at Taku, out on the open sea. No one sings, "A life on the ocean wave," or "Murmuring sea," for our "day of youth went yesterday." The enthusiasm of early years is gone. Instead, I read reverently the 107th Psalm, verses 23,31. Then with the strong, glad, spray-laden breeze on one's face, it is fitting to read, "The Lord on high is mightier than the noise of many waters, yea, than the waves of the sea." "Let the sea roar, and the fullness thereof. Let the floods clap their hands * * before the Lord.' "The sea is his and he made it." "The earth is full of thy riches: so is this great and wide sea. There go the ships; there is that leviathan whom thou hast made to play therein."

Five days, and we steam up through the low, flat, fertile shores of Woo Sung River to Shanghai.

Ho for the land of the rising sun! Two days we sail over a silver sea; yonder is Nagasaki, and now a heavy rain reminds us that this is Japan. On through the Inland Sea. How surpassingly beautiful are the green hills and mountains on every side.

At Kobe we receive a delightful welcome from Mr. C. H. Gulick's family, and on the morrow we meet our former co-laborer in the Kalgan work, Rev. J. T. Gulick. Ten days of rest, and our little Anna is herself again. She is round and fair and sweet, and every one laughingly says she is more like our hostess than like me.

Again away, in a floating palace, fitly named City of Tokio. We glide out of sight of Japan, with hearts strangely stirred by God's work in that land.

One sail after another disappears until we are alone on the great ocean. Water, water, water everywhere.

Our days are all alike. Constant care of the children, and thoughts of home and beloved ones keep hand and heart busy. The events of each day are breakfast, tiffin and dinner, daintily prepared, and faultlessly served by deft and noiseless waiters. We think it a pleasant variety when a stiff breeze makes the waves run high. The table racks are on, yet once and again a glass of water or a plate of soup goes over. We turn our plates at the proper angle, when the long roll begins, and unconcernedly go on.

One day of waves mountain high, which sweep us on to our desired haven. On the 18th day we see the shore of beautiful America. How the heart beats! So soon to see father, brothers and sisters! Thank God. Aye, thank him, too, for the manifold mercies of our journey.

How strange and yet familiar are the sights and sounds of San Francisco. The children's eyes shine as they plan and execute raids on a toy store.

There is yet the land journey of thousands of miles. By night and by day we speed on; across gorge, through tunnel and snow-shed, over the alkali plains, over fertile fields, to Omaha.

At last we arrive in Yankton, and a cheery voice makes weary hearts glad. 'I am Mr. Ward. Your brother Henry is here.' Ah, is that Henry? How he has changed, from boyhood to manhood!

"Over the hills and far away." Here we are! How beautiful the mission houses look! And the dear familiar faces! Rest and home at last for a little while. "For here have we no continuing city, but we seek one to come."

But journeying may be done much more quickly by thought; and spirit may go as quick as thought. So here is the account of Horace E. Warner's thought journey to the family meeting:

If there has seemed to be any lack of interest on my part in the Family Reunion, it is only in the seeming. For my decision to stay at home was made with deep regret, and after the slaying of much strong desire. But aside from the gratification which it would have given me to see you all, and which I hope it would have given you to see me, I do not think the idea of the meeting is impaired by my absence. Only this—I feel as though I had, not willfully nor willingly, but none the less certainly, cut myself off from that sympathy—in the Greek sense—which I stood in much need of, and can ill afford to miss.

I suppose you are now all together with one accord in one place, so far as that is possible. To be ALL together would require the union of two worlds. And this may be, too,—shall we not say it is so? But if the dear ones from the unseen world are present, though you cannot hear their speech nor detect their presence by any of the senses, cannot you feel that I am really with you in some sense too? Of course the difference is great, but so also the difference is great between the meeting of friends in the natural body and the spiritual body. If the mind, the soul, constitutes the man rather than the animal substances, or the myriad cells which make up his physical organization, why may not I leap over the insignificant barrier that divides us? As I write, this feeling is very strong with me. It is vague and indefinite but yet it seems to me that I have been having some kind of communication or communion with you. At all events, my heart goes out strongly toward you all with fervent desire that the meeting will be full of joy and comfort—of sweetest and spiritual growth—the occasion of new inspiration, new courage, new hopes. It is not likely that there can be any repetition of it this side of the "city which hath foundations."

So the memories of this meeting should be the sweetest, and should cluster thick around you in the years of separation. This much I must perforce miss. For though I do truly rejoice in your joys, and partake with you of the gladness of the meeting after so long a time; yet it is only by imagination and sympathy that I make myself one with you, and of this the future can have no recollection.

Now we will let others give their thoughts of the meeting, as it seemed to them from outside. And first, a few words from Rev. John P. Williamson, of Yankton Agency:

The first week in September, 1879, will long be remembered by the Riggs family, and by one or two who were not Riggs'. From the east and the west, from the north and the south, and from across the mighty Pacific, they gathered at the eldest brother's house, at Santee Agency, Nebraska, for a Family Reunion. It was forty-two years last February since Stephen Return Riggs married Mary Ann Longley and came out as a missionary to the Dakotas; and now in his sixty-eighth year, his step still light, and his heart still young; he walks in to his son's house to find himself surrounded by nine children, three sons-in-law, two daughters-in-law, and nineteen grandchildren; with himself and wife making a company of thirty-five, and all present except one son-in-law.

This roll may never be as interesting to universal mankind as that in the tenth chapter of Genesis, but it is almost extended enough to evolve a few general truths. If we were to pick these up our first deduction would be that *like begets like*. This man has certainly given more than his proportion of missionaries. And why, except that like begets like. He was a missionary, his children partook of his spirit and became missionaries. We heard some mathematical member of the company computing the number of years of missionary service the family had rendered. The amount has slipped our memory, but we should say it was over one hundred and fifty.

Our other deduction would be that the missionary profession is a healthy one. Here is a family of no uncommon physical vigor, and yet not a single death occurred among the children who are in goodly number. True the mother of the family has finished her work and crossed the river to wait with her longing smile the coming children, but another ministers in her room, who has added little Aunt Edna to the list, to stand before her father when the rest are far away.

Next we have the observations of Rev. Joseph Ward, of Yankton:

Families have their characteristic points as well as individuals. The family of Rev. S. R. Riggs, D. D., is no exception to this. Their characteristics all point in one direction. It is notably a missionary family. It began on missionary ground forty-two years ago at Lac-qui-parle, Minnesota. From that time until the present the name of the family head has always appeared in the list of missionaries of the American Board. One after another the names of the children have been added to the list, until now we find Alfred, Isabella, Martha, Thomas, Henry, attached to the mission; and doing genuine missionary work, though not bearing a commission from the Board, are two more, Robert and Cornelia.

What place more suitable for the meeting together of father, children, and children's children—thirty-four all told, counting those who have joined the family by marriage—than Santee Agency, Nebraska, a mission station of the A. B. C. F. M.

Though not of the family, I was honored by an invitation to attend the meeting, assured that a "bed and a plate would be reserved for me;" and so, on the first Tuesday of September, I stood on the bank of the Missouri, opposite the Agency, waiting for the ferryman to set me across. I came at the right time, for presently the delegation from Ft. Sully drove their two teams to the landing, and in a moment more Rev. J. P. Williamson, with his oldest daughter, from Yankton Agency, were added to our number.

They came from the east, and the west, and the north. These from Sisseton, these from Sully, and these from the land of Sinim, for the oldest daughter and her husband, Rev. Mark Williams, have been for thirteen years in Kalgan, Northern China, and now for the first time come back to see the father and the fatherland. The personal part of the meeting I have no right to mention. I speak only of its missionary character. The very Prudential Committee itself, in its weekly meetings, cannot be more thoroughly imbued with a missionary spirit than was every hour of this reunion. And how could it be otherwise? All the reminiscences were of their home on missionary ground, at Lac-qui-parle, at Traverse des Sioux, and at Hazelwood. Did they talk of present duties and doings? What could they have for their theme but life at Kalgan, at Good Will, at Santee and at Sully! Did they look forward to what they would do after the family meeting was over? The larger part were to go two hundred miles and more overland, to attend the annual meeting of the Indian churches at Brown Earth. And besides, how to reach out from their present stations and seize new points for work was the constant theme of thought.

Wednesday evening there was a gathering of the older ones and the larger children. The father read a sketch recalling a few incidents of the family life. The reading brought now laughter and then tears. Forty-two years could not come and go without leaving many a sorrow behind.

The mother who had lived her brave life for a third of a century among the Indians, was not there. A beautiful crayon portrait, hung that day for the first time over the piano, was a sadly sweet reminder of her whose body was laid to rest only a year ago among the Teetons, on the banks of the Upper Missouri. Then another paper of memories from one of the daughters, lighted with joy and shaded with sorrow, a few words of cheer and counsel from the oldest son, and a talk in Chinese from the Celestial member, were the formal features of the evening.

As I sat in the corner of the study and heard and saw, there came to me, clearer than ever before, the wonderful power there is in a consecrated life. Well did one of them say that if they had gained any success in their work, it was by singleness of purpose. "This one thing I do" could well be the family motto. They have not been assigned to a prominent place in the work of the world, but rather to the most hidden and hopeless part. But by their persistence of purpose, they have done much to lift up and make popular, in a good sense, missionary work in general, and particularly work for the Indians. It is a record that will shine brighter and brighter through the ages. Eight children and thirteen grandchildren born on missionary ground, and a total of one hundred and fifty-eight years of missionary work.

But the end is not yet. They have just begun to get their implements into working order. Their training schools are just beginning to bear fruit. Most fittingly, a few days before the gathering began, came a large invoice of the entire Bible in Dakota, the joint work of Dr. Riggs and his beloved friend and fellow-worker, Dr. Williamson, who has just gone home to his rest. At the same time came the final proof-sheets of a goodly-sized hymn and tune book for the Dakotas, mainly the work of the eldest sons of the two translators of the Bible. The harvest that has been is nothing to the harvest that is to be. Dr. Riggs may reasonably hope to see more stations occupied, more books made, more churches organized in the future than he has seen in the past. When the final record is made he will have the title to a great rejoicing that he and his family were permitted by the Master to do so much to make a sinful world loyal again to its rightful Lord.

MARTHA'S PAPER, which was read on that occasion, is a very touching description of a missionary journey made under difficulties, six years before, from Sisseton to Yankton Agency.

GOING TO MISSION MEETING.

As I sit on the doorsteps in the twilight, the little ones asleep in their beds, I hear a solitary attendant on the choir-meeting singing. His voice rings out clearly on the night air—

"Jesus Christ nitowashte kin
Woptecashni mayaqu"—

singing it to the tune Watchman.

That tune has a peculiar fascination and association for me, and my thoughts often go back over the time when I first heard it.

It was in the month of roses—in the year seventy-three, that, in company with some of the Renvilles and others I undertook a land journey to the Missouri. I had with me the lad Harry, then five years old, and a sunny-haired boy of nearly a year, little Philip Alfred. He never knew his name here. Does he know it now? Or has he another, an "angel name"?

The rains had been abundant, and the roads were neither very good nor very well traveled. So, some unnecessary time was spent in winding about among marshes, and we made slow progress. More than once we came to a creek or a slough where the water came into the wagons. The Indian women shouldered their babies and bundles as well, and trudged through, with the exception of Ellen Phelps and Mrs. Elias Gilbert. Their husbands were so much of white men as to shoulder their wives, and carry them across. Being myself a privileged person, I was permitted to ride over, first mounting the seat to the wagon, holding on for dear life to the wagon bows with one hand, and to the sunny-haired boy with the other.

By the end of the week we had only reached the Big Sioux, which we found up and booming. I was crossed over in a canoe with my two children, the stout arms of two Indian women paddling me over. Then we climbed up the bank, and waited for the wagons to come around by some more fordable place down below. While waiting, I talked awhile with Mrs Wind, who had been a neighbor of ours on the Coteau. Her lawful husband, a man of strong and ungoverned passions, had grown tired of her and taken another woman. So Mrs. Wind, who had borne with his overbearing and his occasional beatings, quietly left him. This was an indignity her proud spirit could not brook. She went to the River Bend Settlement to live with her son, and there I saw her. I said to her, "Shall you go back to the hill country?" "No," she said, "the man has taken another wife, and I shall not go." I have since heard of her from time to time, and she still remains faithful.

The Sabbath over, we went on again reinforced by the delegation from Flandreau. Reaching Sioux Falls in the afternoon, we avoided the town, and went on to a point where some one thought the river might be fordable. But alas! we found we had been indulging in vain expectations. The river was not fordable, and canoe or ferry boat there was none. But necessity is the mother of invention. The largest and strongest wagon box was selected, the best wagon cover laid on the ground, the boat lifted in, and with the aid of various ropes, an impromptu boat was made ready. Long ropes were tied securely to either end, poles laid across the box to keep things out of the water, and then the boat was launched. The men piled in the various possessions of different ones and as many women and children as they thought safe. Then four of the best swimmers took the ropes and swam up the river for quite a distance, coming down with the current, and so gaining the other shore. This occupied some time, and was repeated slowly until night came on, finding the company partly on one side, and partly on the other. The wagon in which we had made our bed o'nights, not being in a condition for sleeping in, as the box lay by the river side all water soaked, Edwin Phelps, and Ellen his wife, kindly vacated theirs for our benefit, themselves sleeping on the ground. When the early morning came, the camp was soon astir, and breakfast being hastily dispatched, the work of crossing over was renewed. I watched them drive over the horses; the poor animals were very loth to make a plunge, and some of them turned and ran back on the prairie more than once before they were finally forced into the water. When most of the others were over it came my turn to cross. The so-called boat looked rather shaky, but there was nothing to do but to get in and take one's chance. So I climbed in, keeping as well as I could out of the water, which seemed to nearly fill the wagon-box. Some one handed the two children in, and holding tightly to them, I resigned myself to the passage. At one time I heard a great outcry, but could not distinguish any words, and so sat still, unconscious that one of the ropes had broken, rendering the boat more unsafe still. At last I was safely over, thankful enough. When finally everything, and everybody was across, and the boat restored to its proper place, we started on our way at about ten o'clock in the morning. To make up for the late starting, the teams were driven hard and long, and the twilight had already gathered when we stopped for the night. After

I had given my children a simple supper, and they were hushed to sleep, I looked out on the picturesque scene. The great red moon was rising in the sky, and in its light the travelers had gathered around the camp fire for their evening devotions. As I walked across to join them they were singing

"Jesus Christ nitowashte kin
Woptecashni mayaqu—
*Jesus Christ, Thy loving kindness
Boundlessly Thou givest me;*"

to the tune Watchman. It struck my fancy, and I seldom hear it now without thinking of that night, and of the sunny-haired boy who was then taking his last earthly journey, and who has all these years been learning of the goodness of the Lord Jesus Christ, in all its wonderful fullness. An incident of one day's travel remains clear in my mind. The lad Harry often grew tired and restless as was not strange, and so sometimes he was somewhat careless too. In an unguarded moment, he fell out and one of the hind wheels passed over his body. How I held my breath until the horses could be stopped and the boy reached. It seemed a great marvel that he had received no injury. It was surely the goodness of the Lord that had kept him from harm.

On Wednesday we came into Yankton, where I bought a quantity of beef, wishing to show my appreciation of the labors of the men in our behalf. So when camp was made at night, the women had it to make into soup, and almost before it seemed that the water could have fairly boiled, all hands were called to eat of it, and it was despatched with great celerity.

The next afternoon a fierce storm broke over us, and we were compelled to stop for an hour or more, while the rain poured down in torrents, and the heavens were one continual flame of light. When again we started on, every hole by the road-side had become a pool, and the water was rushing through every low place in streams. The rain retarded our progress greatly, yet we came in sight of the Yankton Agency before noon of the next day. Just as we reached it we found a little creek to cross, where a bridge had been washed away the night before. The banks were almost perpendicular, and we held our breath as we watched one team after another go down and come up, feeling sure that some of the horses would go down and *not* come up again. But to our great relief, all went safely over. And very soon we had arrived at the Mission House occupied by Rev. J. P. Williamson and family, and were receiving the kindly welcomes of all. The hospitality there enjoyed was such as to make us almost forget our tedious journey thitherward.

From my traveling companions I had received all possible kindness, yet in many ways I had found the journey quite trying. It was not practicable to vary one's diet very much with the care of the little one, just large enough to get into all mis chief imaginable. So I remembered with especial gratitude Edwin and Ellen Phelps, who used now and then, at our stopping places, to *borrow* the boy, so helping me to get a little rest, or to do some necessary work which would otherwise have been impossible. At that time Edwin and his wife had no children, and their eyes often followed my boy with yearning looks. Since then the Lord has given them little ones to train up for his kingdom, and they are happy.

But of that little sunny-haired baby boy, we have naught but a memory left—and this consolation,

"*Christ the good Shepherd carries my lamb to-night,
And that is best.*"

And this—

"*Mine entered spotless on eternal years,
Oh how much blest!*"

During the meeting the tastes and needs of the children were not forgotten, but AUNT ANNA held them attent to her

MEMORIES OF THE OLD HOME LIFE WRITTEN FOR THE GRANDCHILDREN.

Shut your eyes, and see with me the home place at Lac-qui-parle—a square house with a flat roof, a broad stone step before the wide open door—cheery and sunshiny within. Welcome to grandfather's home!

To the right, in the distance, is the lake Mdeiyedan, where, like a tired child, the sun dropped his head to rest each night. Between us and the lake was a wooded ravine, at the foot of which, down that little by-path, was the coolest of springs, with wild touch-me-nots nodding above it, and a little further on, a large boulder on which we used to play.

It seems to us as if we had but just come in from a long summer's walk, with our hands full of flowers, and each and every one must have a bouquet to set in his or her favorite window. The wind blowing softly brings with it a breath of sweet cleavers, and— well I must tell you what I remember.

I can not stop to tell you of all the little things that made our home pleasant and lovely in our eyes; or of the dear mother who had it in her keeping, for I know all the grandchildren are waiting for their stories.

Well, I will begin by telling the wee cousins about the family cat, Nelly Bly, and one of her kittens, Charlotte Corday. Kittens have some such cunning ways, you know, but Nelly Bly was one of the knowingest and best. She and her kitten were as much alike as two peas in a pod—jet black, and with beautiful yellow-green eyes. Nelly Bly used to curl herself up to sleep in grandpa's fur cap, or sometimes in grandma's work-basket; and if she could do neither she would find a friendly lap. One day poor pussy chose much too warm a place. Grandma had started up the kitchen fire and was making preparations for dinner when she heard pussy mewing piteously, as she thought, in some other room. She went to the doors one by one to let pussy in, and no pussy appeared, but still she heard her mewing as if in pain. What could grandma do? She was neither down cellar nor up stairs. She would look out of doors—but no—just then pussy screamed in an agony of pain. Grandma ran to the stove, opened the door, and pussy, as if shot out from a cannon's mouth, came flying past us--her back singed and her poor little paws all burned. I can't tell whether she learned the moral of that lesson or not, but I know she never was shut up in the oven again.

Yet not so very long after, when the old house was burned, Nelly Bly and Charlotte Corday found a sadder fate. Poor little kittens!—we spent hour after hour searching for their bones but with small success, and then we buried them with choking sobs and eyes wet with childish tears.

Do not let me forget to tell you of Pembina and Flora, nor of the starry host that bedecked our barnyard sky—every calf however humble was worthy of a name. There were our oxen, Dick and Darby, George and Jolly, and Leo and Scorpio, who used to weave along with stately swinging tread under their burden of hay. Then Spika and Denebola, Luna and Lyra—all worthy of honorable mention. Flora, gentle, but with an eye that terrified the little maid who sometimes milked her,—so with wise forethought, a handful of salt was sometimes thrown into the bottom of her pail. You will hardly believe it, but she grew to be so fond of her pail that she found her way into the winter kitchen and anticipated her evening meal. How she ever got through two gates and two doors is a mystery still.

And there was Pembina—how well we remember the day when grandpa brought home a new cow, and how we all went down to meet him and named her and her calf, Little Dorrit, on the spot. She was the children's cow *par excellence*. and blessings on her, we could all milk at a time. She had several bad habits, one of which was eating old clothes and paper, or rubbish generally. Once I remember she made a vain attempt at swallowing a beet, and if grandpa had not come in the nick of time to beat her on the back she would have been dead beat.

Our horses, too, were a part of the family. There were Polly and Phenie, short for Napoleon Bonaparte and Josephine—Fanny and Tattycoram (we had been reading Dickens then).

I remember hearing our own mother tell of the ox they had when they lived at Traverse des Sioux, their only beast of burden, and how he used to stand and lick the window panes, and how when the Indians shot him she felt as if she had lost a friend and companion.

If these stories of our dear animal friends grow too tiresome I might remember about the Squill family at Hazelwood—how

A MONOGRAPH.

they all, including Timothy and Theophilus, contributed something every week to a family paper. I wonder if Theophilus remembers writing an essay for —— with red ink from his arm —— and how Isabella said, "Now be brave, Martha, be brave!'. when she was letting herself down from the topmost round of the ladder—and how Isabella when beheading the Pope in her fanatical zeal, split her forefinger with a chisel.

These are a very few only of the rememberings—some of them are too sacred and too dear to speak about—but even these little incidents seem endeared by the long stretch of years.

Some memories of former days were *revived* for the older children, and *imparted* to the younger ones, by the FATHER'S PAPER:

I REMEMBER.

As one grows old memory is, in some sense, unreliable. It does not *catch and hold* as it once did. But many things of long ago are the things best remembered. Often there is error in regard to dates. The mind sees the things or the events vividly, but the surroundings are dim and uncertain. What is aimed at in this paper is to gather up, or rather select, some events lying along the family line and touching personal character.

The family commences with the mother. I remember well my first visit to Bethlehem, Indiana, where I first met Mary, with whom I had been corresponding, having had an introduction through Rev. Dyer Burgess. That was in the spring. My second visit to the same place was in the autumn of 1836, when the school-mistress and I went on to New England together.

FIRST VISIT TO MASSACHUSETTS.

Of that journey eastward, and the winter spent in Hawley, I should naturally remember a good many things: How when the stage from Albany and Troy put us down in Charlemont, we hired a boy with a one-horse wagon to carry us six miles to Hawley. But when we came to going up the steep, rough, long hill such as I had never climbed before, the horse could only scramble up with the baggage alone. How we reached the Longley homestead in a real November storm only a few days before Thanksgiving, and were greeted by the grandparents ninety years old, and by the father and mother and brothers and sister—all of whom, except Moses, have since gone to the other side. How only a day after our arrival I was waited upon by a committee of the West Hawley church, and engaged to preach for them during the winter. How every Saturday I walked down to Pudding Hollow and preached on Sabbath and usually walked up on Monday, when I did not get snowed in. How the first pair of boots I ever owned, bought in Ohio, proved to be too small to wade in snow with, and had to be abandoned. How the old family horse had a knack of turning us over into snow-drifts. How on our first visit to Buckland, the grandfather Taylor, then about ninety-five years old, when he was introduced to Mary Ann's future husband, a young minister from the West, asked, "Did you ever think what a good horseman Jesus Christ was? Why he rode upon a colt that had never been broke." How the old meeting-house on the hill, with its square pews and high pulpit, creaked and groaned in the storm of our wedding day, Feb. 16, 1837. How we left in the first days of March, when the snow-drifts on the hills were still fifteen feet deep.

March, April, May passed, and the first day of June we landed at Fort Snelling in the land of the Dakotas.

When another three moons were passed by, and we had seen St. Anthony and Minnehaha, and made some acquaintance with the natives, I remember we took passage, with our effects on board a Mackinaw boat for Traverse des Sioux. The boat was in command of Mr. Prescott, who accommodated us with tent room on the journey, and made the week pass comfortably for us. From Traverse des Sioux to Lac-qui-parle we had our first experience of prairie traveling and camping. It was decidedly a new experience. But we had the company of Dr. Williamson and Mr. G. H. Pond, while we commenced to learn the lesson.

AT LAC-QUI-PARLE.

The long, narrow room, partly under the roof of Dr. Williamson's log house, which became our home for nearly five years from that September, is one of the memories that does not fade.

On the 6th of December I remember coming home from Mr. Renville's where we had been all the afternoon obtaining translations. Then there was hurrying to and fro, and the first baby came into our family of two. From that time on we were three, and the little Zitkadanwashta, as the Indians named him, grew as other children grow, and did what most children don't do—viz., learn to go *down* stairs before he did *up*, because, we lived up stairs, and all children can manage to go away from home, when they can't or won't come back of themselves.

In those years our annual allowance from the treasury of the Board was $250. This was more than the other families in the mission had proportionally. But it required considerable economy and great care in expenditure to make the ends meet. Not knowing the price of quinine, and thinking four ounces could not be a great amount, we were much surprised to find the bill $16. But Dr. Turner, of Fort Snelling, kindly took it off our hands.

Once we were discussing the question of how much additional expense the baby would be, when I said, "About two dollars." Thereafter Mr. S. W. Pond, who was present at the time, called the boy " Mazaska nonpa."

A PLEASANT TRIP.

In the second month of 1840, our *three* became *four*. And when the leaves came out and the flowers began to appear, the mother had a great desire to go somewhere. But the only place to go was to Fort Snelling. And so, leaving *Chaskay* and taking *Hapan*, we crossed the prairie to the Traverse des Sioux, in company with Mr. Renville's caravan. The expectation was that the Fur Company's boat would be there. But it was not; nor even a canoe, save a little leaky one, which barely aided us in crossing the St. Peters. The journey through the Big Woods was over logs and through swamps and streams for seventy-five miles. We had two horses but no saddle. Our tent and bedding and such things as we must have on the journey were strapped on the horses. The mother rode one, not very comfortable as may be supposed, but the baby girl had a better ride on a Dakota woman's back. At the end of ten miles "La grand canoe" was found, in which they took passage. That ten miles was destined to be remembered by our return also; for there, where the town of Le Sueur now stands, our bark canoe finally failed us, and without an Indian woman to carry the baby, we walked up to the Traverse, through the wet grass. All together that was a trip to be remembered.

One other thing comes to my mind about our first "little lady." There was only one window in our up-stairs room. On the outside of that the mother had a shelf fixed to set out milk on. One morning when every one was busy or out, the little girl, not two years old, climbed out of the window and perched herself on that shelf. It gave us a good scare.

JOURNEY TO NEW ENGLAND.

In the first month of 1842, our family of *four* was increased to *five*. And when the summer came on we took a longer journey, which extended to New England. This time Hapan was left behind and Hapistinna and Chaskay were the companions of our voyage. The grandmother in Hawley saw and blessed her grandchild namesake Martha Taylor. "Good Bird" says he remembers picking strawberries in the Hawley meadow, where his Uncle Alfred was mowing, in those summer mornings.

NEW STATION AT TRAVERSE DES SIOUX.

A whole year passed, and we came back to the land of the Dakotas, to make a new home at Traverse des Sioux, to experience our first great sorrow, and to consecrate our Allon-bach-uth for the noble brother, Thomas Lawrence Longley. That was a garden of roses but a village of drinking and drunken Sioux; and more of trial came into our life of a little more than three years spent there, than in any other equal portion. There our *Wanskay* was born, and started in life under difficulties. Our family of *five* had now become *six*. Provisions of a good quality were not easily obtained. But it happened that wild rice and Indian sugar were abundant, and the laws of heredity visited the sins of the parents on our third little lady child. But with all the disadvantages of the start, the little "urchin" grew, and grew, like the others.

SENT BACK TO LAC-QUI-PARLE.

Trouble and sorrow baptize and consecrate. The many trials attendant upon commencing our station at Traverse des Sioux and the oaks of weeping there had greatly endeared the place to the mother; and when, in September of 1846, the mission voted that we should go back to Lac-qui-parle, she could not see that it was duty, and went without her own consent. It was a severe trial. In a few months she became satisfied that the Lord had led us. What of character the boy *Hake*, who was born in the next June, inherited from these months of sadness, I know not, but as he came along up, we called him a "Noble Boy." The family had then reached the sacred number *seven*.

In the year that followed we built a very comfortable frame house—indeed two of them—one for Mr. Jonas Pettijohn's family—comfortable, except that the snow would drift in through the ash shingles. Some of the older children can, perhaps, remember times when there was *more snow inside than outside* We were up on the hill, and not under it, where Dr. Williamson and Mr. Huggins had built a dozen years before; and consequently the winter winds were fiercer, though we all thought the summers were pleasanter. In this house our *sixth* child was born who has no Dakota cognomen. We shall call him *Ishakpe*. The half dozen years in which we made that house our home were full of work, broken in upon by a year spent in the east—myself in New York city chiefly. Henry, who could say to enquirers, "I was two years old last September," and Isabella were with their mother in Massachusetts and Brooklyn—Martha and Anna in the capital of Minnesota, and Thomas at the mission station of Kaposia; Alfred, I believe, was at Galesburg, Illinois.

EDUCATING THE CHILDREN

It had been a question that we often discussed, How shall we get our children educated? The basis of allowance from the Treasury of the Board had been on the principle of the Methodist Circuit Riders. The $250 with which we commenced was increased $50 for each child. So that at this time, our salary was either $500 or $550. It was never greater than the last sum until after the outbreak in 1862. We lived on it comfortably but there was very little margin for sending children away to school. And now we were reaching that point in our family history when a special effort must be made in that direction. Before we went on East in 1851, the mother and I had talked the matter over—perhaps some good family would like to take one of the children to educate. And so it was more than one good offer was received for the little boy Henry. But our hearts failed us. Mrs. Minerva Cook, of Brooklyn, said to me, "You are afraid we will make an Episcopalian of him." So near was he to being a Bishop!

MISSION HOUSE BURNED.

Many remembrances have to be passed over. The last picture I have of those mission houses at Lac-qui-parle is, when, on the 3d of March, 1854, they were enveloped in fire. The two little boys had been down cellar to get potatoes for their mother, and holding the lighted candle too near to the dry hay underneath the floor, the whole was soon in a conflagration, which our poor efforts could not stop. The houses were soon a heap of ashes, and the meat and many of the potatoes in the cellar were cooked. The adobe church was then our asylum, and the family home for the summer.

BUILD AT HAZELWOOD.

While occupying the old church and making preparations to rebuild, Secretary S. B. Treat visited us. After consultation, our plans were changed, and we erected our mission buildings at Hazelwood, twenty-five miles further down the Minnesota, and near to Dr. Williamson's and the Yellow Medicine Agency. During the eight years spent there many things connected with the family life transpired. First among them worthy to be noted was, the rounding out of the number of children to *eight*—"Toonkanshena," so called by the Indians—just why I don't know—and Octavia the hakakta. In those days our Family Education Society had to devise ways and means to keep *one* always, and sometimes *two* away at school. By and by, *Zitkadan washta* graduated at Knox College, and *Hapan* and *Hapistinna* at the Western Female Seminary and College Hill respectively. How we got them through seems even now a mystery. But I remember one year we raised a grand crop of potatoes, and sold 100 barrels to the government for $300 in gold. That was quite a lift. And so the Lord provided all through—then and afterward. Nothing was more remarkable in our family history for twenty-five years than its general health. We had very little sickness. I remember a week or so of doctoring on myself during our first residence at Lac-qui-parle. Then the summer after our return there, the fever and ague took hold of two or three of the children. The mother also was taken sick suddenly in the adobe church, and Dr. Williamson and I had a night ride up from Hazelwood. At this place (Hazelwood) the baby boy *Toonkanshena* was sick one night, I remember, and we gave him calomel and sent for the doctor. But the most serious sickness of all these years was that of my "urchin" and Henry, both together of typhoid fever. I have always believed that prayer was a part of the means of their recovery.

QUARTER OF A CENTURY.

When the summer of 1862 came it rounded out a full quarter of a century of missionary life for us. Alfred had completed his seminary course, and in the meantime had grown such a heavy black beard, that when he and I sat on the platform together in a crowded church in Cincinnati, the people asked which was the father and which the son.

While waiting in Ohio for the graduating day of *Hapistinna* to come, I ran up to Steubenville, where I was born, and walked out into the country to the old farm, where my boyhood was spent. The visit was not very satisfactory. Scarcely any one knew me. Every thing had greatly changed.

THE OUTBREAK.

The memories of August 18, 1862, and the days that followed are vivid, but must in the main be passed over. I cannot forbear however, to note what a sorry group we were on that Island, on the morning of the nineteenth! How finally the way appeared, and we filed up the ravine and started over the prairie as fugitives! How the rain came on us that afternoon, and what a sorry camping we made in the open prairie after we had crossed Hawk River! How the little Hakakta girl, when bed time came, wanted to go home! How, when the rain had leaked down through the wagon bed all night upon them, Mrs. D. Wilson Moore thought it would be about as good to die as to live under such conditions! How Hapistinna and Wanskay wore off their toes walking through the sharp prairie grass! How we stopped on the open prairie to kill a cow and bake bread and roast meat, with no pans to do it in! And how, while the process was going on, we had our picture taken! How many scares we passed through the night we passed around Fort Ridgley! How, thus, we escaped, like a bird from the snare of the fowler—the snare was broken and we escaped! How, when the company came to adjust their mutual obligations, nobody had any money but D. Wilson Moore! How those women met us on the top of the hill by Henderson and were glad to see us because we had white blood in us! How on the road we met our old friend Samuel W. Pond, who welcomed our family to his house at Shakopee!

FAMILY IN ST. ANTHONY.

The memories of the campaign of the next three months may be passed over, as having little connection with the family. But I remember the night, when, with more than *three hundred condemnations* in my carpet bag, I had a long hunt at midnight for the little hired house in which the mother and children had recommenced housekeeping. The three years in St. Anthony were ones of varied experiences. Wanskay had gone down to Rockford. Hapan and Hapistinna taught school and kept house for the mother by turns. The three boys went to school.

The war of the Rebellion was not over, but it was nearing its end as we soon knew, when one day the noble boy Thomas brought in a paper for me to sign, giving my permission for his enlistment. I had heard and read so much of boys of sixteen going almost at once into the hospital, that I threw the paper in the fire.

WHAT WILT THOU HAVE ME TO DO?

The missionary work among the Dakotas was so broken up, the clouds hung so heavily over it, that I very seriously entertained the question of giving up my commission as a missionary of the American Board, and turning my attention to work among white people. In my correspondence with Secretary Treat, I proposed a kind of half-and-half work, but that was not approved. Finally I wrote a letter of withdrawal and sent it on to Boston. But the Prudential Committee were slow to act upon it. In the meantime Rev. G. H. Pond came over and gave me a long talk. He believed I should do no such thing—that the clouds would soon clear away—that the need of work such as I could give would be greater than ever before. And so it was. To me Mr.

Pond was a prophet of the Lord sent with a special message. I wanted to know the way. And the voice said, "This is the way —walk in it." With new enthusiasm I then entered upon the work of meeting the increasing demand for school books and for the Bible.

At the very beginning of the year 1865, having completed my three months' work at the Bible House in New York, in reading the proof of the entire New Testament in Dakota and other parts of the Bible, as well as other books, I returned to our home in St. Anthony to find the mother away at the Water Cure establishment. We remember that as a year of *invalidism—of sickness*. But the skillful physician and the summer sun wrought such a cure that in the autumn we removed to Beloit. Here, with comparative health, she had three and a half years of added life.

THE MOTHER CALLED AWAY.

Among the new things that took place in Beloit in the year 1866, was the marriage of *Hapan* and *Hapistinna*, the one starting off for the far off land of the celestials—so called—and the other to the frontier of Minnesota. *Wanskay* was then our housekeeper and the three boys were in school. By and by the time came for the mother to be called away. It was a brief sickness and she passed from us into the Land of Immortal Beauty. It was a comfort to us that our first born—Zitkadan Washta—was residing near by that winter and spring of 1869. As I remember it, three children were far away and five gathered around the mother's grave. Now, looking back over the ten years passed since that time, I seem to say:

"My thoughts, like palms in exile,
    Climb up to look and pray
For a glimpse of that heavenly country,
    That seems *not* far away."

This is a good point to close and seal up the Memories. For the rest a few words may be sufficient. Manifestly, as a family, God has been with us all the way, and the blessings of the Lord Jehovah have been upon us. Forty two years ago we went out— two alone—into the wilderness of prairie; and now we have become *one, two, three, four, five, six*, or more bands.

Sabbath, September the seventh, wound up the precious weeks; and Sabbath evening was the transfiguration of the whole. May its blessed memories tenderly abide in all our hearts. For a year or more, we had looked forward to the Family Meeting that was to be; but now we look back and remember with growing pleasure the meeting that was. As the wagons clattered away on Monday morning, they broke the charmed spell, but each one went their own way richer than they came. A. L. R.

THE END.